TC
Against simple
fragmentation as
wc weakness – strides
against it; and
other conditioning
factors (state and
capital identity).

The Working Class in American History

Editorial Advisors

David Brody
Alice Kessler-Harris
David Montgomery
Sean Wilentz

In Chi — forerunners of 1930s
industrial unionism

A list of the books in the series appears at the end of this volume.

Work and Community in the Jungle

Work and Community in the Jungle

Chicago's Packinghouse Workers,
1894–1922

James R. Barrett

UNIVERSITY OF ILLINOIS PRESS
Urbana and Chicago

Publication of this work has been supported by a grant
from the Oliver M. Dickerson Fund. The Fund was established
by Mr. Dickerson (Ph. D., Illinois, 1906) to enable the
University of Illinois Press to publish selected works
in American history, designated by the executive
committee of the Department of History.

This book is printed on acid-free paper.

Library of Congress Cataloging-in-Publication Data

Barrett, James R., 1950–
Work and community in the jungle : Chicago's packinghouse workers,
1894–1922 / James R. Barrett. — Illini Books ed.
p.   cm. — (The Working class in American history)
ISBN 0-252-06136-5 (pb : alk. paper).
ISBN 978-0-252-06136-3 (pb : alk. paper).
1. Packing-house workers—Illinois—Chicago—History.
2. Community organization—Illinois—Chicago—History. 3. Quality
of work life—Illinois—Chicago—History. 4. Mass production—
Illinois—Chicago—History. 5. Trade-unions—Packing-house
workers—Illinois —Chicago—History. 6. Working class—Illinois—
Chicago—History. I. Title. II. Series
HD8039.P152U53   1990
331.7'6649'00977311—dc20   89-20691
                                    CIP

For Thomas E. Barrett and Catherine M. Barrett
and for the working people of the city of Chicago

Contents

Tables

Maps

Acknowledgments

I started this book as a dissertation at the University of Pittsburgh around the time my son Sean was born, and the two have grown up together. I am proud of both and rather reluctant to let either of them go. I can hold on to Sean for a while, but it is time to send the book out into the world, and I would like to thank all of those who helped me along the way.

My oldest and deepest intellectual debts are to David Montgomery and the late Gilbert Osofsky. Osofsky encouraged me to become a historian by pointing out that American working people had a fascinating history of their own which was well worth the time it takes to piece it together. Montgomery is well known, of course, as a gifted scholar, but he is also a fine teacher and advisor. His enthusiasm and ideas provided the inspiration for this study, and his support over the past decade has been crucial to my development as a historian.

Now that I have achieved journeyman status, I would also like to thank a number of other teachers who offered encouragement to an untried apprentice. David Brody, whom I first met at the University of Warwick in England, acted as editor for the book and helped to improve its quality through his careful reading and criticisms. He is a demanding editor and a good one. I also met Royden Harrison and James Hinton at Warwick, and both of them nurtured my interest in the problems of comparative labor history. Support from Al Young and Carroll Moody of Northern Illinois University has been consistent from a very early stage, and I appreciate it. Edward Thompson has had an enormous impact on my generation through his remarkably original scholarship as well as his commitment to democracy and justice. I was fortunate to know him as an inspiring teacher as well. He too provided solid encouragement at an early date, and I will always be grateful. John Bodnar's most direct input came from his suggestions for revising the manuscript, but I have also learned a great deal from his own writing.

Old friends in Pittsburgh, Chicago, and North Carolina and new ones at the University of Illinois read various parts and versions of the manuscript, and I thank them all heartily. The dissertation was read by Joe White, Maurine Greenwald, Peter Gottlieb, Elizabeth Higginbotham, and Steve Sapolsky. These people and others made Pitt a very stimulating place to study labor history. I am particularly grateful to Sapolsky for his brilliant insights but even more for his friendship.

In Chicago, Bob Slayton made some helpful suggestions, and in Raleigh, Jerry Surh offered searching criticisms. In Chapel Hill, Sue Levine and Leon Fink were not only helpful critics but also wonderfully supportive friends. Here in Urbana-Champaign, Diane Koenker put aside Russian strikers in the throes of revolution and David Prochaska exotic French North Africa to read about the grittier aspects of life on Chicago's South Side. Stan Nadel saved me from some errors in analyzing the quantitative data. Nadine Rutledge did a wonderful job typing the manuscript.

At various stages of the project, I also received help and encouragement from Hartmut Keil, John Jentz, Joseph Hobbs, Dirk Hoerder, Jan Reiff, Nora Faires, Adam Walazsek, Steven Vincent, Jim Crisp, Tony LaVopa, Joseph Hapak, Dan Soloff, Milton Derber, Gail O'Brien, Josh Brown, Sam Hays, Dick Oestreicher, and members of social history reading groups in Pittsburgh, the Research Triangle of North Carolina, and Urbana-Champaign. I am grateful to these and to the other scholars, coworkers, and students, unnamed here, who commented constructively on my work. And I suppose that I am even a little grateful to those who were less than constructive in their criticisms.

A few people from Chicago's labor movement helped to keep the book in proper perspective. The late Hilton Hannah and Robert Ford provided firsthand experiences with some of the problems with which I was concerned. Likewise, Les Orear of the Illinois Labor History Society reminded me through his own work that there is or should be a close relationship between labor history and the people who made it.

For allowing me to read their unpublished works, I thank Rich Schneirov, Claude Lightfoot, Roger Horowitz, and Steve Sapolsky.

At the University of Illinois Press, my thanks are due to Dick Wentworth, who guided me through the production process, and Lee Erwin, who did a nice job of editing the manuscript. Jim Bier, a cartographer at Illinois, is responsible for the maps, and the Chicago Historical Society provided the photographs.

A number of agencies helped me to put bread on the table while I did my research and writing. A graduate fellowship from the Illinois State Historical Society and a predoctoral fellowship from the Andrew Mellon Foundation provided early support, and since then I have been aided by the National Endowment for the Humanities, the Exxon Foundation, and the Newberry Library, as well as the Graduate College Research Board and the Center for Advanced Study at the University of Illinois. My colleagues in the Department of History at Illinois have encouraged me throughout and provided time off from teaching responsibilities so that I could complete the manuscript. I would especially like to thank Chip Burkhardt and Bill Widenor, who were particularly effective department chairpersons.

My parents, my brothers and sister, my in-laws, Shew and Mary Wong, and many friends provided meals, good cheer, and a roof over our heads during the long research trips to Chicago. Steve and Jeanine Brundage did the same in Washington, D.C., and Rob Ruck, Maggie Patterson, Pam Harding, and Paul Boas in Pittsburgh. The research itself was facilitated by the skill and efforts of librarians and archivists at the State Historical Society of Wisconsin at Madison; the University of North Carolina, Chapel Hill; North Carolina State University; the University of Illinois at Chicago and at Urbana-Champaign; the National Archives in Washington and Suitland, Maryland; the University of Chicago;

the Newberry Library; and the Chicago Historical Society. I am particularly grateful to Archie Motley, director of the Historical Society's manuscript collection.

The editors of the *Journal of Social History* and Northern Illinois University Press graciously allowed me to include material here which appeared in earlier publications. Full citations are provided at appropriate points in the notes.

All of these people deserve part of the credit for whatever value the book has for its readers; I accept responsibility for its flaws.

This book is dedicated to my mother and father in recognition of their love and support over the years. They will no doubt be surprised to hear this, but their own values and ideas shaped it as much as any other influences. From my father, I derived a love for the city in all of its complexity and for its people in all of their diversity. I hope that my mother's sense of justice has not been lost in the welter of statistics and the thick description. The book is also dedicated to Chicago's working people. It is exactly one hundred years since they gathered at Haymarket Square to demand their rights and to demonstrate their support for the eight-hour strikes which were sweeping the city and the nation in 1886. A great deal of labor history has been made in Chicago since then, and too much of it has been forgotten. I am especially concerned that this heritage be passed on to our children. If this book helps some of them to understand better who they are and where they came from, I will be more than satisfied.

I have saved my heaviest debts till the end. Sean Eugene Barrett brought the whole enterprise back down to earth on more occasions than I care to remember by asking countless questions about what I was trying to do and by reminding me through his very presence that this book was really not the most important thing in my life after all. Jenni has made many sacrifices and has taught me a great deal since we got together. I would like to pay her back somehow for all of her love and support, as well as for her ideas and ideals, but all I can really do is to tell her how grateful I am for her being there.

Champaign, Illinois, May 1986

Work and Community in the Jungle

Introduction

In the fall of 1904, young Upton Sinclair set out for Chicago, determined to write the great labor novel of the twentieth century. As Harriet Beecher Stowe had done with her description of life under chattel slavery in *Uncle Tom's Cabin*, so Sinclair would spark a storm of protest over the conditions facing the "wage slaves of the Beef Trust," Chicago's immigrant packinghouse workers. For seven weeks the young writer lived among the butcher workmen and -women and their families, carefully studying their work and their community. Dressed in overalls and carrying a metal lunch pail, Sinclair haunted the killing floors and canning rooms, the saloons and tenements of Packingtown. His research paid off in remarkably vivid descriptions of its residents' living and working conditions. *The Jungle* caused an immediate sensation and is often given credit for prompting passage of the Meat Inspection Act of 1906 by highlighting the filthy conditions under which America's food was produced.[1]

As an exposé of corrupt corporate practices, *The Jungle* was a striking success. The plight of the immigrant worker, however, was lost somehow in the uproar over tainted meat. "I aimed at the public's heart," Sinclair later wrote, "and by accident I hit it in the stomach."[2]

Sinclair's classic fictional indictment of American big business has left us with powerful images of early twentieth-century labor and capital. On one side stood the giant "meat trust," drawing on huge wealth, producing its commodities with assembly-line precision, and distributing them throughout the world with complicated marketing arrangements. On the other side stood the great mass of unskilled packinghouse workers—weak, badly divided by race and nationality, thoroughly demoralized. Sinclair's workers are beaten, degraded men and women. Dehumanizing metaphors abound as the people of Packingtown are consumed by the giant technology which surrounds them. They become "cogs in the great packing machine."

The real-life context for Sinclair's story was a dramatic transformation of the American political economy which took place between the end of the nineteenth century and the early 1920s. During these years the economy itself sustained a second industrial revolution, while progressive political reforms enlarged the role of the state considerably.

The structural aspects of this revolution and its political implications are clear. Productivity, manufacturing output, and profits all soared. Through a matrix of mergers, the nation's largest banking houses increasingly concentrated capital in each industry into a few large firms that dominated their respective markets. These efforts left the economy more streamlined and manageable but also less competitive. By comparison to nineteenth-century entrepreneurial firms, these new corporate giants were intricate systems, each integrating a wide range of functions into a single highly structured and centralized bureaucracy. As production outran domestic demand at the end of the nineteenth century, corporate leaders turned their attention increasingly abroad, not only for commodity and investment markets, but also for new sources of labor. As they became more dependent on the international market and more concerned with regulating and planning economic development, businessmen also relied increasingly on federal government intervention to carry out necessary reforms and coordinate a policy which ensured stable growth. Thus, big business and big government became more closely integrated. While many historians might not accept Lenin's formulation that these "imperialist" characteristics represented the highest stage in capitalist development, most would concede that the American political economy entered a new era during the early twentieth century.[3]

But what were the social implications of this transformation? What did the "rise of big business" mean for those who produced the system's wealth? By comparison to our finely textured view of workers' lives during earlier periods of industrialization, the labor history of the early twentieth century is far less developed.[4] One of the ironies of the field, for example, is that scholars have turned their attention only recently to the sort of work which became characteristic of twentieth-century American industry. A new interest in management and worker consciousness and behavior in the workplace has helped to balance labor historians' strong interest in working-class culture with an emphasis on the social relations of production.[5] Yet even the most sophisticated analyses of mass-production work and scientific management reforms fail to gauge the full impact of this transformation of work because they have largely ignored its effects on standards of living and on family and community life.

Local community studies have been somewhat more successful in this regard. The few we have for the early twentieth century have provided important empirical data on the relationship among work, community, and family life. Nearly all of these studies, however, deal with workers living in towns and small cities dominated by a single industry. In steel and textile mill towns and in coal company towns, corporations were often able to exercise control quite directly through manipulation of politics, police, and even cultural institutions. Many of the nation's workers continued to live in such communities during the early years of this century, but an increasingly large number lived in neighborhoods like the one Sinclair portrayed in his novel—ethnic enclaves in Detroit, Cleveland, Chicago, and other large industrial cities. While the impact of industry on workers' lives was often dramatic, the employer's influence was generally less decisive than in a company town. Chicago's immigrant workers, for example, created their own ethnic communities in the midst of a cosmopolitan industrial city with a strong labor movement and a long tradition of working-class solidarity, and these factors had an important effect on class relations in industry.[6]

Work and Community in the Jungle concerns itself with this world of the big-city neighborhood and the large mass-production factory and, more broadly, with the social implications of early monopoly capitalism for the lives of American workers. The book focuses on slaughtering and meat-packing workers in what Sinclair called "the Jungle," Chicago's Union Stockyards and the working-class neighborhoods which grew up around them in the early years of this century. It has four broad themes: the experience of mass-production work; the quality of working-class life; the process of class formation and fragmentation; and the changing character of class relations.

Chicago's packinghouse workers provide an excellent case study of the remaking of the American working class during the early twentieth century. The packing companies' strong market position, their sophisticated corporate bureaucracies and highly rationalized production systems are representative of the "trusts" which came to dominate many sectors of the American economy in this era. The situation of the butcher workmen and -women themselves raises many of the most fundamental questions facing scholars of twentieth-century American workers. How did changes in the structure of the economy affect the experience of work; relations within the family and among groups in the community; the prospects for one's children under the system? How did the increasing ethnic and racial diversity among workers shape working-class organization and the character of class conflict? How were recent immigrants and rural migrants acculturated in the context of large-scale industry and ethnic neighborhoods? What changes can we see in the patterns of working-class organization, protest, and accommodation? What role did the state play in class relations?

Any answers to these questions must concern themselves with both the workplace and the community and with the dynamic relationship between these two crucial dimensions of working-class life. The starting point here, however, is not with the myriad ethnic cultures which characterized the butcher workmen and other groups of workers in this era, but rather with an experience which so many of them shared—mass-production work.

MASS-PRODUCTION WORK

Popular images of mass-production work often center on the personal effects of assembly-line manufacture. Perhaps one of the most familiar is the situation portrayed in Charlie Chaplin's 1936 film *Modern Times*, in which a lone operative struggles to keep up the pace in a factory dominated by big machines. The human spirit wilts in a blur of levers and cogs.

Some recent studies of the early twentieth-century transformation of work, while far more sophisticated than Chaplin's, have also emphasized this technological dimension.[7] But the introduction of mass-production techniques was not simply a matter of getting machines to do the work of people; it involved a change far more fundamental than the mechanization of specific production tasks. Indeed, in the case of packing, the first real assembly-line industry, one finds precious little mechanization of the actual slaughtering and cutting operations. Nor was the assembly line a natural product of some faceless, inevitable process of "modernization."[8] Rather, it represented a major offensive in the ongoing struggle over the character of work.[9] What is described as management "rationalization" of work was often a much more complex, dialectical process involving worker initiatives as well as those of management. This was a political conflict in the broadest sense of the term because it revolved around the crucial problem of power relations at the workplace, specifically the power to decide what constituted proper behavior and then to enforce those norms. How much work? How fast? In meat packing recurrent conflicts erupted between management and workers over production levels, work rules, and a wide range of other issues. The first chapter of this book analyzes the assembly line and other mass-production processes as part of this struggle for control and places them within the context of the meat-packing industry, with its large-scale bureaucratic corporations and the peculiar market forces which helped to shape management psychology.

COMMUNITY, FAMILY, AND THE QUALITY OF LIFE

How did these changes in the character of work affect the quality of peoples' lives in the community? Part of the answer lies in analyzing working-class living standards under early monopoly capitalism.[10] Because a rising standard of living is often advanced as an explanation for the relative conservatism of American workers in the twentieth century, some assessment of the problem is crucial to understanding not only the impact of economic change, but also the evolution of class relations. Economic historians, approaching the problem from the perspective of rapid economic growth, have generally taken an optimistic view. Pointing to aggregate statistics which show rising real wages and per capita income and a decline in average working hours, they have concluded that, while American worker and capitalist may not have shared equally in the fruits of high productivity, both benefited. [11]

Clearly there are limitations to the approach economic historians have taken. One consequence of the increasing complexity of production processes was the diffusion of job hierarchies with a wide range of wage rates for skilled and semiskilled workers and a disparity within the working class between these groups and the great mass of common laborers. [12] National averages for earnings and per capita income may mask all sorts of disparities in wages, working conditions, and wealth. Even if we could refine the figures to reflect the experience of the armies of common laborers whose incomes must have fallen considerably below the mean, we would still miss vital aspects of workers' lives which were affected by their status in society but are not shown clearly by such gross economic indicators.

In order to capture the full impact of new production methods beyond the walls of the packing plants, I have followed workers into their neighborhoods and even into their homes. The most comprehensive analysis of this community dimension is contained in chapter 3, but I have kept my sights trained on the neighborhood as well as on the workplace throughout this study.

I have approached the problem of the standard of living by considering a very broad range of conditions which might more properly be grouped under the term "quality of life." These include not only such factors as working hours and wages but also the physical environment in which workers and their families lived— housing, population density, pollution, and sanitation—and the relationship between these factors and health. My analysis relies heavily on empirical data, but I am most concerned with the subjective problem of human motivation and behavior. The data are important because they provide a crucial backdrop for understanding the tenacity with which communities around the stockyards fought during strikes. Packinghouse workers joined unions and struggled for employment security and higher wages because unionization was linked in their minds with improving the quality of life and creating a viable community.

Converging with the optimism of the economic historians are many recent studies by scholars of the family which have emphasized its importance as an "independent variable" in the process of industrialization. Citing ethnic cultural influences and the economic strategies available to such families, these writers have explained working-class life primarily in terms of the "life choices" concept employed by modernization theorists. It is wrong, they argue, to see families simply as "products" of economic conditions. Families were subject to a whole range of demographic and cultural influences that affected their structure and behavior as much as or more than did economic conditions.[13]

This research has influenced me, and I have considered such factors as family cycle in my analysis. If I have tended to emphasize work and work-related problems—low wages, irregular employment, industrial accidents, and illnesses—in describing Packingtown's families, it is because these were the critical factors in this particular case. Since it was so heavily composed of common laborers, Packingtown is representative of only one type of working-class community in this era, but there should be a place for its families in the developing historical synthesis of American family life.

UNITY AND FRAGMENTATION

The impact of new work methods went beyond the walls of the factory to affect the composition of the labor force and relations among workers. In meat packing and in many other industries, the laboring population was fundamentally reconstituted in the first two decades of the twentieth century. The resulting ethnic, racial, gender, and skill diversity considerably complicated the process of working-class formation. Chicago's Union Stockyards provide a case study of class formation and fragmentation within an extremely diverse working-class population. Here, thousands of young peasants and laborers only recently arrived from the towns, forests, and farms of the Russian and Austro-Hungarian empires mingled with seasoned Irish and German butchers and black migrants from the Deep South. While men did most of the industry's heavy work, they were joined by a growing stream of young, single women and later, during World War I, by thousands of married women and mothers. Packed into the crowded neighborhoods of Chicago's vast industrial South Side, these workers exemplify the divisions within the American working class during this era.

How did workers from such diverse backgrounds interact with one another, as they undoubtedly did in some circumstances? Is it possible to distinguish factors which contributed to class cohesion from those which led to disintegration? In short, what can the experience of Chicago's butcher workmen and -women tell us about the problems of class formation and fragmentation in the early twentieth-century United States?

CORPORATE LIBERALISM AND CLASS CONFLICT

A history of Chicago's packinghouse workers can also tell us much about the broader problem of relations between capital and labor during these years. While labor historians have concentrated on divisions within the working class, business and political historians have started at the other end of the social structure. They stress the tremendous power and growing sophistication of the corporate elite who guided the nation's largest business institutions and often its political affairs as well. Some have explained this group and its labor relations largely in terms of ideology, postulating a pervasive "corporate liberal" consensus among important business and labor leaders gathered around the National Civic Federation. These historians emphasize the increasingly conservative and bureaucratic character of the dominant American Federation of Labor (AFL) leadership on the one hand, and on the other the attempt by progressive corporate executives to co-opt the labor movement through relatively high wages, welfare programs, and, if necessary, collective bargaining. Underlying such formulations is the notion that the largest and most profitable firms could afford to take this more enlightened view because of their dominance in the marketplace.[14]

The state's role in labor relations is central to this analysis of corporate liberalism. The idea of a maturing and increasingly close relationship between big business and the government during the early twentieth century provides a perspective too often missing from labor history studies, which frequently deal only with employer-employee relations. Local, state, and federal governments all played an important role in disciplining the labor force and breaking strikes throughout the late nineteenth century. But the federal government also tried to stabilize industrial relations in the early twentieth century through various forms of mediation, arbitration, and labor reform legislation.

Scholars of corporate liberalism have been important in linking the relations between labor and capital to a coherent analysis of the American political economy as a whole in the early twentieth century, and I have tried to relate my analysis to this broader context. But this top-down approach, with its emphasis on the writings and pronouncements of corporate executives and union officials, may be misleading. What did corporate liberalism look like and how effective was it from the vantage point of the shop floor rather than the boardroom? How well can the corporate liberal analysis explain management behavior in the Chicago context? And what effects did government intervention have on labor organization, negotiation, and conflict?

In part, this book is an attempt to reconstruct the complex microcosm of workers' lives at the factory and in the community. In this sense the story might help us better understand what life must have been like for such people. But the book is also an argument for the importance of such lives in the broader stream of American history. Despite its vivid descriptions of work and living conditions, *The Jungle* is not an entirely accurate portrayal of working-class life in early twentieth-century America. The main element missing from much of Sinclair's historic drama is any notion of human agency, and yet in real life the behavior of the workers themselves constituted a crucial dimension of the story. Chicago's packinghouse workers were not the hopeless, animal-like creatures described in Sinclair's novel, but rather active agents in the transformation which swept urban industrial America in the early part of this century. Their personal lives are of interest to any sympathetic observer, but it is their role as agents of social change that makes their experiences historically significant.

NOTES

1. Upton Sinclair, *The Autobiography of Upton Sinclair* (New York, 1962), 108–10; Leon Harris, *Upton Sinclair, American Rebel* (New York, 1975), 70, 83–90; Christine Scriabine, "Upton Sinclair and the Writing of *The Jungle*," *Chicago History* 10 (Spring 1981): 26–37.

2. Scriabine, 36–37; Sinclair, *Autobiography*, 126.

3. Elliott Brownlee, *The Dynamics of Ascent: A History of the American Economy* (New York, 1977); Gabriel Kolko, *The Triumph of Conservatism: A Reinterpretation of American History, 1900–1915* (New York, 1967), and *Main Currents in Modern American History* (New York, 1976); James Weinstein, *The Corporate Ideal in the Liberal State: 1900–1918* (Boston, 1968); Thomas C. Cochran, *The American Business System: An Historical Perspective, 1900–1915* (Cambridge, Mass., 1957); Richard Edwards, *Contested Terrain: The Transformation of the Workplace in the Twentieth Century* (New York, 1977), chap. 3; Naomi Lamoreaux, *The Great Merger Movement in American Business, 1895–1914* (New York and London, 1985); Alfred Chandler, *The Visible Hand: The Managerial Revolution in American Business* (Cambridge, Mass., 1977); Christopher Tomlins, *The State and the Unions: Labor Relations, Law, and the Organized Labor Movement in America, 1880–1960* (New York and London, 1985), chap. 1; V. I. Lenin, *Imperialism, the Highest Stage of Capitalism* (Peking, 1973).

4. Some of the most influential of the works dealing with early industrialization include Herbert Gutman, *Work, Culture, and Society in Industrializing America: Essays in Working-Class and Social History* (New York, 1977); David Montgomery, *Beyond Equality: Labor and the Radical Republicans* (New York, 1967); Alan Dawley, *Class and Community: The Industrial Revolution in Lynn* (Cambridge, Mass., 1975); Thomas Dublin, *Women at Work: The Transformation of Work and Community in Lowell, Massachusetts, 1826–1860* (New York, 1979); Bruce Laurie, *The Working People of Philadelphia, 1800–1860* (Philadelphia, 1980); Sean Wilentz, *Chants Democratic: New York City and the Rise of the American Working Class, 1788–1850* (New York, 1984); and Daniel Walkowitz, *Worker City, Company Town: Iron and Cotton Worker Protest in Troy and Cohoes, New York, 1855–1884* (Urbana, Ill., 1978). For critical assessments of recent work in the field of labor history, see David Brody, "The Old Labor

History and the New: In Search of an American Working Class," *Labor History* 20 (1979): 111–26; and David Montgomery, "To Study the People: The Working Class," *Labor History* 21 (1980): 485–512.

5. David Montgomery, *Workers' Control in America: Studies in the History of Work, Technology, and Labor Struggles* (New York and London, 1979); Daniel Nelson, *Managers and Workers: Origins of the New Factory System in the United States, 1880–1920* (Madison, Wis., 1975); Harry Braverman, *Labor and Monopoly Capital: The Degradation of Work in the Twentieth Century* (New York, 1974); Edwards, chap. 6; Stephen Meyer III, *The Five-Dollar Day: Social Control in the Ford Motor Company, 1908–1921* (Albany, N.Y., 1981).

6. John T. Cumbler, *Working-Class Community: Work, Leisure, and Conflict in Two Industrial Cities, 1880–1930* (Westport, Conn., 1977); Tamara K. Hareven, *Family Time and Industrial Time: The Relationship between the Family and Work in a New England Industrial Community* (New York and London, 1982), and "The Laborers of Manchester, New Hampshire, 1919–1922: The Role of Family and Ethnicity in Adjustment to Industrial Life," *Labor History* 16 (Summer 1975): 249–65; Tamara K. Hareven and Randolph Langenbach, *Amoskeag: Life and Work in an American Factory-City* (New York, 1978); John Bodnar, *Immigration and Industrialization: Ethnicity in an American Mill Town* (Pittsburgh, 1977); David Corbin, *Life, Work, and Rebellion in the Coal Fields: The Southern West Virginia Miners, 1880–1922* (Urbana, Ill., 1981). Unfortunately, Ewa Morawska's *For Bread with Butter: The Life-Worlds of East Central Europeans in Johnstown, Pennsylvania, 1890–1940* (New York and London, 1985), which is perhaps closest to my own study in subject matter, appeared after this manuscript had gone to press.

7. David Landes, *The Unbound Prometheus: Technical Change and Industrial Revolution in Western Europe, 1750 to the Present* (New York and London, 1969), 290–326; Nelson, 3–23; Siegfried Giedion, *Mechanization Takes Command: A Contribution to Anonymous History* (1948; reprint, New York, 1969), 77–121 and, for meat packing, 209–46.

8. Peter Stearns, *Lives of Labor: Work in a Maturing Industrial Society* (New York, 1975).

9. Edwards, 11–22; Montgomery, *Workers' Control in America*, passim.

10. Peter Shergold, *Working-Class Life: The "American Standard" in Comparative Perspective, 1899–1913* (Pittsburgh, 1982), is the best systematic study of the problem for this era.

11. Brownlee, chap. 9; Douglas C. North, *Growth and Welfare in the American Past: A New Economic History* (Englewood Cliffs, N. J., 1966), 161–64; Harold G. Vatter, *The Drive to Industrial Maturity: The U.S.*

Economy, 1860–1914 (Westport, Conn., 1975), 245–46, 299–305; Stanley Lebergott, *The Americans: An Economic Record* (New York, 1984), 377–83.

12. See Shergold, chap. 3; and David Gordon, Richard Edwards, and Michael Reich, *Segmented Work, Divided Workers: The Historical Transformation of Labor in the United States* (New York and London, 1982), 149–50.

13. See, for example, Virginia Yans-McLaughlin, "Patterns of Work and Family Organization: Buffalo's Italians," *Journal of Interdisciplinary History* 2 (1971): 200–214; and Tamara K. Hareven, "Introduction" and "Family Time and Industrial Time: Family and Work in a Planned Corporation Town, 1900–1924," and John Modell and Tamara K. Hareven, "Urbanization and the Malleable Household: An Examination of Boarding and Lodging in American Families," all in *Family and Kin in Urban Communities, 1700–1930*, ed. Tamara K. Hareven (New York, 1977).

14. Kolko, *The Triumph of Conservatism* and *Main Currents in Modern American History;* James Weinstein, "The IWW and American Socialism," *Socialist Revolution* 1 (1970): 3–42, and *The Corporate Ideal in the Liberal State;* Ronald Radosh, "The Corporate Ideology of American Labor Leaders from Gompers to Hillman," *Studies on the Left* 6 (1966): 66–88, and "Labor and the American Economy: The 1922 Railroad Shop Crafts Strike and the 'B & O Plan,' " in *Building the Organizational Society: Essays on Associational Activities,* ed. Jerry Israel (New York, 1972), 73–87. See also Tomlins, 60–95.

1

The Meat-packing Industry: Monopoly Capital and Mass Production

Jurgis went down the line with the rest of the visitors, staring open-mouthed, lost in wonder. He had dressed hogs himself in the forest of Lithuania; but he had never expected to live to see one hog dressed by several hundred men.

Upton Sinclair, *The Jungle*

Charles Edward Russell called it "the greatest trust in the world." For millions of American farmers, industrial workers, and professional reformers throughout the late nineteenth and early twentieth centuries, the meat-packing industry and its corporate giants symbolized the growth of monopoly capitalism in the United States. Some historians have questioned whether this "Meat Trust" and its counterparts in other industries possessed the sort of decisive control that has been attributed to them. Certainly these were not monopolies in the purest sense of the term. Yet the industry was a model of what Alfred Chandler has described as "oligopolistic" industrial growth. The grip which the "Big Five" packers—Swift, Armour, Morris, Cudahy, and Schwarzschild and Sulzberger (later Wilson)—held on the developing national and international markets shaped the character of labor relations in the industry from the late nineteenth century on. [1]

The formation of a mass market for meat products pressed the packers to rationalize packinghouse work, creating in the process one of the earliest mass-production industries. While their dominance in the marketplace made them imposing adversaries of any workers' movement, their reorganization of work brought them greater control over the system of production and the labor market.

The Big Five were in many respects characteristic of corporations in highly concentrated markets, but the packers were not omnipotent. The peculiarities of their product placed constraints on technology and forced them to cut costs. In the midst of a developing monopoly system, wages and basic work rules provided the source for recurrent conflicts, and the packinghouses remained battlegrounds through much of the era of "corporate liberalism."

THE CORPORATE OLIGOPOLY

As early as the mid-nineteenth century, a fairly high degree of geographic concentration was achieved in the hog-slaughtering industry around Cincinnati. By the 1842–43 season nearly half of all commercially dressed hogs were packed in the ten largest packing centers, located along the rivers of Ohio, Indiana, Illinois, and Kentucky. Cincinnati became the center of by-product manufacturing and of a lucrative pork export trade. But the various stages in the production process—slaughtering, packing, marketing, and distribution—remained separate, and the scale of production remained small. Even after the rise of the railroad shifted the focus of production to larger houses in Chicago during the 1850s and 1860s, few if any plants had more than 100 employees. As late as 1880, the average number of workers in Illinois plants was 190, and most still had considerably fewer than 100. The industry also remained highly competitive. In 1863 Chicago had at least forty-five packinghouses, including several which killed more than 100,000 cattle and hogs per year, and by 1880 the number of houses in the city had actually increased.[2]

Competition in the industry, its unintegrated business structure, and its small-scale production facilities were all products of its seasonality. Meat was highly perishable. Until an efficient means of refrigerated transportation was perfected, slaughtering, packing, and shipping could be carried on only during cool weather. The market remained regional at best.

The origins of the modern packinghouse lie in the growth of a national urban market for dressed meat from the late 1870s through the 1890s. The men who built this market and the modern business organizations that serviced it were classic nineteenth-century entrepreneurs. Most, like Philip Danforth Armour and Gustavus Swift, were from old-line Yankee families in the Northeast. They had made some money in commerce in the period after the Civil War and were willing to take a risk in making their fortunes. In pursuit of this goal, they created some of the most modern business organizations of the era. From its inception, the market structure and corporate organization of the industry, perfected by Gustavus Swift, provided a model for highly rationalized growth through vertical integration. The leading packers integrated all major economic functions within their firms: purchasing of raw materials, manufacturing, distribution, and finance.[3]

The packers developed their market through a network of branch houses, each with its own storage facilities and sales organization, while railroads brought the firms' products to more remote towns. As their system grew, the range of their products also expanded. The packers sought to drive prices down by fully utilizing their raw material—the animals they slaughtered. This meant not only the marketing of more meat products but also the development of an extensive by-product industry. Glue, fertilizer, soap, and oil and tallow works grew up within or around the packinghouses to transform what was once refuse—blood, bone, horn, and hoof—into valuable commodities. A measure of the packers' success in this area is the fact that by the early twentieth century the return on dressed meat was lower than what it cost to produce it, but by-product utilization still allowed the packers high profits.[4]

The range of packinghouse commodities generated from the time the animal was knocked unconscious to the final distribution of meat and by-products demanded an elaborate marketing operation. The complexity of the production process itself called for a sophisticated cost-accounting system. The emphasis on expanding the product line led the packers to establish some of the earliest research and development departments. All of these features were components of a highly structured corporate bureaucracy which showed the way for many newly developing consumer goods industries.[5]

Rationalization shaped the organization of markets as much as it did the structure of the industry's major corporations. The independent local packinghouse might hold its own in the small-town market; in fact, the number of meat-packing plants actually increased from 1,080 to 1,641 between 1899 and 1909. But the big profits lay in domination of the national urban market, and that market was carefully carved up and shared by the largest firms. Combinations followed soon after the first successful shipment of refrigerated meat. Marketing pools functioned throughout the 1880s, and by the mid-nineties an even more sophisticated system was in place, producing some range in prices while allowing for very similar profit margins, and establishing fines for violators of the various marketing agreements. When a federal injunction broke up the pools in 1902, the packers turned to the idea of a merger. The three largest corporations—Swift, Armour, and Morris—established the National Packing Company in 1903 and merged many of the largest independents into the new holding company. At this point the "Big Six" (now including National) slaughtered almost 90 percent of all meat inspected east of the Rockies. The ultimate aim, according to Gustavus Swift, was to have National absorb the three parent companies, creating one giant corporation which could eventually control the entire market. This plan was hobbled by a federal antitrust suit, however, forcing the liquidation of the holding company in 1912.[6]

Nevertheless, combination of the big firms persisted. When the Federal Trade Commission launched a large-scale investigation during World War I, researchers found that the Big Five had increased their influence over virtually every aspect of the industry. Their share of the national trade had grown between 1908 and 1916, by which time they were killing about 70 percent of all livestock slaughtered by packers engaged in interstate commerce—and the proportion was even higher in the major packing centers like Chicago, Kansas City, and Omaha. Hundreds of independents competed for a share of the rest of the market, but none of them controlled more than 1 percent.[7]

The big packers were joined not only through their marketing agreements, but also through joint ownership or control of hundreds of subsidiary and affiliated packing companies, stockyards, financial institutions, and other businesses. Among them, they owned 91 percent of all refrigerator cars in the country and held controlling interests in most of the major stockyards, making it extremely difficult for the independents to compete effectively. Of about sixty thousand towns serviced by railroad car routes in 1918, the Big Five accounted for more than fifty-eight thousand. The two largest companies, Swift and Armour, serviced almost forty-eight thousand of the towns between them.[8]

Capital was highly concentrated within each corporation as well as over the industry as a whole. With the exception of Swift, which had six thousand shareholders as early as 1903, the major packing concerns were closed corporations. None listed its stocks on either of the major exchanges, and most shares were held by the families which had started the businesses. By the period of the First World War, part of the empire was brought under the control of the nation's largest and most active banking houses. In 1916 Wilson was taken over by Kuhn, Loeb and Company, Guarantee Trust (part of the House of Morgan), and the Chase National Bank. The Federal Trade Commission noted a "maturing relationship" between the Big Five and the highest reaches of finance capital by 1918.[9]

As the packers extended their control over the interstate trade, they turned their attention toward the world market. The last two decades of the nineteenth century brought a dramatic expansion of U.S. exports in spite of European protective legislation and the reputation of American "embalmed beef." Because the largest packers controlled refrigerated steamers even more tightly than they did railroad cars, the American export trade fell under their domination from its inception. Marketing pools were now extended to the international sphere. The Bureau of Corporations reported in 1905 that the Big Five sold about 95 percent of all beef exports. Such exports did not represent a large proportion of beef production, however, and this proportion fell from around 5 percent to less than 1 percent between 1907 and 1913. Exports rose sharply during World War I, reaching almost 10 percent of production by 1918, but fell once again in the early 1920s. [10]

Yet such figures underestimate the large packers' influence in the world market. From about 1907 on, the American firms concentrated export production in their Latin American subsidiary plants, and Argentina replaced the United States as the world's largest meat exporter. From 1910 through World War I the four largest American packers controlled more than half and at times as much as two-thirds of the beef export trade from Argentina and Uruguay, and a partial list of foreign companies operated by the Big Five in 1916 totalled thirty-eight in twelve countries. [11] Control of the market for fresh meat implied control of much of the canned meat and by-product trade as well. "The Armour Canning Company label is well-known throughout the world," an Armour publication boasted. "Armour's corned beef cans mark the desert and Nile routes to Khartoum; you will find them on the banks of the Amazon, the Ganges, and the Volga. They are equally a stand-by in Hudson's Bay posts and the gold fields of South Africa." [12]

Many of the cans littering the banks of the Ganges and the South African gold fields were made in factories on the South Side of Chicago. Perhaps more than any other industrial giant of the era, the Meat Trust had a world-renowned capital—the nerve center for its corporate bureaucracies and a huge workshop where much of the actual production was carried on. Standing between the endless herds of the Great Plains and the industrial Northeast, tied to both through a network of rail lines, Chicago was a natural marketplace for the richest agricultural hinterland in the nation.

The refrigerator car was the key which opened the national market for dressed meat and made Chicago its vital link. With the car's perfection in the late 1870s, Chicago assumed its role as "hog butcher for the world." Immigrants poured into the city, more then doubling its population between 1870 and 1890 and providing the industry with a labor force. In the same years Chicago's meat-packing industry grew by more than 900 percent. At the turn of the century it was the city's largest manufacturing employer, accounting for 10 percent of wages and a third of total manufactured goods in this highly developed and diversified metropolitan economy. In the next two decades Chicago's importance as a packing center declined gradually as the industry shifted further west, closer to western feedlots, and the newer packing centers like Omaha, Kansas City, and Sioux City, Iowa, garnered an increasing proportion of the slaughtering business; but within Chicago the packinghouses continued to employ a large proportion of the city's workers. [13]

Union Stockyards, the center of the industry, dominated the southwestern corner of the city. Between its opening in 1865 and the turn of the century, 400,000,000 animals valued at $5,500,000,000 passed through the stockyards' gate. By 1900 daily capacity had reached 75,000 cattle, 80,000 sheep, and 300,000 hogs. Although many smaller independent firms shared the stockyards with the Big Five, the giants accounted for most of the slaughtering. Armour, Swift, Morris, National, and Schwarzschild and Sulzberger slaughtered 95.8 percent of all livestock in 1903. [14]

Popular antimonopoly sentiment and some government legislation meant that the packers' control was not as extensive as they might have hoped. The government took action in 1921 with the

Table 1. The Slaughtering and Meat-packing Industry in Chicago, 1889–1923

Year	Plants	Average Wage Earners*	Capital (000)	Wages (000)	Value Added (000)
1889	57	17,875	39,222	11,006	30,038**
1899	38	25,345	67,138	12,876	38,287**
1904	32	22,613	70,265	12,388	32,542**
1914	37	26,408	194,434	16,311	64,475
1919	46	45,695	395,716	69,864	125,304
1921	41	27,209	+	35,219	57,799**
1923	50	30,282	+	39,334	+

*Average Wage Earners = number employed on 15th of each month, divided by 12

**Value Added = value of products, less cost of materials

+ No data

Source: Alma Herbst, *The Negro in the Slaughtering and Meat Packing Industry in Chicago* (Boston: Houghton Mifflin, 1932), 151.

passage of the Packer and Stockyards Act, which forced the Big
Five to divest themselves of some of their holdings, notably their
controlling interests in the various stockyards. In the face of
widespread hostility toward the "Meat Trust," the packers insisted that the industry was competitive and that the FTC,
spurred on by "demagogues and professional agitators," had conducted an unfair and biased investigation. Regulation such as
this, the packers maintained, was uncalled-for in an industry as
volatile as meat packing.[15]

To some extent, they had a point. Despite all their efforts to
abolish competition in the industry, the packers were always
under pressure to keep production costs down. Many local markets remained competitive. Even in Chicago, independents accounted for about a fourth of the local sales.[16] While few American companies could compete with the Big Five in the international arena, economy was also critical here for competition with
British, Australian, and Latin American firms.

The packers operated on a fairly tight profit margin because
their raw material made up such a large proportion of costs. In
1919, when the average material cost for all U.S. industries ran
about sixty cents on the dollar, leaving forty cents for manufacturing and profit, the same margin for packing was only eleven cents.
Elaborate marketing and distribution operations ate up some of
this margin, but the largest proportion went to payroll because of
the labor-intensive character of the work.[17]

In an industry where uncontrollable material costs made up so
large a proportion of manufacturing expense, as was the case with
the livestock market, labor costs assumed a critical importance in
management psychology. Throughout the late nineteenth century, the packers transformed the organization of packinghouse
work in order to cut these costs to the bone.

PACKINGHOUSE WORK

Historians have deprived the packers of their rightful title of
mass-production pioneers, for it was not Henry Ford but Gustavus Swift and Philip Armour who developed the assembly-line
technique that continues to symbolize the rationalized organization of work.[18] The popular notion of the assembly line is rather

vague: machines take over the work of humans to increase output. Both elements—automation and speed—are characteristic of mass-production work. But the introduction of assembly-line methods and the peculiar character of work organization in meat packing draws our attention away from mechanization and toward the division of labor and continuous-flow production methods. It was through these strategies that the packers transformed the work experience of those who labored in their plants.

As in most industries undergoing rapid expansion, a dialectic developed in meat packing between market and work process. As new production methods allowed for lower prices, the market for dressed meat grew; then work was further "rationalized" in the continuing search for new markets. In meat packing this dialectic was strongest in the late nineteenth century. Having created a thriving national market and branched out into the international trade, the packers built the most sophisticated production process in the United States before the turn of the century. By this time, two-thirds of all slaughtering was done in factories rather than in retail shops or on farms.[19] Meat-packing work had already been reorganized as factory work before most other mass-production industries were born. But in the early twentieth century, when young industries like automotive, electrical, and rubber were exploiting the methods pioneered in meat packing and harnessing them to new sources of power, the packers were already reaching the limits of technological innovation in their own industry.

During the first two decades of this century, while most manufacturing industries experienced tremendous increases in productivity, and the capacity of the whole economy grew faster than in any previous era, packing lagged behind. Output per man-hour declined steadily between 1909 and 1919, rose briefly in the early twenties, and then dropped off once again as meat consumption fell. The number of wage earners actually rose faster than output, yielding an increase of 12 percent in wage earners per unit of product between 1899 and 1937. In a list of fifty-one industries ranked by productivity over these same decades, packing was thirty-second. Most impressive, however, is the static quality, the small degree of change in the industry's productivity over the years.[20]

This stagnation resulted from the limits imposed by work organization and technology. Because of the problems involved in handling irregular-sized material and a wide range of perishable products, packinghouse work was highly labor-intensive. In packing, then, we have the incongruous situation of a few large, modern corporate bureaucracies achieving a high degree of control in the commodity market but remaining dependent to a considerable extent on hand labor.

What is particularly striking in any description of meat-packing work is the lack of mechanization in the actual slaughtering and cutting operations. "Of all the large industries in this country," the *Monthly Labor Review* noted, "slaughtering and meat packing ranks as the one which is probably least susceptible to mechanization." Unlike most other manufacturers, meat packers dealt with raw material—cattle, sheep, and hogs—which varied greatly in terms of size, weight, and quality. Sometimes they were able to construct a machine that could adjust to the size and shape of the animal. The hog scraper, patented in 1876, is an example. But this proved impossible for most other operations. "Even when dead," Siegfried Giedion observed, "the hog largely refuses to submit to the machine."[21]

The problem was the same on the cattle-killing floor. When a British economist toured American steel mills in 1903 he was particularly struck by "the very conspicuous absence of labourers in the American mills." In steelwork employers eliminated production bottlenecks "by replacing men with machines at every opportunity." An observer in the gallery above Swift's cattle-killing floor in the same year, however, was bound to be struck by the welter of human activity on the floor below. Studying productivity in the 1920s, U.S. Commissioner of Labor Ethelbert Stewart discovered that every process currently employed in the killing of cattle was still done by hand, much as it had been by farmers and small-town butchers before the coming of the modern packinghouse. There had been many changes since then in the way the work was organized, but these had all come in the handling of the meat and the division of labor. As late as the 1930s, a survey of 974 workers in five packing plants found that only 197 of them (20 percent) were machine operators or helpers. The rest all worked by hand.[22]

Meat packing became the first assembly-line industry precisely because the packers were not able to mechanize their production operations. This forced them to turn their attention to the division of labor. Here the packers made their most significant contribution to the development of mass-production work.

A kind of primitive assembly line had been introduced as early as the 1830s in Cincinnati's hog slaughterhouses. Harriet Martineau, touring these plants in 1837, was reminded of Adam Smith's classic illustration of the division of labor in a Birmingham pin factory. She marveled at how twenty men were able to slaughter and dress six hundred and twenty hogs in eight hours. The roots of what we now call assembly-line production can be traced to these early slaughterhouses. Hogs entered at the roof and then slid along on overhead rails, propelled by their own momentum and an occasional shove by laborers standing along the way. Sliding from one floor to another, they were "disassembled" as they moved.[23]

The important groundwork for mass production in pork packing, then, was already laid by the mid-nineteenth century, almost as soon as the industry began to concentrate in cities. Later changes came in the *extent* of the division of labor, in the mechanical conveyance of the carcass, and in minor improvements like the substitution of steel for wood in the construction of the overhead rails. The minute subdivision of the task and the rapid flow of the process are both captured in Upton Sinclair's description of hog slaughtering in Chicago just after the turn of the century.

> It was a long, narrow room, with a gallery along it for visitors. At the head there was a great iron wheel, about twenty feet in circumference, with rings here and there along its edge. Upon both sides of this wheel there was a narrow space, into which came the hogs at the end of their journey; in the midst of them stood a great burly Negro. . . . [The wheel] began slowly to revolve, and then the men upon each side of it sprang to work. They had chains which they fastened about the leg of the nearest hog, and the other end of the chain they hooked into one of the rings upon the wheel. So, as the wheel turned, a hog was suddenly jerked off his feet and borne aloft. . . . At the top of the wheel he was shunted off upon a trolley, and went sailing down the room. . . . One by one they hooked up the hogs, and one by one with a swift stroke they slit their throats. There was a long line of hogs, with squeals and life-

blood ebbing away together, until at last each started again, and
vanished with a splash into a huge vat of boiling water. . . . The
carcass hog was scooped out of the vat by machinery, and then it
fell to the second floor, passing on the way through a wonderful
machine with numerous scrapers, which adjusted themselves. . . .
It was then again strung up by machinery, and sent upon another
trolley ride; this time passing between two lines of men, who sat
upon a raised platform, each doing a certain single thing to the carcass as it came to him. One scraped the outside of the leg; another
scraped the inside of the same leg. One with a swift stroke cut the
throat; another with two swift strokes severed the head, which fell
to the floor and vanished through a hole. Another made a slit down
the body; a second opened the body wider; a third with a saw cut
the breastbone; a fourth loosened the entrails; a fifth pulled them
out. . . . There were men to scrape each side and men to scrape
the back; there were men to clean the carcass inside, to trim it and
wash it. Looking down this room, one saw . . . a line of dangling
hogs a hundred yards in length; and for every yard there was a
man, working as if a demon were after him. [24]

This description refers only to the handling of the hog carcass.
As the animal moved along the rail, intestines, fat, and other materials to be used in the manufacture of sausage and by-products
"vanished through a hole" and were conducted to the proper
work area via chute or pipe. In each of the by-product departments—lard refinery and tank room, pickling cellar, hide cellar,
canning room, and others—as well as in sausage making, the division of labor was comparable, though it was the more recently
developed by-product departments which employed the greatest
amount of machinery. [25]

Technological advances also quickened the pace on the cattle-
killing floor. At one time the stunned animal had simply fallen on
the ground, where it was "stuck" (for bleeding) and then labori-
ously dragged by three or four men and attached to a cross tie
high enough to allow its head to swing free. This often took more
than fifteen minutes. By the turn of the century, one "shackler"
could hoist seventy carcasses each minute, "simply clipping the
shackle around the hind foot, while steam power does the rest."
Once shackled, the animal was pushed along an overhead rail
which conveyed it from one group of workers to another. But in
addition to hoists, overhead rails, and endless chains, long

pointed poles called "pritchers" were also used to move the carcass *by hand* at various stages of the process. After 1908, some cattle-killing beds were equipped with moving dressing tables run on a conveyor system. Rather than being pushed by workers to the next operation, the carcass was conveyed automatically and the work was done as it moved by. Generally, however, cattle killing was even less adaptable to mechanization than hog slaughtering, and the result was greater emphasis on the division of labor.[26]

As late as the early 1880s in some houses, the entire slaughtering and cutting operation was frequently done by one man—the "all-round butcher"—with the aid of a young helper, often his son.[27] Up to this time, the journeyman butcher was still a craftsman, often earning twenty-five to thirty dollars or more per week. In the course of a workday, he could expect to handle a wide variety of animals in terms of size, weight, and quality of meat. He not only controlled the pace of work and conducted the whole slaughtering and cutting process; he also made all decisions about just how the cutting was to be done. But by the early 1880s, division of labor had allowed the packers to introduce a large number of unskilled workers, and this clearly undermined the butcher's power. By the mid-1880s many changes in the organization of work had already taken place, but the speedup on the killing floors seems to date from that period and was related to a change in the system of pay. As in the case of many other trades, these skilled butchers had been paid by output, with the "price" fluctuating between seventy-five cents and a dollar per head. This system ended in 1886, however, with the introduction of the eight-hour day and payment by the hour, "and since that time," a veteran concluded in 1903, "butchers have worked by the hour and been driven like slaves."[28]

By the turn of the century, the job was still done by hand, but the all-around butcher had been replaced by a killing gang of 157 men divided into 78 different "trades," each man performing the same minute operation a thousand times during a full workday. Bureau of Corporation investigators wondered at

the remarkable extent to which the division of labor is carried. In the old-fashioned small slaughterhouses one man, or at most a few men, performed all the tasks from the dealing of the death blow to the final preparation of the carcass for sale. In the largest slaughtering plants of today will be found hundreds, or even thousands, of workmen, each of whom performs a very small, narrowly defined task, in which by innumerable repetitions he becomes expert. [29]

"It would be difficult to imagine another industry where division of labor has been so ingeniously and microscopically worked out," the labor economist John R. Commons observed. "The animal has been surveyed and laid off like a map." [30]

The packers achieved three important and interrelated accomplishments through this subdivision of labor. First, by grossly reducing the amount and quality of skill required to do the job, they destroyed the control which the all-around butcher had exercised over the slaughtering and cutting processes. A few highly skilled positions remained, but these were very specialized. In fact, mass production created a new, more narrowly defined notion of skill. Splitting the backbone of a steer, for example, required great dexterity as well as strength, and only a few men could do the job. Thus, splitters and a few other trades earned high wages under the new system. Although these butcher aristocrats also enjoyed high status, however, even they had little, if any, control over the character or pace of the work. "There is no room for individuality or artistry in beef butchering," a management text explained. "The worker does not decide where or how to make his cut; he does not look at the animal and make an appropriate decision. All cuts are by the book; the instructions are very exact." [31] The creative dimension of cattle slaughtering—the planning and decision making exercised by the old all-around butcher—had been stripped away, appropriated by the packers, and embedded in the technology and organization of the assembly line. [32]

Technological innovations which facilitated the flow of production were prized largely because they strengthened this control. In 1908 the industry journal saw the introduction of the endless chain in hog slaughtering as a major breakthrough because it prevented the slowest worker from regulating the speed of the entire gang. When Armour introduced a conveyor system on their cattle-killing floor that year, the journal hailed the innovation as the harbinger of a new era in the industry. The emphasis, once again, was on speed and control. "Instead of the men going to the work," the journal explained, "the work comes to them. And they must keep steadily and accurately at work, for it keeps coming, and each man must complete his task in an appropriate time or confess himself incompetent for the job."[33] In the modern packinghouse, David Brody concludes, "Management, not the men, set the pace of work on the cutting line."[34]

This control, in turn, allowed the packers to increase production speed greatly. In hog slaughtering, the killing-floor foreman controlled the line with a lever. "If you need to turn out a little more," one superintendent confided, "you speed up the conveyors a little and the men speed up to keep pace."[35] The result was a striking intensification of work which affected the skilled butcher as much as the common laborer. Output for splitters, the most skilled men in cattle killing, increased by 100 percent within a decade. In 1884, five splitters had handled eight hundred cattle in the course of a ten-hour workday; by 1894 four of them were handling twelve hundred at a lower hourly rate. This meant an average of thirty animals per man-hour; by 1900, the average was up to thirty-five.[36] "They worked with a furious intensity," Sinclair observed of the cattle butchers, "literally upon the run."[37] It was this speedup more than any other aspect of the work which contributed to labor organization among the skilled workers.

Speed was maintained in a variety of ways. Some workers, perhaps ten in a gang of two hundred, were "steady time" men who were guaranteed a full six days' pay, regardless of how much they actually worked. Naturally, such positions were prized and, by fostering competition, they tended to divide the workers. Since retaining steady-time status depended upon one's speed and efficiency, the packers could cultivate "pacers" in each gang by awarding steady time to the fastest. These men were usually placed at critical points in the flow of production, and were thus in a position to set the pace for the rest of the gang.[38]

Perhaps the most direct method of maintaining speed was through close supervision by men with a vested interest in production. In the sausage department the superintendent received a bonus figured on the basis of profit. Companies cooperated, exchanging data on line speed and other factors. Daily, foremen faced the fact that their jobs depended on trimming a little more off the production costs, and an intense rivalry was set up—between houses within the same firm and among foremen within the same house. A retired foreman explained the system for journalist Ernest Poole. "In those [pre-union] days, if I could save 1/25th of a cent on the expense of killing each beef I knew that I would be preferred over other foremen. I was constantly trying to cut down wages in every possible way by driving bargains with separate men. The other foremen were doing the same. Some of them got a commission on all expenses they could save below a certain point."[39]

Finally, the transformation of work produced a thorough recomposition of the labor market. The small group of remaining butcher aristocrats was dwarfed by an army of common laborers who made up two-thirds of the industry's labor force by the turn of the century. These unskilled workers were paid a common labor rate, which fluctuated with the supply of labor and general economic conditions.[40] When the size of this group and the narrow margin within which the packers operated are considered, the critical importance of maintaining a low common labor wage rate becomes clear. Squeezed between a low margin and a large payroll, the packers were always under pressure to keep labor costs down. In addition to maximizing production speed, they also reduced costs through a system of casual hiring.

Reorganization of work meant not only a deskilling of occupations but also irregular employment. Without the "artificial" pressure of unions, the packers could employ their workers flexibly, taking men and women on for a week, a day, or even for a few hours. When they were no longer needed, the workers were sent home. A great advantage of Chicago over country towns, an industry journal explained, is the availability at Union Stockyards of "all the labor you want for which you pay by the hour, and only use the labor as long as necessary."[41]

Packinghouse work was casual in two ways. Like many other industries of the era, packing was seasonal, though the severity of its seasonal fluctuations was greater than that in many other industries. While refrigeration reduced its impact somewhat, a slack season of two or three months settled in every summer, and with it came layoffs. Short-term lapses in consumer demand at various points throughout the year could also bring idleness. Whenever cattle shipments or the demand for meat products fell off, those on the lower rungs of the job ladder were thrown out of work, while some of the more skilled took laborers' jobs at the lower wage rate in order to keep their places. Thus both skilled and unskilled suffered under the system.

The problem was more severe in some departments than in others. At the turn of the century, for example, time lost in one of the largest plants varied from a low of five weeks in the sausage department to a high of nearly twelve weeks in the pickling cellar, where the cheapest cuts of meat were soaked in brine. Although some companies, notably Swift, experimented with guaranteed time schemes designed to reduce the effects of seasonality, these did not apply to many common laborers. Throughout the period up to the twenties, the problem persisted and perhaps even worsened. There were probably as many workers affected by seasonality in the twenties as had been the case at the turn of the century.[42]

But even during the busy season, packinghouse employment was unreliable. Working hours varied considerably during the week because the packers organized the workday in relation to the size and timing of cattle shipments. Killing gangs and workers in many other departments reported early in the morning and hung around until they could find out how much work there would be for the day. They were called to work as the batches of animals entered the pens, but the actual workday did not begin until the animals were ready for the slaughter, which might not be until much later in the morning. Then the gang was driven hard until the slaughtering and dressing were done. On a Monday or Tuesday, when most cattle arrived in the yards, quitting time might be 10:00 P.M. or even midnight. On a Friday, when shipments were light, it might be noon. Butcher workmen were paid only for the hours they actually worked, excluding time lost for mechanical breakdowns; and they worked only when they were needed. As of 1910, average pay for all workers in cattle-killing gangs was about eight dollars per week. Laborers, of course, averaged much less—about six or seven dollars for three full and two or three "broken" days (thirty-five to forty hours) per week. Laborers' families could not rely on even this amount, however, because of the casual hiring system. As economist John C. Kennedy told the Commission on Industrial Relations, "A man never knows if he is hired for an hour or a week."[43]

Even skilled workers had to report by seven in the morning to have a chance for work, but many common laborers were hired on a short-term basis. The foreman or a yards policeman would simply go out to the gate and choose the required number of laborers from among those who looked strongest. A young Lithuanian laborer described one of his early experiences with the casual hiring system.

> Men and women were walking in by thousands as far as we could see. There was a crowd of about 200 men waiting there for a job. They looked hungry and kept watching the door. At last a special policeman came out and began pointing to men, one by one. Each one jumped forward. Twenty-three were taken. Then they all went inside, and all the others turned their faces away and looked tired. I remember one boy sat down and cried, just next to me, on a pile of boards. Some policemen waved their clubs and we walked on.[44]

The lucky men received numbered brass checks which were deposited at the end of the workday and picked up again each morning for as long as they remained employed. Estimates suggest that from one-fifth to one-third of the industry's workers were casual laborers hired in this way.[45]

The key to the system and the low wage rate was the crowd of unemployed who gathered each morning outside the yards' gates and the employment offices of the various firms. The hiring of common labor was strictly a supply and demand proposition. "They will be glad to take 15 cents an hour," one superintendent reasoned. "Why should we pay more than we have to?"[46] Although the crowds at the gates were greatest during periods of high unemployment, some two hundred to one thousand people were always outside. Thus, wages and working conditions were affected as much by "the man at the gate" as by what was happening inside the packinghouses.[47]

But the packers' control derived not only from the new technology and work processes. It rested also on a social transformation of their labor force. The development of mass-production work required massive recruitment of unskilled labor and resulted in a racial, ethnic, and gender diversity which became characteristic of many American industries during the early twentieth century. It is to a profile of the butcher workmen and -women that we now turn.

NOTES

1. Charles Edward Russell, *The Greatest Trust in the World* (New York, 1905) is the classic muckraking exposé of the industry's monopoly character. For a revisionist account, see Gabriel Kolko, *The Triumph of Conservatism: A Reinterpretation of American History, 1900–1915* (New York, 1967). See also Mary Yeager, *Competition and Regulation: The Development of Oligopoly in the Meat Packing Industry* (Greenwich, Conn., 1981); Alfred Chandler, "The Origins of Big Business in American Industry," *Business History Review* 33 (Spring 1959): 1–31. Louis Galambos, *The Public Image of Big Business in America* (Baltimore, 1975), demonstrates the link between the packers' public image and antimonopolism among a wide range of social groups over several decades.

2. Yeager, 5–18; Illinois Bureau of Labor Statistics, *Third Biennial Report* (Springfield, 1884), 19–20. See also Margaret Walsh, *The Rise of the Midwestern Meat Packing Industry* (Lexington, Ky., 1982).

3. Yeager, 58–64; Chandler, "The Origins of Big Business," 6–7, and *The Visible Hand: The Managerial Revolution in American Business* (Cambridge, Mass., 1977), 299–301. On the first generation of meat-packing entrepreneurs, see Frederick Cople Jaher, *The Urban Establishment: Upper Strata in Boston, New York, Charleston, Chicago, and Los Angeles* (Urbana, Ill., 1982), 476–77, 482–83, 491, 498–99; and Jocelyn M. Ghent and Frederick C. Jaher, "The Chicago Business Elite, 1830–1930: A Collective Biography," *Business History Review* 50 (Autumn 1976): 288–328.

4. Chandler, *The Visible Hand*, 299–301; U.S. Bureau of Corporations, *Report of the Commissioner of Corporations on the Beef Industry* (Washington, D.C., 1905), 21–24.

5. Yeager, chap. 3; Alfred Chandler, *Strategy and Structure* (Cambridge, Mass., 1962), 25–27, 40; L.D.H. Weld, "The Packing Industry: Its History and General Economics," in *The Packing Industry*, ed. Institute of American Meat Packers (Chicago, 1924), 79–81. See also Chandler, *The Visible Hand*, 392–400.

6. Kolko, *The Triumph of Conservatism*, 51–53; Richard Arnould, "Changing Patterns of Concentration in American Meat Packing, 1880–1963," *Business History Review* 45 (Spring 1971), 23–24; U.S. Senate, Select Committee on the Transportation and Sale of Meat Products, *Report and Testimony*, 51st Cong., 2d sess., 1–2, 6, 12–13; David Brody,

The Butcher Workmen: A Study of Unionization (Cambridge, Mass., 1964), 3; Louis F. Swift, *The Yankee of the Yards* (London, 1927), 209. See also Dorothy Einbecker, "Investigations of Chicago Packing House Combinations, 1898–1906" (M.A. thesis, University of Chicago, 1943), 29–32 and passim.

7. Federal Trade Commission, *Report on the Meat Packing Industry, Summary and Part 1* (Washington, D.C., 1919), 121–23, 128–29. (Hereafter FTC, *Summary and Part 1*.)

8. Federal Trade Commission, *Summary of Report on the Meat Packing Industry* (Washington, D.C., 1918), 16–18; Arnould, 21.

9. Arnould, 10.

10. U.S. Senate, Select Committee on the Transportation and Sale of Meat Products, *Report and Testimony*, 31–32; Bureau of Corporations, *Report on the Beef Industry*, 66; Rudolf Clemen, *The American Livestock and Meat Industry* (New York, 1923), chap. 13, especially 281–82 and graph, 291.

11. FTC, *Summary and Part 1*, 12, 33–35, 164, 168, 174–77, 185–99. In *The Triumph of Conservatism*, Kolko stresses the importance of this developing trade in the efforts of the major packers to secure federal meat inspection (98–108).

12. Armour and Co., *Souvenir* (Chicago, 1893), n.p.

13. J. Paul Goode, *The Geographic Background of Chicago* (Chicago, 1926), 41–49; Bessie L. Pierce, *The History of Chicago* (New York, 1957), 2:108–11, 119–21; *Twelfth U.S. Census, 1900, Manufactures, Part 2* (Washington, D.C., 1902), 184–85; *Thirteenth U.S. Census, 1910, Manufactures* (Washington, D.C., 1923), 364; John C. Kennedy et al., *Wages and Family Budgets in the Chicago Stockyards District* (Chicago, 1914), 2–3; Mary Yeager Kujovich, "The Refrigerator Car and the Growth of the American Dressed Beef Industry," *Business History Review* 44 (Winter 1970): 460–82.

14. Charles J. Bushnell, *The Social Problem at the Chicago Stockyards* (Chicago, 1902), 7; Amalgamated Meat Cutters and Butcher Workmen of North America, *Official Journal* 5 (Oct. 1903): 6–8.

15. Weld, 75–76, 91–95.

16. Bureau of Corporations, *Report on the Beef Industry*, 60.

17. *National Provisioner* 66 (Feb. 18, 1922): 20; E. A. Cudahy, Jr., "Financing the Packing Industry," in *The Packing Industry*, 205.

18. Henry Ford acknowledged in his autobiography that he derived his own ideas about assembly-line manufacture from watching the slaughtering process in a Chicago packinghouse. See Henry Ford, *My Life and Work* (Garden City, N.Y., 1923), 81.

19. Solomon Fabricant, *The Output of Manufacturing Industries, 1899–1937* (New York, 1940), 131.

20. Elliot Brownlee, *The Dynamics of Ascent: A History of the American Economy* (New York, 1977), chap. 8; Thomas C. Cochran, *The American Business System: An Historical Perspective, 1900–1950* (New York, 1967), chap. 2; "Productivity of Labor in Slaughtering and Meat Packing and in Petroleum Refining," *Monthly Labor Review* 13 (Nov. 1926): 30–34; Solomon Fabricant, *Employment in Manufacturing, 1899–1939* (New York, 1942), 83–85, 90–91, 99; John Kendrick, *Productivity Trends in the U.S.* (Princeton, N.J., 1961), 162. See also *National Provisioner* 68 (Mar. 10, 1923): 27.

21. "Productivity of Labor," 31; Arthur Cushman, "The Packing Plant and Its Equipment," in *The Packing Industry*, 108–11, 122–23; Siegfried Giedion, *Mechanization Takes Command: A Contribution to Anonymous History* (New York, 1948), 93–94, 224. See also *National Provisioner* 126 (Jan. 26, 1952): 236, and 68 (Mar. 10, 1923): 27.

22. Frank Popplewell, *Some Modern Conditions and Recent Developments in Iron and Steel Production in America* (Manchester, 1906), 103, quoted in Katherine Stone, "The Origins of Job Structures in the Steel Industry," *Radical America* 7 (1973): 29; Ethelbert Stewart, "Labor Productivity in Slaughtering," *Monthly Labor Review* 18 (Mar. 1924): 14–21; Harry Jerome, *Mechanization in Industry* (New York, 1934), 116–17. For an excellent description of the scene as it might have appeared to a contemporary visitor, see Upton Sinclair, *The Jungle*, with introduction and notes by James R. Barrett (Urbana, Ill., 1987).

23. Giedion, 43–45, 217–18, illustrations on 89, 97, and 217; Clemen, 122.

24. Sinclair, *The Jungle;* Oscar Mayer, "Pork Operations," in *The Packing Industry*, 179–84. For a detailed description of each job in the hog-killing and cutting process in 1917, see U.S. Department of Labor, Bulletin no. 252 (Washington, D.C., 1919), 1075–114, which provides the same detail for other departments of a packing plant as well. Comparing this with virtually identical descriptions for 1927 (U.S. Department of Labor, Bulletin no. 472 [Washington, D.C., 1929], 131–63) suggests how little the work had changed after the turn of the century. See also Frederick W. Wilder, *The Modern Packing House* (Chicago, 1921), 251–65, and the vivid description in Rudyard Kipling, *American Notes: Rudyard Kipling's West* (London, 1891; reprint, Norman, Okla., 1981), 145–48.

25. For detailed descriptions of this work, see U.S. Department of Labor, Bulletin no. 472, 142–46. See also U.S. Employment Service,

Descriptions of Occupations: Slaughtering and Meat Packing (Washington, D.C., 1918).

26. Stewart, 15; Wilder, 92–105, and for pritching sticks, 97; *National Provisioner* 39 (Dec. 5, 1908):18–20, 22.

27. Stewart, 15; Bureau of Corporations, *Report on the Beef Industry*, 17.

28. *Official Journal* 2 (Mar. 1901): 8; 2 (May 1901): 11. See also the reminiscences of another veteran butcher workman, Neil Carbray, in *National Provisioner* 65 (Aug. 27, 1921): 41, (Sept. 20, 1921): 41, and (Oct. 1, 1921): 41. While the workday reverted to ten hours later the same year, payment by the hour remained. (See chapter 4.)

29. U.S. Department of Labor, Bulletin no. 252; Bureau of Corporations, *Report on the Beef Industry*, 17–18.

30. John R. Commons, "Labor Conditions in Slaughtering and Meat Packing," in *Trade Unionism and Labor Problems*, ed. John R. Commons (Boston, 1905), 224.

31. Paul Aldrich, ed., *The Packers' Encyclopedia* (Chicago, 1922), 20, quoted in James R. Grossman, "A Dream Deferred: Black Migration to Chicago, 1916–1921" (Ph.D. diss., University of California, Berkeley, 1982), 254.

32. David Montgomery, "Workers' Control of Machine Production in the Nineteenth Century," in his *Workers' Control in America: Studies in the History of Work, Technology, and Labor Struggles* (New York and London, 1979); Benson Soffer, "A Theory of Trade Union Development: The Role of the Autonomous Workman," *Labor History* 1 (Spring 1960): 141–63.

33. *National Provisioner* 39 (Oct. 17, 1908, and Dec. 5, 1908). See also Mayer, 180, 184–5.

34. Brody, 5.

35. *National Provisioner*, Nov. 17, 1900, 17, quoted ibid.

36. Stewart, 15; Commons, 227. See also *Chicago Socialist*, July 30, 1904.

37. Sinclair, *The Jungle*.

38. Commons, 227, 236.

39. Alma Herbst, *The Negro in the Slaughtering and Meat Packing Industry in Chicago* (Boston, 1932), 7; *National Provisioner* 66 (Jan. 14, 1922): 28; Charles J. Bushnell, "Some Social Aspects of the Chicago Stock Yards," part 1, *American Journal of Sociology* 7 (1901): 165–67; *Official Journal* 5 (Aug. 1904): 17; Ernest Poole, "The Meat Strike," *The Independent* 57 (July 28, 1904): 181.

40. Commons, 243, 245–46.

41. *National Provisioner*, Mar. 10, 1894, 16, quoted in Brody, 5.

42. Charles J. Bushnell, "Some Social Aspects of the Chicago Stockyards," part 3, *American Journal of Sociology* 7 (1902): 458; U.S. Commission on Industrial Relations, *Final Report and Testimony*, vol. 4 (Washington, D.C., 1916), 3467; Clemen, 707; Herbst, 111.

43. Clemen, 608–9, 71–81; Kennedy et al., 9–19; Commission on Industrial Relations, *Final Report*, 4:3513–14.

44. Antanas Kaztauskis, "From Lithuania to the Chicago Stockyards—An Autobiography," *Independent* 57 (Aug. 4, 1904), 241–48. Although the journalist Ernest Poole published this piece as a legitimate autobiography, he later admitted that there was no Antanas Kaztauskis and that the piece was a composite of various characters. Because Poole based the piece on six weeks' research in the community and on extensive interviews, I have accepted it as representative of the experiences of such an immigrant laborer. (See Ernest Poole, *The Bridge: My Own Story* [New York, 1940], 95.) Antanas Kaztauskis's story is reprinted in *Plain Folk: The Life Stories of Undistinguished Americans*, ed. David M. Katzman and William M. Tuttle, Jr. (Urbana, Ill., 1982); quotation on p. 109.

45. On the casual hiring system at the Union Stockyards, see Charles J. Bushnell, *Social Problem at the Stockyards* (Chicago, 1902), 26–27; and Commission on Industrial Relations, *Final Report*, 4:3463–64. For varying estimates on the number of casual laborers in the work force over time, see Commons, 243, 245; U.S. Immigration Commission, *Reports*, part 11, *Immigrants in Industry*, vol. 13, *Slaughtering and Meat Packing* (Washington, D.C., 1911), 229; and Commission on Industrial Relations, *Final Report*, 4:3504–5, 3510. Women were also employed irregularly, but they did not stand out in front of the packinghouses, perhaps because this was considered degrading. Women were most often referred by friends or relatives already employed.

46. Quoted in Poole, 180.

47. Commission on Industrial Relations, *Final Report*, 4:3463.

2

The Packinghouse Workers

Afterward, as cheaper labor had come, these Germans had moved away. The next were the Irish—there had been six or eight years when Packingtown had been a regular Irish city. . . . The Bohemians had come then, and after them the Poles. . . . The Poles, who had come by tens of thousands, had been driven to the wall by the Lithuanians, and now the Lithuanians were giving way to the Slovaks. Who there was poorer and more miserable than the Slovaks, Grandmother Majauszkiene had no idea, but the packers would find them, never fear.

Upton Sinclair, *The Jungle*

The advent of mass-production methods, as in packing, was characteristic of many industries in the United States during the first two decades of the twentieth century. As they reorganized production processes, employers also restructured labor markets, drawing their workers from a much wider social and geographic spectrum than they had in the nineteenth century.

As a result, the American working-class population was transformed and workers as a social group were probably more heterogeneous during this era than at any other time in the nation's history. An earlier generation of "old immigrant" and native-born workers remained dominant in most skilled occupations, but the "new immigrants"—largely unskilled farmers and farm laborers from southern and southeastern Europe—were rapidly displacing them from the ranks of common laborers and machine tenders.

Although the number of women entering the manufacturing sector leveled off after the turn of the century, they entered clerical and retail positions in increasingly large numbers, and thus their overall proportion in the wage-earning population continued to rise. Finally, blacks secured positions in many manufacturing industries for the first time during World War I, as a result of war production and the shortage of immigrant labor. Racial diversity grew, considerably complicating the process of class formation.[1] While the heterogeneity of the American working class may not make its history unique, such complexity undoubtedly shaped the experience of American workers in profound ways.

Nowhere was such diversity greater than in Chicago's Union Stockyards and the surrounding slaughtering and meat-packing plants. The most sweeping effects of the reorganization of packinghouse work can be seen in the emergence of an international labor market which drew a succession of migrant peoples from around the world into Chicago's slaughterhouses. When Immigration Commission investigators studied the industry in 1908-9, they found more than forty nationalities represented. The work force was demographically diverse not only in terms of ethnicity but also in terms of race, age, gender, and work experience. Mixed in with older, skilled Irish and German butchers were thousands of young, recently arrived eastern European peasants and laborers. These butcher workmen were joined by an increasingly large proportion of women. Thousands of black migrants from the South arrived during the war, making the packing industry one of the most important employers of black labor in U.S. manufacturing.

The economic functions of this migration are important. The expanding market for meat products, together with the labor-intensive character of the work process, forced the packers to secure new sources of labor. The flood of immigrants and black migrants into the labor force as common laborers and machine tenders provided the packers with enough workers to keep up with the expanding market, while stabilizing labor costs at the lowest possible level.

The social implications of this diversification of the packinghouse labor market, however, are equally significant. The labor force that evolved exemplifies the complexity of working-class formation in the United States during this era. The skill divisions inherent in the mass-production process between common laborers and the more skilled "knife men" were compounded by the social and cultural differences among the successive groups that entered the labor force—black and white, male and female, old immigrant and new.[2]

For this reason, it is difficult to provide a composite sketch of the "typical" packinghouse worker of the early twentieth century. Drawn from throughout Europe and North America, the butcher workmen and -women exhibited a striking diversity of experiences. Even among the new immigrants from eastern Europe there were important differences in terms of prior work, marital status, age, and time of arrival. These demographic factors as well as the objective differences in work experience among common laborers, machine tenders, and skilled butchers provided the context for social relations among the workers themselves and influenced the character of class relations in the industry.

Yet the same forces which created such a socially diverse labor pool also provided considerable common ground among the packinghouse workers. The nature of the work process and employment practices in packing not only produced shared grievances and goals among people from various social backgrounds but also brought them into close contact with one another. This contact facilitated the acculturation of newer groups and enhanced class solidarity.

THE BUTCHER ARISTOCRACY

If we could walk through a large Chicago packinghouse of 1909 and talk to the butcher workmen and -women as they went about their work, the Germans and the Irish and their offspring would probably impress us as the most "American."[3] About three-fourths of the Irish and about two-thirds of the Germans still in the industry at that time had come to the United States in the 1880s or earlier. Most of the Irish had been small farmers or agricultural laborers in Ireland, though a few had been artisans or industrial workers of some kind. The Germans had considerably more industrial work experience than the Irish at the time of their arrival. A few even had slaughterhouse experience and about one

Table 2. Nationality of Employees in the Slaughtering and
Meat-packing Industry of Chicago, 1909 and 1928

	1909 (N = 15,489)	1928 (N = 13,194)
Native-born:	*Proportion*	*Proportion*
White	18.9	27.3
Black	3.0	29.5
Foreign-born:		
Bohemian and Slovak*	10.0	4.2
German	10.4	2.9
Irish	7.5	3.0
Lithuanian	12.0	7.8
Mexican	—	5.7
Polish	27.7	11.9
Russian	2.9	2.9
Other	7.6	4.8
TOTAL	100.0	100.0

*Includes "Austrian" and "Czechoslovakian"

Sources: Data for 1909 were taken from the U.S. Immigration Commission,
Reports, part 11, *Immigrants in Industry*, vol. 13, *Slaughtering and Meat Packing*
(Washington, D.C.: GPO, 1911), 204. The 1928 data are from Paul S. Taylor,
Mexican Labor in the United States: The Calumet Region (Berkeley: Univ. of
California Press, 1930), 40.

in four had been an artisan or factory operative. Still, perhaps
one-third of them had also been involved in agricultural work.
Few from either group had come to Chicago after 1900.[4] Whatever problems they had experienced in adjusting to the rigors of
packinghouse work were only a dull memory for most of them by
the early twentieth century.

Most of these Irish and German butchers were older married
men; about half were forty-five or older and very few were under
thirty. Practically all husbands in both groups had either brought
their wives with them or married in the United States. By 1909
more than a third of the Germans and over half of the Irish owned
their own homes in the region of the stockyards or, increasingly,
in more desirable neighboring communities. German butchers
lived among their Irish coworkers and fraternized with them.
Though their own ethnic culture continued to flourish, nearly all
German packinghouse workers spoke English. By the turn of the

century, then, the Irish and Germans were the most experienced, stable, and homogeneous portion of the work force. Many had worked their way into the skilled knife jobs, planted roots in one or another working-class neighborhood, and raised families. Clearly, they were the veterans, the "first generation," in the industry.[5]

The Bohemians stood between these "old immigrants" and the new ones coming from eastern Europe in terms of age, work experience, and time of arrival in the United States. Bohemians began entering the industry around 1880, when the Irish and Germans were already entrenched. By 1900 about 40 percent had been in the United States for more than twenty years. Unlike the German and Irish immigration, however, which had virtually ended by the turn of the century, the flow of Bohemians continued after 1900, mixing with that of the other eastern European groups. About 20 percent of those Bohemians studied by the U.S. Immigration Commission had been in the country for less than five years in 1909 and almost 40 percent had come since 1900. Like most immigrants, Bohemians stayed home during the depression of the 1890s; otherwise they came into the industry constantly from the 1880s through the early years of this century.[6]

Of all the eastern Europeans, the Bohemians had the most varied Old World work experience. Coming from the more industrialized region of what is today Czechoslovakia, only about one-third had been farmers or farm laborers, and over 20 percent had worked as artisans or operatives. Only the Bohemians, of all major ethnic groups in the industry, had much experience in slaughterhouses before entering Chicago's. Almost one in five had been a butcher workman in Bohemia or elsewhere before coming to take up the trade in the Midwest.[7]

Bohemians tended to be a bit younger than the Germans and Irish. Less than a third were over forty-five and nearly as many were under thirty. Many of the younger men who had recently arrived in the country were single, but most Bohemians were married men who had settled in with their families and often owned their own homes. Although nearly all second-generation Bohemian workers in the Immigration Commission study spoke English, many of the immigrants did not. The language barrier encountered by some Bohemians may have isolated them from Irish butchers, though many could probably get by in German. Almost two-thirds of the Bohemian workers were fully naturalized, though a minority of 16 percent had not even taken out second papers in the naturalization process. All of this suggests an ethnic community which was somewhat mixed in terms of age, occupational background, and adjustment to American urban society. Most Bohemians, however, were well established and shared a wealth of work and community experience and grievances with the older groups.[8]

Most of these older immigrants were skilled "knife men." Despite all the advantages that the rationalized work process offered the packers, the complicated character of slaughtering required the use of some skilled workers. Among the one-third of those considered skilled, management erected an elaborate job hierarchy. Each of the seventy-eight "occupations" in a cattle-killing gang had its own wage rate. Promotion from one grade to another was not done in any systematic fashion, and there were many claims of corruption and favoritism. But the significant point is that, on the surface at least, the butcher workmen and -women were divided up on the basis of status and wages.[9]

Most of the more skilled men worked in the actual slaughtering and cutting operations, though even in these departments their proportion was shrinking. Commons found in 1905 that in a cattle-killing gang of 230 men, 139 were common laborers paid from fifteen to eighteen cents an hour. Of the remaining 98 men, only 11—7 floormen and 4 splitters—were paid the top rate of fifty cents an hour, while the average for the gang as a whole was twenty-one cents, just a few cents above the common labor rate. The work of the splitters and floormen was the most intricate on the killing floor. As a result, they became the aristocrats of the industry. One generally recognized division between "butchers' work" and common labor was use of the knife. Most of the men holding knife jobs were drawn from the older ethnic groups— Irish, Germans, and, increasingly in the course of the early twentieth century, Bohemians.[10]

Alma Herbst has described how in one sense modernization of the work process actually enhanced the status of the most skilled men.

For those whose natural aptitudes lay in the direction of dexterity with the knife, division of labor facilitated the development of greater skill. Their technique became localized and concentrated. The most efficient cattle butchers in the world lived in the community. A prerogative of family groups, though changing with successive immigrant waves, the tradition was passed on from father to son. An aristocracy was created.[11]

Admittedly, the whole concept of skill had changed. The "all-round butcher" had given way to the specialized "knife man," and in the process much of the intellectual component inherent in old-fashioned butchering had been lost. Repeating the same task hundreds of times each day at extreme speed and under constant supervision was undoubtedly alienating work. But by virtue of their pay, craft solidarity, traditions of organization, and other considerations, the most skilled men indeed came close to the classical conception of a "labor aristocracy."

George Schick's career was probably comparable to that of many other German and Irish butchers. After emigrating to the United States from Germany with his family, he started work at the age of thirteen in Farmer House, one of several small packinghouses in Chicago at the time. He dressed his first bullock at the age of fifteen in 1876, and in the late 1870s went to work for Swift, where he was earning twenty-seven dollars a week in 1881. But Schick became involved in the great eight-hour strike of 1886, joined the Knights of Labor, and was fired after the organization's decline. By the turn of the century, he had worked in all of the city's major houses and had three brothers who were also butchers.[12]

Some occupations were dominated by a single ethnic group. Livestock handlers, for example, were Irish Catholic almost to a man and most were drawn from the same parish—St. Gabriel's, just east of the yards. Sausagemaking was the traditional preserve of aging German butchers, too old to keep up with the pace of the killing floor, but this control broke down during an unsuccessful strike in 1903. Such ethnic continuity suggests that neighborhood and kinship ties may have been important in hiring and promotion.[13]

Work groups in most departments, however, were quite mixed ethnically. Here packing differed markedly from the situation in steel. Many of the departments in a steel plant were dominated by one ethnic group or another, so that workers from various social backgrounds were often physically isolated from one another. In addition, the process of steel making tended to divide skilled from unskilled, with laborers toiling on furnaces or in the yards and skilled men in the rolling mills. Steelworkers were not only socially diverse; they were literally separated from one another. The lack of contact and shared experiences and grievances at work reinforced cultural divisions within the laboring populations of mill towns and contributed to a bitter hostility between old immigrant and native-born skilled workers on the one hand and Slavic laborers on the other.[14]

Cattle butchers held on tenaciously to their craft pride. They still owned and cared for their tools well after 1900 and floral pieces at a butcher's funeral were apt to be made in the shape of these cutting tools. Long after the decline of the all-around butcher, cattle-dressing contests were a common form of entertainment. Here one house (or, after unionization, one local) pitted its fastest man against another's. Even in the modern packinghouse, then, there was room for a "fellowship of the knife" among the small group of skilled workers who remained in the industry.[15]

Yet one of the peculiar aspects of the packinghouse job hierarchy was the ease with which seemingly rigid divisions between jobs melted away when they became obstacles to controlling production costs. The "go-between," an essential element within the job structure, illustrates this fluid quality. The go-between divided his time between a lower-wage job and one of the more skilled positions, providing the packer with a number of crucial advantages. By allowing the foreman to fill in with go-betweens in the event of absenteeism, rather than hire full-time skilled men, the system directly reduced costs. In the meantime, the less skilled man learned the job "above" him and was available as a replacement for the skilled butchers, whose organizational strength was thereby reduced. One management text explained how the go-between system could be used to cultivate a certain number of men who could be used to fill in on any job. These new all-around men, however, unlike their nineteenth-century counterparts, were essential elements in the extensive division of labor rather than impediments to it. In addition to minimizing production costs, the go-between system also reminded the knife men that many of their new, more specialized skills were rather easily acquired. In this way as well, their fate was tied to that of the common laborers who toiled alongside them. The go-between strategy was clearly a threat to the skilled men, but its significance also lies in what it meant for those at the other end of the job ladder. Filling in on more skilled work not only offered the un-skilled worker a chance to earn extra money; it also represented a bridge from one job to another.[16]

THE NEW IMMIGRANTS

By the first decade of the twentieth century, common laborers represented at least two-thirds of the industry's workforce. Their wages ranged from fifteen cents an hour at the turn of the century to eighteen and a half cents at the height of the union's power in 1904 and back down to sixteen and a half cents from 1904 until the First World War. At this point, wartime inflation, unioniza-tion, and labor shortages combined to bring substantial increases for the first time. The proportion of common laborers varied from one department to another. In by-product manufacturing it was often much higher than in the killing gangs. In 1905, 95 percent of all oleo and glue workers earned less than twenty cents an hour. But even in killing gangs and in the various cutting depart-ments most workers were laborers. In beginning to understand the conditions faced by these workers, it is important to remember that they suffered not only from relatively low wages but also from chronic job insecurity. Many were casual laborers.[17]

After the turn of the century, most of the people standing out-side of the packing plants were recent immigrants from eastern Europe. Streaming into the common labor market in the years preceding the First World War, scrambling for any jobs they could find on the killing floor, in the cutting rooms, or even in the hide cellars and fertilizer plants, they assured the packers of an ade-quate supply of strong arms and backs and kept the common la-bor rate depressed. How did these new immigrants compare to those who had preceded them into the industry?

Poles entered the industry in large numbers for the first time after a strike and riot in 1894, and by 1905 they were the largest foreign-born group in the labor force. By 1909 a small group of Polish workers had been in the country since the turn of the century, but the vast majority had come since then, about half after 1904. There were a few artisans and industrial workers among them, but over half had been small farmers or farm laborers and many of the others had been general laborers of some kind. [18]

The Poles were much younger than the earlier immigrants, over half under thirty and two-thirds under thirty-five. Fewer were family men and many husbands had left their wives and families in the old country. Almost 60 percent of the under-thirty group and more than a third of the total number studied by the Immigration Commission were single. The fact that the earliest Polish immigrants had arrived in the late nineteenth century meant that many Poles could speak English, and the most recent arrivals could learn from those who had worked in the industry for a while. By 1909, almost two-thirds of the Polish packinghouse workers could speak English, a proportion as high as that of the more established Bohemian butchers. [19]

All of the characteristics which made the Poles different from earlier immigrant groups—their youth, mobility, and newness to the urban environment and mass-production work—were even more pronounced in the case of the Slovaks and Lithuanians. Like the Poles, the vast majority of these immigrants came after the turn of the century, but even fewer had lived in the United States longer than nine years. About three-fourths of all Lithuanians and Slovaks had been farmers or farm laborers, a proportion considerably higher than that of the Poles, and few of them had industrial work experience. Although they were generally around the same age as the Poles, there were fewer middle-aged men among the Slovaks and Lithuanians. [20]

By contrast even to the other Slavic groups, the Lithuanians were relatively unattached. The overwhelming majority of those under thirty (more than half of the total group) and almost two-thirds of those between thirty and forty-five were single. A third of the husbands had left their families in the old world. Of the fourteen major ethnic groups in the industry, only the Russians had proportionally more husbands living alone. The youthful and unattached character of the Lithuanians suggests mobility, or at least an unsettled quality, though even they were not rootless. [21]

Lithuanians and Slovaks were comparable, however, in terms of the language barrier which divided many of them from their fellow workers; nearly half of those in each group were not able to speak English.[22] The implications of this problem for social relations among workers in the plants and community can only be imagined, but certainly shop-floor conversations between these recent immigrants and the more "Americanized" Irish, Germans, and Bohemians must have been problematic. On the other hand, since one of every two Slovak or Lithuanian laborers and an even higher proportion of Poles did speak English, presumably these more articulate workers acted as interpreters, linguistic and cultural bridges, between the older and the newer immigrants.

Within all this diversity we can discern some general characteristics of the Slavic immigrants as a group. Most were young and had only been in the United States a few years by 1909. Some had picked up a variety of work experience in the regions from which they came or along the way to this country, but most had spent their working lives as farmers or agricultural laborers and were facing large mass-production factories for the first time. The longer they stayed here, the more likely they were to send for their families, and, as in the case of steel and probably other industries as well, this move tended to stabilize them, to plant them more firmly in the community and the industry.[23]

The most important bond among all the eastern European immigrant groups was the situation facing the common laborer in the meat-packing industry, for the vast majority of Poles, Lithuanians, and Slovaks worked at unskilled jobs and earned the common labor rate. Average wage rates for all of these groups were remarkably similar in 1909. While about 80 percent of the Irish, German, and Bohemian butchers earned more than seventeen and a half cents an hour, the corresponding proportion was less than 50 percent for Poles, Lithuanians, and Russians, and just over 50 percent for Slovaks. While native-born whites averaged between $2.20 and $2.30 per day, and the small group of settled blacks $2.07, the average daily rate for Polish and Lithuanian laborers was $1.79.[24]

Wage rates for ethnic groups at various stages in their work lives suggest that advancement was also slower for the newer immigrants. About one-fourth to one-third of the Irish and the Germans who had been in the United States less than five years at the time of the Immigration Commission study in 1909 already earned more than the common labor rate, but among both Poles and Lithuanians who had arrived around the same time more than two-thirds were still common laborers. Even the seasoned workers among the newer immigrants tended to remain in the common labor ranks. Of 1,692 Polish and Lithuanian workers who came to this country between 1900 and 1905, about 40 percent were still earning the common labor rate in 1909, whereas three-fourths of the Germans and Bohemians and over 80 percent of the Irish who had arrived in the same period had already begun to climb toward the more skilled knife jobs. The Bohemians rose most quickly and were disproportionately represented among the skilled. The Irish were something of an anomaly. Although well represented among the skilled because of their long tenure in the industry, they also contributed fairly large numbers of older immigrants to the common labor pool. These veterans were left to toil alongside the new Slavic immigrants in the ranks of the unskilled. The contact which this suggests between older, more experienced Irish workers and younger recent immigrants was important in the process of acculturation and socialization that led to labor organizing.[25]

The contrast in conditions between the older and more recent immigrants can also be analyzed in terms of regularity of employment. While about two-thirds of the German and Irish household heads surveyed by the Immigration Commission worked a full twelve months of the year, the figure for Poles and Slovaks was less than half.[26]

THE BLACK MIGRANTS

A few black workers were in Chicago's packing plants as early as 1880, but blacks did not enter the industry in any significant numbers until after the turn of the century. Some of those who came as strikebreakers in 1904 stayed on after the strike, but by 1910 there were still only 178 black men and 8 black women, about 1.4 percent of the work force, at Chicago.[27]

Between 1910 and 1920 Chicago's black population mushroomed from 44,103 to 109,458, an increase of 148 percent. The bulk of this growth resulted from massive migration from the South which peaked during the acute wartime labor shortage between 1916 and 1919. Most migrants came from the "Black Belt" areas of Mississippi, Georgia, Alabama, South Carolina, and Louisiana. The majority were sharecroppers, agricultural laborers, or the children of such families, forced from the land by natural or financial calamity and drawn to the northern industrial cities by high wages and the chance to escape the stifling atmosphere of the Deep South.[28]

In 1915 only 1,100 blacks were in the Chicago packing plants, but by 1918 the number had jumped to 6,510. Just how quickly this transformation of the work force took place is suggested by table 3, showing the growth of black employment at one of the largest Chicago plants between the beginning of 1916 and the end of 1918. Within two years the number of blacks at this plant rose from about 300 to more than 3,000, an increase from 3.7 percent to over 22 percent of the work force.

While the Chicago labor force as a whole was expanding rapidly throughout these years, black employment was growing much faster. After tripling in the first six months of 1916, the number of black workers more than doubled again during the following year. At the height of war production, blacks made up as much as 70 to 80 percent of the workers in some of the smaller plants. After falling a little at the end of the war, when production dropped, black employment rose once again, reaching almost 20 percent by 1920. During the depression year of 1921, large numbers of black common laborers were laid off, but with the return of prosperity black employment climbed once again, to its highest level, more than one-third of the labor force in the city's two largest plants by the end of 1923.[29]

Demographically, black migrants bore a strong likeness to those who had preceded them into the common labor pool. They were disproportionately young and unattached, either because they were single or because they had left their families back home in their search for work and their efforts to save money. Having worked most of their lives in agriculture, they now faced the regimentation and alienation of mass-production work and the problems of adjusting to life in a big industrial city. Yet in other respects their situation differed from that of the new immigrants.

Table 3. The Growth of Black Employment in One Major
Chicago Packinghouse, January 1916 to December 1918

	Total Employment	Negro Employment	Percent Negro
January 1916	8,361	311	3.7
July 1916	8,062	733	9.1
January 1917	10,255	1,657	16.2
July 1917	10,679	2,278	21.3
January 1918	10,878	3,069	22.1
July 1918	15,336	2,323	15.1
December 1918	17,434	3,621	20.8

Source: George E. Haynes, *The Negro at Work During the World War and During Reconstruction*, U.S. Department of Labor, Division of Negro Economics (Washington, D.C.: GPO, 1921), 54–55.

By the period of the First World War and the early twenties, as some Poles and other eastern Europeans began to climb toward the more skilled jobs, blacks were still nearly all relegated to those chronically insecure positions paying the least. Together with the growing number of women in the industry, black and immigrant white, black men provided the critical nucleus of shifting, casual laborers upon which the industry depended. Excluded entirely from some departments, they were often placed in the least desirable jobs in the others.[30]

Even more than the recent Slavic immigrants, black migrants were confined to unskilled jobs. Of 7,957 in eight different Chicago plants during 1922, almost 99 percent were doing unskilled work. Black workers complained of discrimination in advancement and many lost what they called "hope on the job." Still, by 1920, the Meat Trust had become the largest employer in Chicago's Black Belt, engaging more than one-half of all the community's manufacturing workers. By comparison, the steel industry, the next most important employer of black labor, took on less than one-fourth the total in meat packing. If it were possible to count all those who stayed in the industry only briefly and then moved on to other work, it is likely we would find that most black men in Chicago had some experience in the packing plants by the 1920s. Throughout this era when many industries remained

closed to blacks because of employer or union hostility, the packers offered them relatively high wages and continued to employ
them even during economic decline. The implications of this extreme reliance on packinghouse employment for conditions in the
black community and for the consciousness of black butcher
workmen were one reason why labor organization was particularly
difficult among these migrants.[31]

While black employment in meat packing remained high
through the twenties, working *conditions* deteriorated. The industry entered a period of decline as the demand for meat fell off,
and work became even more seasonal. A smaller proportion of the
labor force was kept on during the slack period, and this situation
translated into more layoffs for blacks.[32]

Slack periods gave the packers an opportunity to reconstitute
their work force because such a large proportion of it was laid off.
In the early years of the twentieth century, the proportion of
Slavic immigrants increased at the expense of the older immigrant
groups. To some extent, this was the natural outcome of a gradual
process due more to broader social changes than to conscious
planning on the packers' part. The situation was different, however, during the depression of 1921. Here the packers clearly
made a choice to replace Slavic and especially Polish immigrants
with blacks and Mexicans. This shift was part of a strategy to
break down labor organization, and the trend was reversed following the destruction of the union. Beginning with the summer of
1923, the proportion of blacks in the industry was gradually reduced. In her study of black employment and work conditions in
the packing industry, Alma Herbst concluded that "the companies count upon the Negroes as an ever-present group of job-
seekers who may always be found loitering around the employment office."[33] The same remark might have been, and was,
made about the Poles or Lithuanians a few years earlier or of the
Mexicans a few years later.

The Mexicans arrived in the early twenties to round out the
ethnic composition of the industry. Although they entered in
small numbers during the First World War, and did not make up
a significant proportion of the work force until about 1923, from
that point on their numbers rose until by 1928 they represented
about 6 percent of the workers in Chicago's plants. Like previous

migrant groups, most had not been in the United States long when they went to work in the industry. They were also young and single. Of several thousand studied by Paul Taylor in 1928, almost 80 percent had been in the U.S. five years or less. Over 60 percent were under thirty and more than half unmarried. As Mexicans entered the industry, often after some experience in railroad construction gangs, they were concentrated in the common labor ranks, as other migrants had been before them.[34]

THE WOMEN WORKERS

Women were already an important labor source in some packinghouse departments, notably by-products and canning, before the 1890s, and their representation in the work force grew consistently from the late nineteenth century through the First World War. The most rapid increase, however, came during the 1890s and the first five years of this century, when extreme division of labor and the mechanization of some operations diluted the degree of skill required for most jobs, reducing them to tasks that women were deemed capable of performing. By the 1920s women could be found in most departments of a modern packinghouse—making, labeling, and filling cans; trimming meat; making sausage casings; packing lard, butter, butterine, chipped beef, cheese, and other items; and even working on the hog- and cattle-killing floors of a few houses. In 1890 women represented 1.6 percent of Chicago's packinghouse workers; by 1920, 12.6 percent.[35]

Yet even as women came to play a more important role in the industry, their work tended to be different in a number of ways from that done by most men. In those departments where they replaced men, women worked in the most poorly paid positions, while men retained the few coveted jobs. In sausagemaking, for example, women twisted, linked, and tied, while men tended the steam-driven stuffing machines—and received a higher rate of pay.[36] Moreover, while lines of progression were established for men in some departments during the late nineteenth century, advancement was virtually nonexistent for women as late as the 1920s. Occasionally a production worker might make the giant leap to a clerical job or even become a "forelady," but most spent their careers in unskilled work.[37]

Table 4. The Growth of Women's Employment in the Chicago
Meat-packing Industry, 1890–1920

		Men		Women	
Year	Total*	N	(%)	N	(%)
1890	15,523	14,875	(95.8)	243	(1.6)
1900	25,141	23,205	(92.3)	1,421	(5.7)
1905	22,391	19,857	(88.7)	2,477	(11.1)
1910	22,064	19,384	(87.9)	2,647	(12.0)
1920	45,011	39,341	(87.4)	5,649	(12.6)

*Figures include small proportions of children.

Sources: Eleventh U.S. Census, 1890, Manufactures (Washington, D.C.: GPO,
1895), 144–45; *Twelfth U.S. Census, 1900, Manufactures* (Washington, D.C.:
GPO, 1902), 184–85; *U.S. Census of Manufactures, 1905*, part 2 (Washington,
D.C.: GPO, 1906), 236; *Thirteenth U.S. Census, 1910, Manufactures*
(Washington, D.C.: GPO, 1912), 298; *Fourteenth U.S. Census, 1920,
Manufactures* (Washington, D.C.: GPO, 1923), 364.

Women also contended with different pay systems from those
for men. While very few men worked for piece rates, these were
common in departments with large numbers of women. Packers
sometimes tried to increase productivity by organizing the women
into small piece-rate teams. Wages for women packinghouse
workers compared unfavorably not only with those of their male
counterparts, but also with working women in other Chicago industries. In 1906 over 84 percent of the women in packing studied by the Illinois Bureau of Labor Statistics earned less than the
common labor rate, i.e., the lowest rate for men, and this pattern
persisted over the next two decades.[38]

In an industry famous for its casual hiring practices and extremely erratic employment patterns, women were also far less
secure in their jobs than were male employees. As a group,
women in packing and by-product departments were laid off for
shorter periods of time than men on the kill floors, but the problem of seasonal layoffs affected a larger proportion of them than of
the men. Even after the packers made attempts to stabilize their
work force, women still suffered disproportionately from seasonal
unemployment. In her careful study of payroll records for the
1920s, Alma Herbst found that much of the industry's high labor
turnover was concentrated within a fairly small segment of the la-

bor force consisting largely of foreign-born women and blacks.[39]

Until World War I the vast majority of women workers (from 80 to 95 percent) were single and most were young, the average age remaining about twenty. Changes in the racial and ethnic composition of the female labor force paralleled those for men. Up to the turn of the century about half were foreign-born, while the rest were primarily the American-born daughters of Irish, German, and Bohemian butchers. By the 1890s there was a slight shift from Irish and German to Bohemian and Polish, paralleling the more general shift in the ethnic composition of the labor force as a whole. Over 90 percent of a large sample (N = 206) investigated in 1892 were single. Most had entered the industry quite young (mean = 14 years, 8.2 months) and had been working in it for several years (mean = 5 years, 2.7 months).[40]

The ethnic makeup of the labor force continued to change after the turn of the century, so that the constituency for women's unionism in 1901-4 was quite heterogeneous, a mixture of more experienced second-generation Irish women and a mass of younger recent Polish and Lithuanian immigrants. A 1906 Illinois Bureau of Labor Statistics study of 456 women found that nearly two-thirds (62 percent) were native-born and well over half of the foreign-born were from eastern Europe, most of them Polish. While many of the native-born were daughters of immigrants, the fathers were now more apt to be Polish laborers than skilled Irish butchers. Still, most of the women were single (85.4 percent) and lived at home (78 percent). More women walked to work in packing than in any other Chicago industry considered in the 1906 study.[41]

During the next two decades, the ethnic shift continued. By 1911 Edith Abbott and Sophinisba Breckinridge of the University of Chicago found very few Irish women in the packinghouses except in forelady positions. A 1918 study conducted by the packers themselves (N = 600) discovered that about 40 percent of the white women questioned were first- or second-generation Polish and another 25 percent were Lithuanian. During the war and the early 1920s black women entered the industry in large numbers so that by 1928 they accounted for over 25 percent of the female labor force.[42]

Few married women entered the packing plants until World

War I. As late as 1914, for example, almost 90 percent of the women working in Armour's Chicago plant were single. During the war, however, the combined effects of conscription, increased production, and a dramatic decline in immigration produced a severe labor shortage in packing as in many other industries. As a result, thousands of married women, including many with small children, joined the industry's labor force.[43] One characteristic which most of these married women shared with their single sisters was the need to work in order to ensure the economic survival of their families.[44]

COMMON LABOR IN MASS-PRODUCTION INDUSTRY

Many social historians have emphasized the problems employers faced in disciplining and socializing "pre-industrial" people in the formation of a modern labor force.[45] One might expect that the problem would be particularly severe in a highly rationalized industry like packing, which depended for its labor supply on underdeveloped regions of eastern Europe and the American South. But the image of both the black migrants and the new immigrants as ignorant peasants torn from the land with little or no work experience beyond the soil has been challenged recently by research which has uncovered the complicated process by which both groups made their way to the American industrial city.

During the late nineteenth century traditional eastern European peasant economies were in decay. Demographic changes, continual subdivision of land, and the gradual erosion of traditional household industries produced a class of mobile agricultural proletarians in each of the three regions of what is today Poland and in other parts of eastern Europe. These landless farmers migrated throughout Europe and beyond in search of work, hoping always to return with enough money to resume their old way of life. In the case of black migrants, an equally complex system of migration developed with the northern industrial city as the farthest point in an ongoing search for work. Many young blacks migrated seasonally and worked at a variety of jobs to supplement their own incomes or those of their sharecropper parents.[46]

Historian Peter Stearns has argued against drawing too sharply the line between agricultural and other kinds of work in "traditional" societies and common labor in "modern" industrializing society. Like agricultural work, for example, work in many late nineteenth- and early twentieth-century industries was seasonal and hours were irregular. Even some specific tasks that rural migrants encountered in their new environment were not very different from those in the old country. The discontinuity, Stearns argues, was not so great as some historians have thought. [47]

Even if many black and Slavic migrants came into Chicago's packing plants directly from farms, some of the tasks to which they were set—stuffing sausage, shoveling manure, or even slaughtering—were precisely those with which many of them had had some experience. In the packing plants the irregular workweek, fluctuating length of the workday, and seasonal nature of the industry seem to complement what have often been termed "pre-industrial" work habits and lifestyles. Seasonality and irregular employment might allow time for religious observation, weddings, funerals, and other traditional cultural functions, or even for journeys home. When A. L. Jackson of the Wabash Avenue Y.M.C.A. asked a discharged black migrant whether he had gone to work every day, the man replied, "Goodness no! I just had to have some days of the week off for pleasure." Perhaps the very irregularity of packinghouse work as well as the preponderance of hand labor were characteristics which allowed for a period of adjustment in the working lives of black and Slavic migrants. [48]

On balance, however, the confrontation with Packingtown was a real departure in the lives of these workers, in several ways. First, their labor was bought and sold as a commodity within a highly competitive big-city labor market. Seasonality in Lithuania or Mississippi might have meant a respite after harvesting during which one might fish, do odd jobs, or subsist on what had been laid by. In Chicago, however, idleness meant submergence in a flooded casual labor market and the constant pressure of rising commodity prices which left those living on the common labor rate far behind. The black migrant quoted above probably had little trouble finding another job during the severe labor shortage of the war years, but in more normal times he was one face in a large crowd. Even the Polish agricultural laborer who sold his time to the highest bidder did so in Poland within a narrowly demarcated

local market. In Chicago he made the transaction in competition
with an army of other "working stiffs," each with nothing
between him and starvation but his own strength. A young
Lithuanian laborer described his own recognition of the predicament: "I knew that money was everything I needed. My money
was almost gone and I thought that I would die soon unless I got a
job, for this was not like home. Here money was everything and a
man without money must die."[49]

The nature of the work itself and even the physical environment of the packing plants were also markedly different from
anything most newcomers had encountered. Less than half of
those black migrants interviewed in 1920 by the Chicago Commission on Race Relations were utilizing *any* previous training or
experience in their new work. The majority, like the Slavic immigrants studied by the Immigration Commission, had been farmers. Of course, many migrants had worked in various southern
industries—lumbering or tobacco manufacturing, for example—
but even they had done so on a short-term basis. The fact that
black employment remained high in packing and that fifty
thousand migrants were still in Chicago in 1920 suggests that
some sort of adjustment to permanent industrial employment was
necessary for many.[50]

Likewise, the Polish or Lithuanian peasant faced a work environment different from any he or she had known in Europe.
Chicago's packing plants were simply huge. Except perhaps for
steel mills, they were as a class the largest factories in early
twentieth-century America. By the turn of the century Armour
gathered over 6,200 workers together in one establishment; Swift,
more than 5,000.[51] During World War I, the plants grew enor-
mously. The labor force in one of Chicago's largest more than
doubled, from 8,000 workers to 17,000, in the course of the
conflict. Adjacent to the plants themselves, the Union Stockyards
sprawled. "There is over a square mile of space in the yards,"
Upton Sinclair wrote, "and more than half of it is occupied by cattle pens; north and south, as far as the eye can reach there
stretches a sea of pens. And they were all filled—so many cattle
no one had ever dreamed existed in the world."[52] The sheer size
of the yards and slaughterhouses impressed the most sophisticated visitors, who flocked to see them from around the world.

The great stone gate at the main entrance of the Union Stockyards, near the corner of Thirty-ninth and Halsted streets, circa 1905–10. (Courtesy of the Chicago Historical Society, ICHi-19107)

A view across Union Stockyards with the Armour packing plant in the distance, from a sketch by Joseph Pennell, 1917.

Courtesy of the Chicago Historical Society, ICHi-17497)

The casual labor system in the yards: A line of men waiting to be hired in front of the Central Time Station, Union Stockyards, 1904. (Courtesy of the Chicago Historical Society, DN-100)

A group of packinghouse workers seated in front of a saloon along "Whiskey Row" on Ashland Avenue, just across from the packing plants, around the turn of the century. Several of the men hold the metal pails used to transport beer across to the plants. (From a contemporary post card, courtesy of the Chicago Historical Society)

"Knockers" stunning cattle on the killing floor, from a sketch by Joseph Pennell, 1917. (Courtesy of the Chicago Historical Society, ICHi-14903)

A "splitter" cleaves a carcass into halves on the killing floor, from a sketch by Joseph Pennell, 1917. (Courtesy of the Chicago Historical Society, ICHi-04109)

Hog butchers dressing carcasses, from a sketch by Joseph Pennell, 1917. (Courtesy of the Chicago Historical Society, ICHi-17496)

A canning department staffed largely by young women workers, 1917. (Courtesy of the Chicago Historical Society, ICHi-03286)

The impression they must have made on a young, recently arrived peasant can only be imagined.

Within the plants the atmosphere was dominated by the sight, sound, and smell of death on a monumental scale. On the hog-killing floor, the ear was constantly assaulted by the lamentations of dying pigs. "The uproar was appalling, perilous to the ear drums; one feared there was too much sound for the room to hold—that the walls might give way or the ceiling crack. There were high squeals and low squeals, grunts, and wails of agony; there would be a momentary lull, and then a fresh outburst, louder than ever, surging up to deafening climax."[53] In the midst of all this squealing, gears ground; carcasses slammed into one another; cleavers and axes split flesh and bone; and foremen and straw bosses shouted orders in half a dozen languages.

It was not only the size of the packing plants, their cacophany of human, animal, and machine sounds, and their distinctive odor that distinguished them from the migrant's earlier work environments. What made packinghouses really different was the organization of their labor processes and the speed with which the work was performed. It is difficult to imagine an early twentieth-century industry that involved more incessant repetition or closer supervision than did meat packing. Division of labor in rural, agricultural societies, be they in Poland or the Deep South, tended to be what Marx called a *social division of labor,* while the minute subdivision of the task in the packinghouse was *division of labor in detail.*[54] In the former, the various tasks might be sorted out to family members, often on the basis of gender, but any one individual had numerous responsibilities, each of which contributed to the maintenance of the farm and the family. In the giant packinghouse an operation which the peasant or farmer had done once a year—the slaughtering of a hog—was broken down into its constituent elements, each of which was assigned to one or more laborers among the thousands who made up the work force. Jurgis Rudkus, the hero of Upton Sinclair's *The Jungle*, never thought he would "live to see one hog dressed by several hundred men."[55]

It was probably the *pace* of the work which laborers complained of most. The hog butchers and laborers whom Jurgis watched were "working like demons" because they were under the watchful eye of a foreman or straw boss, and they understood that their livelihoods were at stake, for a defining characteristic of mass-production work is that control over the production process is exercised by another person. Through the pacesetter, the endless chain, moving cutting benches, and close supervision, the packers controlled the pace of work.

William Hard, a sympathetic journalist, described the scene on the assembly line in a packing department: "The onlooker himself is so filled with a benumbing sense of the concentrated monotony of life as he observes a girl stuffing pieces of dried beef into a glass can, hour after hour, day after day, year after year, her eyes fixed on the beef, the table, and the can, her fingers moving with the steady regularity of the clicking of a watch. . . . She seems like an assimilated part of automatic nature."[56]

The threat mass production posed to skilled workers, then, was paralleled by the alienation it caused among the unskilled migrants. Whatever control over his or her daily work the individual Polish peasant or black sharecropper had enjoyed on the land was relinquished the moment he or she walked through the stockyards gate.

Each of these groups of workers—the older skilled immigrants, the new immigrant common laborers, the black migrants, and the young women workers—faced different conditions. For the skilled men, the system meant a maddening pace and continued threats to their status; for the immigrant or black common laborer, a wage below subsistence level and a constant search for employment; for the young woman worker, a race against the stopwatch to make her piece rate. To all, the system offered chronic insecurity of employment, domination by superintendents, foremen, and straw bosses, and the personal alienation that is an inescapable product of mass-production work. Like countless generations before and after them, these people worked to live. It is to the quality of their lives that we now turn.

NOTES

1. Philip Taylor, *The Distant Magnet: European Emigration to the USA* (New York, 1972), 48–65; David Montgomery, *Workers' Control in*

America: Studies in the History of Work, Technology, and Labor Struggles (New York and London, 1979), 34–37; Daniel Nelson, *Managers and Workers: Origins of the New Factory System in the United States, 1880–1920* (Madison, Wis. 1975), 81–85, 145–47; David Brody, *Workers in Industrial America: Essays in the Twentieth Century Struggle* (New York, 1980), 14–21; Gabriel Kolko, *Main Currents in Modern American History* (New York, 1976), chap. 3.

2. Richard Edwards, *Contested Terrain: The Transformation of the Workplace in the Twentieth Century* (New York, 1977), especially chaps. 9 and 10; David M. Gordon, Richard C. Edwards, and Michael Reich, *Segmented Work, Divided Workers: The Historical Transformation of Labor in the United States* (London and New York, 1982), 127–62; *Labor Market Segmentation* (Lexington, Mass., 1975), passim; Andrew Friedman, *Industry and Labour: Class Struggle at Work and Monopoly Capitalism* (London, 1978); Jill Rubery, "Structured Labour Markets, Worker Organization, and Low Pay," *Cambridge Journal of Economics* 2 (1978): 17–36.

3. All empirical data regarding immigrant packinghouse workers, unless otherwise specified, are drawn from the U.S. Immigration Commission, *Reports*, part 11, *Immigrants in Industry*, vol. 13, *Slaughtering and Meat Packing* (Washington, D.C., 1911). (The data for the report were gathered in 1908–9.)

4. Immigration Commission, *Reports*, part 11, vol. 13, 202–3, 210.

5. Ibid., 250, 252, 256, 257, 260.

6. Ibid., 202.

7. Ibid., 210.

8. Ibid., 249–50, 252–53, 254, 257, 258–59, 260.

9. For a comparable phenomenon in steel, see Katherine Stone, "The Origins of Job Structures in the Steel Industry," *Radical America* 7 (1973): 19–64.

10. John R. Commons, "Labor Conditions in the Slaughtering and Meat Packing Industry," in *Trade Unionism and Labor Problems*, ed. John R. Commons (Boston, 1905), 224, 237, 246; *Chicago Tribune*, July 26, 1904. See also Fred Wilder, *The Modern Packing Plant* (Chicago, 1905), 118–22, 126–27. On the basis of his 1905 study, Ethelbert Stewart concluded that part of the explanation for the rapid rise of the Bohemians within the job structure was ethnic and kinship ties with foremen. See Ethelbert Stewart, "The Influence of Trade Unionism on Immigrants," U.S. Bureau of Labor Statistics, Report no. 56 (Washington, D.C., 1906), reprinted in *The Making of America*, vol. 3, *Labor*, ed. Robert M. LaFollette (Chicago, 1905; reprint, New York, 1969), 228. Another possible explanation for the Bohemians' success was their slaughterhouse work experience in the Old World.

11. Alma Herbst, *The Negro in the Slaughtering and Meat Packing Industry in Chicago* (Boston, 1932), 7.

12. On the concept of the labor aristocracy, see E. J. Hobsbawm, "The Labour Aristocracy in Nineteenth Century Britain" in his *Labouring Men* (London, 1964), 272–315, and "Debating the Labour Aristocracy" and "The Aristocracy of Labour Reconsidered" in his *Workers: Worlds of Labour* (New York, 1984), 214–51; and J. F. Moorhouse, "The Marxist Theory of the Labor Aristocracy," *Social History* 3 (1977): 61–82. On Schick's career, see Amalgamated Meat Cutters and Butcher Workmen of North America, *Official Journal* 2 (Mar. 1901): 8.

13. *Chicago Tribune*, July 26, 1904; Commons, 246.

14. David Brody, *Steelworkers in America: The Non-Union Era* (New York, 1969), 120–21, 260–61; John Bodnar, *Immigrants and Industrialization: Ethnicity in an American Mill Town* (Pittsburgh, 1977), 35–50; John A. Fitch, *The Steelworkers* (New York, 1910), 31, 142–49.

15. *Official Journal* 1 (Apr. 1900); 2 (Sept. 1901): 15; 5 (July 1904): 28–34.

16. Carl Thompson, "Labor in the Packing Industry," *Journal of Political Economy* 15 (Feb. 1906): 107, 90. See also U.S. Employment Service, *Descriptions of Occupations: Slaughtering and Meat Packing* (Washington, D.C., 1918), 21. The strategy of developing an all-around mass-production worker was not peculiar to packing. See Montgomery, 34–35.

17. Commons, 243, 245.

18. Immigration Commission, *Reports*, part 11, 13:202, 210. See also William I. Thomas and Florian Znaniecki, *The Polish Peasant in Europe and America* (Boston, 1918), 1:156–205.

19. Immigration Commission, *Reports*, part 11, 13:250, 252, 256, 260.

20. Ibid., 200, 202, 210, 256.

21. Ibid., 250, 252.

22. Ibid., 260.

23. Cf. Brody, *Steelworkers in America*, passim.

24. Immigration Commission, *Reports*, part 11, 13:213.

25. Ibid., 216. This point is developed in chapter 4.

26. Ibid., 229. These figures are based on a study of household heads in the neighborhoods adjacent to the Union Stockyards rather than packinghouse employees per se. The vast majority of men questioned, however, in each ethnic group, worked in the industry.

27. Herbst, 16–27; *Thirteenth U.S. Census*, 1910, vol. 4, *Occupations* (Washington, D.C., 1912), 544–46.

28. James R. Grossman, "A Dream Deferred: Black Migration to Chicago, 1916-1921" (Ph.D. diss., University of California, Berkeley,

1982), passim; William Tuttle, *Race Riot: Chicago in the Red Summer of 1919* (New York, 1970), 96. See also Florette Henri, *The Great Migration* (New York, 1975), especially chaps. 1 and 2.

29. Lorenzo Green and Carter G. Woodson, *The Negro Wage Earner* (New York, 1930), 272–74; *Fourteenth U.S. Census*, 1920, vol. 4, *Occupations* (Washington, D.C., 1923), 1076–79; Herbst, xxii.

30. Herbst, 75–80.

31. Walter A. Fogel, *The Negro in the Meat Industry* (Philadelphia, 1970), 29–30. On the problem of organizing the migrants, see chap. 5.

32. Herbst, 99–102.

33. Tuttle, 128; James R. Barrett, Robert L. Ruck, Peter Rachleff, and Steven Weiner, "Race and Class in the Chicago Stockyards, 1900–1939" (University of Pittsburgh, typescript, 1975), 94–95; Herbst, 34, 72, 151.

34. Paul S. Taylor, *Mexican Labor in the United States: Chicago and the Calumet Region* (Berkeley, 1930), 37–38, 40, 51–52, 74, 155.

35. Edith Abbott and Sophinisba Breckinridge, "Women in Industry: The Chicago Stockyards," *Journal of Political Economy* 19 (1911): 637–44; Illinois Bureau of Labor Statistics, *Fourteenth Biennial Report* (Springfield, 1908), 290–300; Mary E. Pidgeon, *The Employment of Women in Slaughtering and Meat Packing*, Bulletin of the U.S. Women's Bureau no. 88, U.S. Dept. of Labor (Washington, D. C., 1932), 17–32.

36. Abbott and Breckinridge, 638–39, 643–44.

37. Pidgeon, 32.

38. Ibid., 639–41, 648–49; *Eleventh U.S. Census, 1890, Manufactures* (Washington, D.C., 1895), part 2, 144–45; Commons, 241; Illinois Bureau of Labor Statistics, *Fourteenth Biennial Report*, 290–300; John C. Kennedy et al., *Wages and Family Budgets in the Chicago Stockyards District* (Chicago, 1914), 12–13; Edith Abbott, "Wages for Working Women in Chicago: Some Notes on Available Data," *Journal of Political Economy* 21 (1913): 154–57. See also Pidgeon, 59–79.

39. Abbott and Breckinridge, 645–47; Herbst, 71–77, 99, 102.

40. U.S. Commissioner of Labor, *Fourth Annual Report: Working Women in Large Cities* (Washington, D.C., 1889), 92–93, 132–33, 178–79, 264–65, 311; Illinois Bureau of Labor Statistics, *Seventh Biennial Report* (Springfield, 1893), 82, 312, 338, 345, 349, 340–42.

41. Illinois Bureau of Labor Statistics, *Fourteenth Biennial Report*, 180, 196, 198, 209, 211.

42. Commons, 238; Abbott and Breckinridge, 635; Stockyards Community Clearing House, "1918 Community Study," Folder 20, Mary McDowell Papers, Chicago Historical Society; Herbst, xxi; George Haynes, *The Negro at Work During the World War and During Reconstruc-*

tion, U.S. Department of Labor, Division of Negro Economics (Washington, D.C., 1921), 52–53.

43. U.S. Commission on Industrial Relations, *Final Report and Testimony*, vol. 4 (Washington, D.C., 1916), 3527; Stock Yards Community Clearing House, "1918 Community Study," n.p.

44. This point is developed fully in the discussion of family economy in the following chapter.

45. For the seminal British scholarship on this problem, see E. P. Thompson, "Time, Work Discipline and Industrial Capitalism," *Past and Present* 38 (1968): 56–97; Sidney Pollard, *The Origins of Modern Management* (Cambridge, Mass., 1965), chap. 5. The implications of a "recurrent tension" between "pre-industrial" work habits and employers' quest for "industrial morality" in the United States are described in Herbert Gutman, "Work, Culture and Society in Industrializing America, 1815–1919," in his *Work, Culture and Society in Industrializing America: Essays in Working Class and Social History* (New York, 1976), 3–78.

46. Ewa Morawska, "'For Bread With Butter': Life Worlds of Peasant Immigrants from East Central Europe, 1880–1914," *Journal of Social History* 17 (1984): 387–91, and *For Bread with Butter: The Life-Worlds of East Central Europeans in Johnstown, Pennsylvania, 1890–1940* (London and New York, 1985), 22–62; Victor Greene, *The Slavic Community on Strike: Immigrant Labor in Pennsylvania Anthracite* (South Bend, Ind., 1968), 13–32; Caroline Golab, *Immigrant Destinations* (Philadelphia, 1977), 75–100; Grossman, passim; Peter Gottlieb, "Making Their Own Way: Southern Blacks' Migration to Pittsburgh, 1916–1930" (Ph.D. diss., University of Pittsburgh, 1977), chaps. 2 and 3; John Bodnar, Roger Simon, and Michael Weber, *Lives of Their Own: Blacks, Italians, and Poles in Pittsburgh, 1900–1960* (Urbana, Ill., 1982), 29–56. See also Joseph Barton's analyses in *Peasants and Strangers* (Cambridge, Mass., 1975), chap. 2; and John Bodnar, *The Transplanted: A History of Immigrants in Urban America* (Bloomington, Ind., 1985), chap. 1.

47. Peter N. Stearns, "The Unskilled and Industrialization," *Archiv für Sozialgeschichte* 16 (1976): 249–82. Andrea Grazziosi, "Common Laborers, Unskilled Workers, 1890–1915," *Labor History* 22 (1981): 512–44, emphasizes *changes* in the nature of common labor tasks during the early twentieth century.

48. Carl Thompson, 93. The black migrant is quoted in Allen Spear, *Black Chicago* (Chicago, 1967), 156.

49. Antanas Kaztauskis, "From Lithuania to the Chicago Stockyards—An Autobiography," in *Plain Folk: The Life Stories of Undis-*

tinguished Americans, ed. David M. Katzman and William M. Tuttle, Jr. (Urbana, Ill., 1982), 108. See chap. 1, n. 44.

50. Chicago Commission on Race Relations, *The Negro in Chicago* (Chicago, 1922), 79, 166–68. See also Grossman, 242–43.

51. Daniel Nelson, *Managers and Workers: Origins of the New Factory System in the United States, 1880–1920* (Madison, Wis., 1975), 7; State of Illinois, *Eighth Annual Report of the Factory Inspectors* (Springfield, 1900), 46–49.

52. Upton Sinclair, *The Jungle,* with introduction and notes by James R. Barrett (Urbana, Ill., 1987).

53. Ibid., 39.

54. Harry Braverman, *Labor and Monopoly Capital: The Degradation of Work in the Twentieth Century* (New York, 1974), chap. 3; Karl Marx, *Capital* (London, 1887; reprint, London, 1976), vol. 1, chap. 3. See also Montgomery, 34–37.

55. Sinclair, *The Jungle.* For a contrast between blacks' wage work in the South and that which they faced in Chicago's packing plants, see Grossman, 249–66.

56. William Hard, "Labor in the Chicago Stockyards," *Outlook* 83 (June 6, 1906): 371.

3

The Families and Communities of Packingtown, 1894–1922

If the rich could pay people to die for them, the poor would make a wonderful living.

Yiddish Proverb

That word "job" came into my vocabulary in 1894 and has since become almost a sacred word. . . . It is the first word learned by the immigrant; the children lisp it; the aged cling to it to the end. A "steady job" or "Please give me a job" is ever at the front of their minds and on the tips of their tongues.

Mary McDowell[1]

Drawn from various parts of the United States and from around the world; separated from one another by previous work experience, as well as by language and custom, Packingtown's residents nevertheless shared a common fate. The vast majority of them worked in the packinghouses, most as common laborers. How did this work shape the lives of those who depended upon it for their livelihoods and how did it affect the communities they created for themselves?

The packers lacked the sort of direct control over their workers' lives which employers achieved in company towns where management not only controlled employment, and often housing and local government, but even churches and other cultural institutions. In contrast, by the early twentieth century Chicago's South Side was a patchwork quilt of vibrant ethnic neighborhoods constituting alternative sources for ideas and values to those of employers and the dominant middle-class culture. The divisions among such communities were real. Indeed, consciousness of nationality seems to have been *increasing* during the early twentieth century, especially among eastern Europeans. But packinghouse workers from these myriad ethnic communities found a common ground—not only in the sense that they came into contact with one another in the packing plants and in the neighborhoods, but also through shared work experiences and grievances, grievances often seen as threats to precisely the traditional values of family and community which lay at the heart of their cultures. It was upon such common ground that working-class formation and organization developed.

The relative cultural autonomy of these communities did not save them from the effects of packinghouse employment. Socially, the South Side's ethnic heterogeneity was itself a product of the constant recomposition of the industry's labor force. The nature of meat packing as an industry meant that it also strongly influenced the *physical* character of Packingtown and the quality of life there.

The industry's negative impact may be seen in pollution, in extreme overcrowding, and in the poor health such conditions produced. In a word, Packingtown was an industrial slum. But to say that the neighborhood was dirty and congested, its people poor, does not tell us what it was like to live in a place like Packingtown. How did low wages and irregular employment influence the way people organized their lives? And how were such problems related to the general struggle for survival? In order to approach these questions systematically, we must take a more intimate look at Packingtown. We need to look into its families' homes and begin to piece together a picture of a local economy based on casual employment and the common labor rate—economic realities faced by millions of workers in industries and communities throughout the country in these years.

THE SOCIAL ECOLOGY OF POVERTY

Like so many other industrial cities, turn-of-the-century Chicago was a study in social contrasts. Nowhere were these more apparent than in two neighboring communities on the city's South Side—Hyde Park and Packingtown. Beginning life as a suburb linked to the city's central business district by Illinois Central commuter trains, Hyde Park was annexed by the city in 1889. The neighborhood underwent a dramatic development as a result of the establishment of the University of Chicago there in 1892 and the opening of the World's Columbian Exposition on the southern shore of Lake Michigan the following year. Laid out with wide, landscaped boulevards and quiet tree-lined residential streets, Hyde Park was a bastion of middle-class respectability in the midst of Chicago's industrial South Side (see map 1).

Though the two communities were within a couple of miles of each other, most Hyde Park residents probably had little reason or desire to visit Packingtown. They could journey downtown for work or shopping without coming near the working-class neighborhood. To those who occasionally made the trip—the students and faculty from the University of Chicago's prestigious department of sociology—Packingtown offered a "social laboratory" at the doorstep of their campus. One of the university's prime motivations in deciding to establish a settlement house in the area was, in fact, to provide its budding social scientists with a window into the world of the immigrant worker.[2] The proximity of the two neighborhoods is partly responsible for the rich picture of life in Packingtown available to us, as University of Chicago investigators produced books and articles on a broad range of social problems, using Packingtown as their case study.[3]

A theme runs through many descriptions of the neighborhood, those of social scientists as well as popular journalists. It conveys an image of Packingtown as a place beyond the pale of normal society, a place which, because of the degraded and volatile character of its population, posed a threat to the metropolitan community as a whole. Ernest Poole's 1904 description captures this view: "Packingtown begins to seem like a little world in itself. You feel that there is a great mass of humanity, the kind that is the hardest to manage, the easiest to inflame, the slowest to understand."[4]

Charles J. Bushnell, a doctoral student at the University of Chicago, saw his dissertation as a study of the dangers inherent in the development of such a degraded population.

> With our cities growing much more rapidly than our country districts, great hordes of population of diverse languages, customs, and habits, are being annually crowded into congested city wards, where . . . [life] becomes a wild, sodden, sickening, inhuman, and infinitely tragical struggle; not only a menace to those finer dreams of noble, joyous, and beautiful national life, but a threat to the very essentials of common and decent civilization itself. [5]

Few of Packingtown's inhabitants viewed their community in this light, but Bushnell was not the only Hyde Parker to see the neighborhood primarily in terms of the threat it seemed to pose to the more respectable elements of the city.

Packingtown was but one portion of a solid industrial belt running north and south along the branches of the Chicago River from the city's central business district. On the South Side the industrial landscape included vast expanses of railroad freightyards with their warehouses and car shops, a network of canals serving a dozen lumberyards, the huge McCormick plant of International Harvester Corporation, a number of foundries and machine shops, breweries, and several coalyards and electrical generating stations to keep the whole complex in operation. Farther south lay the blast furnaces and rolling mills of South Chicago. Just north of Thirty-ninth Street, a number of box manufacturers, packing companies, and rendering plants drew upon the stockyards for their economic survival and on the surrounding neighborhoods for their labor supply. [6]

One became aware of Packingtown long before stepping down from the streetcar near the great stone gate of the Union Stockyards. The unique yards smell—a mixture of decaying blood, hair, and organic tissue; fertilizer dust; smoke; and other ingredients—permeated the air of the surrounding neighborhoods. Smoke belching from the stacks of the largest plants all but obscured the other dominant structures in the South Side skyline, the steeples of the various ethnic churches.

To the white-collar worker or university student passing through on a streetcar, Packingtown's very appearance and physical isolation must have enhanced its image as a world apart. On the north, at Thirty-ninth Street, lay "Bubbly Creek," a long dead arm of the Chicago River that derived its name from the carbolic acid gas rising to its surface from decaying packinghouse refuse. To the west, a stench rose from a series of uncovered city dumps where Hyde Park and other neighborhoods threw their garbage. South of Packingtown, across numerous railroad tracks at Fifty-first Street, lay a more respectable working-class district populated largely by skilled workers from the older immigrant groups. In all directions except south, freightyards cut the area off from the rest of the city. On the east, the entire neighborhood was dominated by the Union Stockyards themselves, which stretched, together with the packing plants and their auxiliary industries, for a full mile south from Thirty-ninth Street to Forty-seventh Street and for a mile west between Halsted Street and Ashland Avenue (see map 2). The yards resembled a small town with its own police and fire protection, banks, hotel and restaurant facilities, hundreds of miles of roads, ramps, and railways and, of course, thousands of animals herded together into pens awaiting their fate.[7]

Just south and west of the yards, tucked amidst the smoke and garbage, packing plants and car shops, was a community of forty thousand people. The advantage to living here was obvious from the common laborer's point of view—one could walk to work. In an industry where employment depended in large part on one's ability to stay close to the plants, waiting for the word from the foreman or special policeman, this was an important consideration. In turn, ethnic communities thrived in this forbidding environment, and so the laborer could expect to find a comprehensible language and familiar cultural institutions there as well as emotional and economic support in the struggle for existence.

Notwithstanding such important considerations, the combined effects of the casual labor system and the close proximity of the neighborhood to the yards and packing plants undermined the quality of life in Packingtown. By 1900 nearly all of the streets in Hyde Park were paved, for example, while Packingtown's roads, with the exceptions of Forty-seventh Street and Ashland Avenue, were dirt. The working-class community also had far fewer sewerage facilities than its neighbors, and its main business district consisted largely of saloons. With an average family income at the turn of the century of less than one-fifth of Hyde Park's, Packingtown had more than fourteen times the number of families on relief. By the First World War, physical conditions had improved somewhat, but the neighborhood remained polluted and unhealthful. [8]

Living in the shadow of the packing plants and working in their damp cellars and cutting rooms meant not only irregular employment at low wages but often disabling illness and death. The industry's effects on the physical environment are best reflected in the health statistics for the neighboring communities. Although Packingtown's population was less than twice the size of Hyde Park's in the years from 1894 to 1900, its deaths from consumption, bronchitis, diphtheria, and other contagious diseases ranged from two and a half to five times those for the middle-class neighborhood. As in so many other urban communities of the era, tuberculosis was the big killer, accounting for more than 30 percent of the 429 adult deaths during 1908 and 1909. Packingtown was widely thought to have the highest tuberculosis rate in the city and one of the highest in the country. Infant mortality rates for the period around the turn of the century were also disproportionately high. Packingtown averaged less than three and a half times Hyde Park's number of children under six but almost five and a half times its mortality figure for those in that age group. By 1909, the situation was actually worse. One of every three infants died before the age of two, a rate seven and a half times that for the lakefront ward that included Hyde Park. [9]

Not included in such health statistics are the thousands of injuries which became a part of the new mass-production process, including many peculiar to meat packing. In one house alone, Swift and Company, 3,500 injuries were reported for the first six months of 1910, and this number included only those requiring a physician's care. According to the director of Armour's welfare department, one of every two of the company's 22,381 workers was injured or became ill at work during 1917. Armour's Chicago plant averaged twenty-three accidents per day. Each job had its own dangers: the dampness and cold of the pickling room and hide cellar; the sharp blade of the beef boner's knife; the noxious dust of the wool department and fertilizer plant; the wild charge

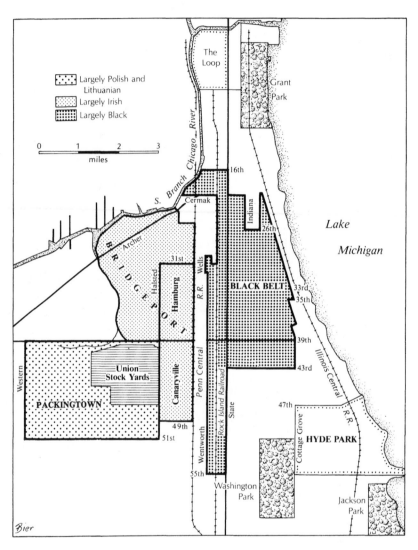

Map 1. Three Working-class Communities on Chicago's South Side, 1920

of a half-crazed steer on the killing floor. And those dangers intrinsic to the work itself were exacerbated by the speed with which it was carried on. The result was frequent idleness due to accidents and disease. In a total of 284 households studied by the U.S. Commissioner of Labor in 1905, thirty-four family heads (12 percent) noted periods of unemployment, averaging about 12.4 weeks, as a result of accidents or illness on the job. At work or at home, a butcher workman or -woman faced death and disabling illness simply by virtue of his or her occupation and social position.[10]

The dismal health of the community can be attributed in part to the pollution of the environment. The neighborhood was known throughout the city for its filth, smoke, and smell. When Robert Hunter set out to study tenement conditions in Chicago for the City Homes Association in 1901, he intentionally chose not to investigate Packingtown, fearing that conditions there were so bad that they might prejudice his sample of the city's slums.

> If the purpose had been merely to select the worst houses and blocks that the city can show, portions of the North and South Sides would have been chosen. The Stock Yards District and portions of South Chicago show outside sanitary conditions as bad as any in the world. Indescribable filth and rubbish, together with the absence of sewerage, make the surroundings of every frame cottage abominably unsanitary.[11]

The housing itself and the congestion within it probably also lowered the community's health standards. While the percentage of all-frame buildings in the city as a whole was only 59.7, the figure for Packingtown was 92.6. Out of twenty-four neighborhoods canvassed in 1909–10 by University of Chicago students, only the South Chicago steel area had more frame homes. The vast majority of Packingtown's, like much of Chicago's working-class housing, were built before the housing reforms of 1902. In practical terms, this meant they were firetraps. In 1923 another University of Chicago investigation found that the condition of many buildings had deteriorated still more since the earlier study. The packers' own attorney concluded in 1918 that the only solution to slum housing was "absolute destruction of the district. You should tear down the district, burn all the houses."[12] Lacking any suitable alternative housing, the citizens of Packingtown could not afford to follow the attorney's advice. Instead, most families made do with what they had.

The typical Packingtown tenement was a dilapidated two-story wooden structure divided into four or more flats. Each flat consisted of four dark, ill-ventilated rooms shared by the family and its boarders. An "average" household included 6.7 people—the parents, two children, and two or three boarders. There were exceptions—a good number of widows; some families who had taken in grandparents; even a flat shared by eight men, one of whom cooked and cleaned while the others worked. But the overwhelming majority of households comprised nuclear families who took in boarders of their own nationality. The degree of congestion in the flat had a direct relationship to the family's economic condition as well as to its stage in the family life cycle. Poorer families with all their children still at home were forced to take in more boarders, thereby aggravating the congestion. Predictably, the most crowded parts of the neighborhood were those inhabited by the greatest number of boarders, and these were also the blocks with the highest rates for tuberculosis and infant mortality.[13]

But boarding was essential to the local economy and had a dual function. For many of the community's families, it represented the margin between economic survival and catastrophe. At least one-third and perhaps as many as half of the Slavic and Lithuanian packinghouse workers in the years before the First World War were bachelors or married men who had left their families in Europe. In addition, a minority were young, single women living away from home. The 1909 University of Chicago housing study indicates that about a third of Packingtown's population consisted of boarders. For them the system offered the cheapest possible accommodation within easy walking distance of the yards. The average rate for room and board was about $10.25 per month, and the rate for women was usually a bit lower than that for men. This was somewhere around one-fourth the average monthly wage for men and about one-third the average monthly wage for women.[14] But the boarding system, by providing a cheap means of existence for the boarder and an important supplement to the family income, helped to subsidize a low-wage economy.

Since it led to overcrowding and disease, it was another way in which the expenses of the industry were assumed by the community.

In the midst of all these figures it is easy to overlook the fact that these crowded frame tenements were people's *homes*. In compiling a manuscript census of the area in 1905, Ethelbert Stewart and his investigators noted the furnishings and appearance of the flats they visited. Apart from suggesting that the middle-class sensibilities of the investigators were offended by much of what they saw, the notations also indicate the range of conditions and a clear effort on the part of many families to bring a touch of humanity to otherwise rather dismal surroundings. Pictures of relatives in the old country, the Madonna and Christ, and patron saints adorned many walls. Some families managed to afford rugs and draperies, while others had to live without them. Plants and flowers fought for their share of the polluted atmosphere. Some of the community's families clearly took great pride in their homes. Such evidence that the human spirit remained alive in the shadow of the slaughterhouse makes the neighborhood's dogged tenacity in subsequent struggles more understandable. [15]

THE SOCIAL RELATIONS OF A SLUM

In the early years of this century Packingtown became increasingly congested under the impact of successive waves of "new immigrants"—unskilled workers from agricultural backgrounds in eastern Europe. Between the turn of the century and the end of the First World War, the original Irish and German pioneers were largely displaced by Slavic people, particularly Poles and Lithuanians.

Table 5 shows how quickly this transformation of the neighborhood took place. The old immigrant (German, Irish, Canadian) groups declined in cumulative percentage of the population from 55.5 in 1900 to 28 in 1910, while the new immigrant groups (Polish, Lithuanian, Slovak, Hungarian) rose from 18.5 percent to 48 percent of the population over these same years. The 1910 sample also included several Slovene and eastern European Jewish families. A 1905 census by the U.S. Commissioner of Labor and a 1909 University of Chicago survey both demonstrate a dispropor-

Table 5. Ethnic Composition of Packingtown Male Family
Heads, 1900–1910

	1900		1910	
	(N = 200)		(N = 200)	
Native-born	4.0%		4.0%	
*Foreign-born:**				
German	34.5 ⎫		16.5 ⎫	
Irish	18.5 ⎬	55.5	9.5 ⎬	28.0
Canadian	2.5 ⎭		2.0 ⎭	
Bohemian	18.0		13.0	
Polish	17.5 ⎫		29.0 ⎫	
Lithuanian	0.5 ⎬	18.5	11.0 ⎬	48.0
Slovak	— ⎭		6.0 ⎪	
Hungarian	0.5 ⎭		2.0 ⎭	
Other	4.0		7.0	
TOTAL	100.0%		100.0%	

*The ethnic categories include immigrants and the children of immigrants.
Source: Systematic sample of 200 family heads, U.S. Bureau of the Census,
Manuscript Census of Chicago, 1900 and 1910.

tionate concentration of eastern European families, notably Poles
and Lithuanians, in those parts of the neighborhood immediately
adjacent to the stockyards. The massive immigration following
the turn of the century transformed the ethnic character of the
neighborhood, then, creating a community which was quite
mixed ethnically but increasingly dominated by new immigrants.
The *size* of the population also grew dramatically, crowding more
and more people into the stifling wooden tenements. In the first
decade of this century population increased by 75 percent and
continued to grow until by 1920 over fifty-seven thousand people
were living "back of the yards."[16]

All of these people lived on about one square mile of land, including streets and parks, surrounded by garbage dumps, stockyards, packing plants, and railroad tracks. Population density in
Packingtown was seventy-five per acre in 1910; the figure for the
less congested working-class community immediately south was
only forty. Some parts of the neighborhood were more crowded
than others. In several of the blocks just west of the yards, for ex-

ample, where boarders were most heavily concentrated, density ranged from two hundred to three hundred and fifty per acre in 1909.[17] (See map 2, p. 80.)

Throughout the early twentieth century social life in the community flowed along paths shaped by a strong ethnic identification among the various nationalities. One striking indication of this division was the almost total absence of interethnic marriages. Of 284 households surveyed in 1905, only five were inhabited by interethnic couples: one Polish/Russian, one Polish/Bohemian, one English/Irish, one German/Bohemian, and one Polish/Slovak. At the most intimate level of social relations, then, ethnicity ruled; sexual contact across nationality lines was extremely rare, at least among the first generation.[18]

If it was rare for someone of one nationality to marry someone of another, this was because people's personal lives were divided from one another, on the surface at least, by the organizations and culture which they created for themselves. Soon after arrival in the community, each ethnic group established its own church, so that despite the neighborhood's overwhelming adherence to Roman Catholicism religion was not a unifying force in Packingtown. In addition, the Lithuanian and Polish Catholic and German Lutheran parishes all maintained their own schools, where children were taught in the native tongue rather than in English. A 1912 study found that the community's nine parochial schools had an enrollment more than twice that of the public elementary schools. As late as 1918, a sample of nine hundred of the community's children showed that about two-thirds were still educated in the parish schools, which were organized along ethnic lines.[19]

Fraternal, economic, and political groups were all characterized by the same ethnic division. The Bohemians in particular were joiners, and they developed an impressive array of voluntary organizations. By 1902 there were over 30 savings and loans and 259 benefit societies, as well as 35 gymnastics clubs, 18 singing societies, 5 bicycling clubs, and 4 drama groups. It seemed to Hull House investigators that every Bohemian man and woman belonged to at least one order or beneficial society; some belonged to several. Many of these organizations maintained their headquarters in the vicinity of the yards, though the real heart of

Chicago's Bohemian community was a couple of miles north in Pilsen, on the near southwest side of the city. The Bohemians were also more divided than other ethnic communities between Roman Catholics and freethinkers, anticlerical radicals who emphasized education and other forms of self-improvement and battled constantly against the Church's influence. Eight Bohemian parishes, including two in Packingtown, enrolled over three thousand children in their schools in 1904, but the freethinkers were also able to maintain a large school network in which children could learn in an environment free of clerical influence. In Packingtown these competitive ideologies were institutionalized in the form of the SS. Cyril and Methodius parish school and a freethought school, which were within two blocks of each other and drew their adherents from the same population. [20]

Each of the other major ethnic groups in the community rivaled the Bohemians in extent of voluntary organization. The eastern Europeans created extensive networks based on their parishes, the focal points of Slavic community life. Both the Lithuanians and Poles established fraternal orders, savings and loans, and nationalist organizations in addition to the array of religious and social groups which knitted each parish together. Both communities were rent by the same clerical/freethought conflict that divided the Bohemians, though the Polish and Lithuanian freethinkers were clearly in the minority. Each community also fostered an active socialist movement. The Lithuanian Socialist Alliance, which eventually became the Lithuanian Language Federation of the Socialist Party, was particularly strong, providing a network of cultural activities for the community's radicals. Every shade of political opinion seemed to be represented, and each faction published its own newspaper. There were local Democratic and Republican organizations among both Lithuanians and Poles, and Bohemian Democratic and Socialist clubs and other groupings, but all conformed to the dominant ethnic divisions within the community. [21]

Finally, there were ties to the old country itself. In some cases the link was too strong to be broken by emigration. For these people the stay in America was a brief sojourn, or perhaps part of a pattern of cyclical migration; one's goals and identification remained focused on the Old World. While the new immigrants of the late nineteenth and early twentieth centuries generally showed a strong tendency toward reemigration, the phenomenon was particularly common among certain Slavic groups. National figures for 1908 to 1923 show that about two Poles left the country for every five who arrived. Chicago *Polonia* had a term to describe those in continual migration to and from the Old World— *obiezyswiaty,* or "globetrotters." Polish reemigration was especially high in the years just before World War I, when the outward flow very nearly approximated that of arrivals. While the figure for Lithuanians in the 1908–23 period was a bit lower than that for Poles (one leaving for every four who arrived), the rate for Slovaks was actually higher (one leaving for every two who arrived). There are no detailed data for Packingtown immigrants in particular, but the fact that there was a complete travel service for immigrants operating out of a neighborhood bank suggests that the paths between Chicago's South Side and eastern Europe were well worn. It was possible to arrange the whole trip right in the neighborhood.[22]

Ethnic national consciousness crystallized in the years preceding World War I, riveting the attention of Poles, Lithuanians, and Bohemians on the gradual emergence of modern, unified nation-states throughout southern and eastern Europe. The stress and conflicts produced by the confrontation with an urban industrial environment, far from weakening ethnic identification, welded together contending factions and isolated peasant subcultures into cohesive nationality groups. Ethnic identification among eastern Europeans was never stronger than in the early twentieth century.[23]

One of the greatest testaments to ethnic cohesion in Packingtown is the slow progress that formal "Americanization"—English instruction and naturalization, for example—made in the community. The Citizenship School at the University of Chicago Settlement was proud of its English and civics classes for adult immigrants, but in 1909 enrollment stood at only 122, a tiny fraction of the community's foreign-born. Studying the problem among packinghouse workers in the same year, Immigration Commission investigators found that only 27.7 percent of the Poles, 21 percent of the Lithuanians, and 11.7 percent of the Slovaks studied were fully naturalized, and the fact that the study included only immigrants who had been living in the country five years or more means that it probably overestimated the number of naturalized citizens in the work force considerably. The packers' own First World War study showed that 32 percent of the men and 67 percent of the women surveyed could not speak English. Only one-fourth of the men were citizens, and 43 percent had not even taken out first papers in the naturalization process, despite the fact that they had lived in the United States an average of fifteen years. Census figures for 1920 suggest that even the nativism of the war years had little effect; the proportion of aliens in most parts of the neighborhood remained high. Clearly, formal efforts at Americanization were not reaching the vast majority of the foreign-born in Packingtown.[24]

Yet a study of ethnic residential segregation suggests important modifications for this view of a community fragmented along ethnic lines. Federal censuses for the era suggest a striking degree of ethnic diversity. Even Poles, the most highly segregated foreign-born group in the city, were far less segregated in Packingtown than in other parts of the city.[25] But such data only show that all these people lived in the same part of the city; it gives us little idea of their chances for coming into contact with one another.

Data from the 1920 federal census, disaggregated on the basis of census tract, allows us to analyze smaller residential units, each not more than fifteen to twenty city blocks. This approach shows concentrations of ethnic groups in particular parts of the neighborhood, often centering on the community's ethnic parishes. Over 56 percent of the Bohemians lived in a single census tract in the extreme southwestern corner of the community, an area bounded by Forty-seventh and Fifty-first streets on the north and south and by Robey Street and the Pittsburgh, Cincinnati, Chicago and St. Louis Railroad tracks on the east and west. Almost three-fourths of all the Lithuanians lived in the neighborhood's least desirable blocks, just west of the stockyards, between Ashland Avenue and the city dumps on the east and west and between freightyards and Forty-seventh Street on the north and south. About a fourth of the large Polish community was contained in one census tract, the sixteen blocks just southwest of the yards. This enclave was bounded by Forty-seventh and Fifty-first streets on the north and south, Centre (now Racine) Avenue on the east, and Loomis Street on the west. But even the census tract is too large a unit of analysis, and the impression of ethnic segregation conveyed is somewhat misleading. The representation of each of these groups in most of the census tracts was, in fact, quite close to its proportion in the total population, suggesting again some degree of ethnic mixture.[26]

Two separate house-to-house canvasses conducted in 1905 and 1909 allow us to gauge ethnic segregation within individual blocks, and both tend to reinforce the impression of an ethnically mixed neighborhood, though there is certainly a degree of ethnic concentration. The 1905 data show that Polish families were distributed evenly over the blocks. Lithuanians were concentrated disproportionately on Paulina Street in the blocks just west of the yards, but these blocks also contained thirty-two Polish families and even one large Irish family. Slovaks were more concentrated on Honore and Laflin than on other streets, but Honore had more Poles than Slovaks and Laflin was quite mixed, with more Irish than any of the other blocks. The clearest example of segregation was on Winchester and Robey streets, which apparently were inhabited only by Bohemians at the time of the 1905 census. These blocks not only had a higher proportion of brick buildings than most of the others, but they were also a little farther away from the noise, congestion, and pollution of the yards. This was clearly the most desirable part of the neighborhood. It was inhabited by families who had been living in the country for a long time and had managed to amass some savings and pay off their homes. The families here had a higher proportion of skilled fathers and more children going into skilled and white-collar occupations. Of all the groups in the neighborhood, only Bohemians could boast these characteristics.[27]

The 1909 data show a greater degree of segregation, particularly on Loomis, Throop, Elizabeth, and Centre streets, which were all in the Polish neighborhood just southwest of the yards. But these blocks also contained many Bohemian, German, and Irish families. These later data confirm the impression conveyed by the 1905 census that the most congested blocks west of the yards were also those containing the highest proportions of recent immigrants. Yet even here, some Irish and Germans remained behind to live alongside the Lithuanians and Poles.[28]

The raw data from the 1905 census even allow us to determine

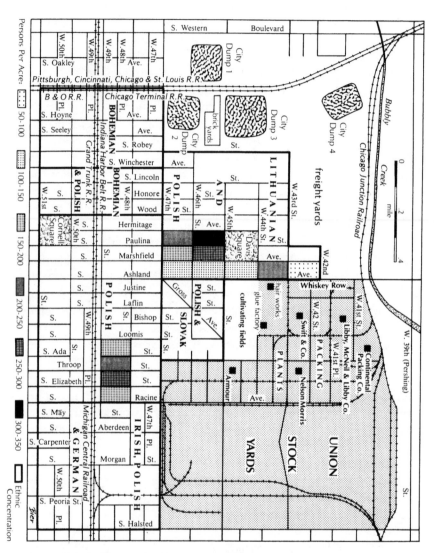

Map 2. Ethnic Residential Concentrations and Population Density in Selected Blocks, Packingtown, 1909. Adapted from Edith Abbott and Sophinisba Breck-inridge, "Housing Conditions in Chicago, III: Back of the Yards," *American Journal of Sociology* 16 (Jan. 1911), map, n.p.

how common it was for families from different ethnic backgrounds to be living together in the same building. Of seventy-six multifamily dwellings in the sample, forty-five (59.2 percent) were shared by families from different backgrounds. The most common mixture was Polish and Lithuanian, in spite of traditional tensions between these groups. In some cases, however, several different nationalities shared the same building. For example, 4429 South Honore Street housed a German widow and her two children, a middle-aged Slovak couple and their four teenagers, a middle-aged Polish couple with their two teenage daughters, and three young Polish couples with their five children. While such diversity was not typical, *some* degree of mixture was quite common.

Photographs of Packingtown in the early twentieth century often show people outside—sitting on stoops, standing on corners, walking to and from work. Even photos of the filthy alleys and flooded dirt roads frequently show groups of children playing. The fact that the people of Packingtown spent so much time out of doors should not be surprising, given the congestion and stifling atmosphere of the wooden tenements. But this characteristic, which Packingtown undoubtedly shared with many other working-class communities, is significant because it increased the potential for interethnic social contact. The implications of this sort of contact will be important when we turn to the question of working-class organization.[29]

At least one social institution certainly bridged some of the ethnic divisions in the community—the saloon. Considerable attention has been focused recently on the obvious cultural importance of the working-class saloon. But it would be difficult to imagine a situation in which it played a more vital role in the life of the community than it did in Packingtown. The Twenty-ninth Ward, which included Packingtown, had five hundred saloons at the turn of the century, twenty-five times the number in Hyde Park. A packer-sponsored study during the First World War found a total of three hundred in a much smaller area immediately around the yards. Many of these were concentrated near the Ashland Avenue and Halsted Street approaches to the yards; others were scattered throughout the residential blocks to the south and west. Although the packers and some contemporary social scientists took the existence of so many saloons as one more indication of the degenerate character of the neighborhood and its inhabitants, an analysis of the saloon's function in the community leads us in a different direction. The saloon played an important role in the social contacts between recent immigrants and the more assimilated butcher workmen who had worked in the industry for decades and provided the leadership for early labor organizations.[30]

As the most important commercial base in the community, saloons provided one of the few avenues of upward social mobility for those hoping to escape the packinghouses. Many saloon-keepers along "Whiskey Row" on Ashland Avenue, for example, were retired butcher workmen who had been financed by breweries. In exchange for an agreement from the prospective saloonkeeper to sell only his brand of beer, the brewer paid the rent and license fee, provided the fixtures and beer, and even helped to find a suitable location. A special assessment was levied on each barrel of beer and in this way the saloonkeeper gradually reimbursed his brewer. By 1907 an estimated 80 percent of Chicago's saloons were brewer-financed. This arrangement made it relatively easy for some better-paid workers to enter the liquor trade.[31]

Saloonkeepers were not only the community's single most important group of businesspeople. They also offered important services for the great mass of packinghouse workers who were not on their way up. Since they provided practically the only halls in the community, saloons hosted weddings, dances, and other festivities and offered meeting places for fraternal groups, other ethnic organizations, and, later, union locals. Another service provided was check cashing. One writer estimated that 95 percent of all stockyards checks were cashed in saloons. The one at Forty-third and Ashland Avenue, for example, cashed over forty thousand dollars' worth of paychecks each month. For such service, the saloonkeeper kept the odd change and the patron was expected to stand a round of drinks. The saloon was also a cafeteria. Since the packers provided none, the worker faced the option of eating his lunch amid the blood and filth of the killing floor or walking across Ashland Avenue to a saloon where he could get a hot lunch for the price of a beer. Then there were the less tangible benefits of saloon socializing—newspapers, fellowship, perhaps even a bit of music. It is not difficult, then, to understand why saloons thrived in the community.[32]

Some saloons provided an informal atmosphere where ethnic divisions began to break down. The distribution of saloons and their function in relation to work and the labor market meant that some of them were ethnically mixed. Spot maps and social surveys show that saloons had different functions depending upon their proximity to the yards. There were saloons scattered *throughout* the community. In the 1909 survey of twelve blocks by University of Chicago students, the ten residential blocks yielded an average of three saloons each. One of the blocks had seven drinking establishments and another six. In two blocks along Ashland Avenue, however, investigators found forty-six saloons, an average of twenty-three per block. This was part of "Whiskey Row," several blocks of Ashland Avenue that stretched between Bubbly Creek and Forty-seventh Street, adjoining most of the major packing plants and related factories. While the buildings along this stretch housed many immigrant families, most of them also contained at least one saloon. This uneven distribution emerges even more clearly in spot maps, which show a fairly broad distribution of saloons in residential blocks "back of the yards" but a heavy concentration of them along Whiskey Row (see map 3). Neighborhood residents called the latter "daytime saloons" because they were filled with crowds of butcher workmen at various times during the workday but deserted in the evening, when the men socialized in their neighborhoods.[33]

Most saloons in the residential blocks occupied corner buildings, often sharing the location with a grocery store or other commercial establishment, as well as apartments. The corner saloon's commercial success was based on its role as a refuge from the stifling little wooden tenements, and those on ethnically mixed blocks may have integrated various nationalities. Most, however, only reinforced the ethnic divisions that existed; there were Polish, Bohemian, and Lithuanian corner taverns.[34]

Whiskey Row, on the other hand, presents a very different picture. Obviously, this was a choice commercial location for such a business. On their way to and from work; during the noontime "can rush," when runners dashed back and forth across Ashland to bring beer back for workers eating in the various plants; and

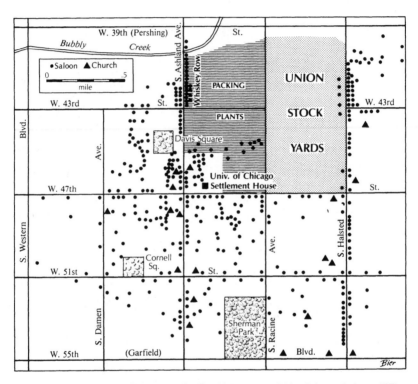

Map 3. Distribution of Saloons in Packingtown, 1908. Adapted from "The Heart of Chicago," map by W. E. McClennan, *Northwestern Christian Advocate,* Apr. 14, 1909, courtesy of the State Historical Society of Wisconsin.

during their respites from the endless search for work, Irish, German, Slavic, and all other manner of butcher workmen rubbed elbows at bars often tended by men who had spent many years in the packinghouses themselves. While Poles entered the saloon trade in increasing numbers during the early twentieth century, the Irish and Germans continued to predominate, and the man behind the bar was apt to be a skilled Irish butcher who had turned in his overalls for a bartender's apron. Some of these saloonkeepers were, in fact, former union activists who had been blacklisted from the industry.[35]

The irregular character of packinghouse work meant that many workers spent a good deal of time in saloons. Outside the workplace itself, these were the points where social contact between "old" and "new" immigrants, particularly those who could speak English, was most likely. It is important to remember, when we visualize thirty thousand workmen streaming out of the packing plants in their bloody overalls and into the saloons along Ashland Avenue, that the world of work provided its own sources for identification, which differed from the ethnic influence which permeated so much of community life. Workers from various houses, regardless of ethnicity, gathered in those saloons closest to their own plants to exchange employment information and discuss common grievances. It is doubtful that even "daytime" saloons were racially integrated, but certainly these institutions, beyond the watchful eye of the superintendent, offered a great potential for contact across ethnic lines. It is no coincidence that the first seeds of labor organization were sown in this fertile ground as the movement spread from the older generation to the younger, from the Irishman to the Pole.[36]

Yet a large proportion of Packingtown's population was excluded from this critical institution. The world of the urban saloon was a man's world, and whatever socialization occurred there did not affect relations among immigrant working-class women in any direct way. There was also at least one common ground, however, for many of the community's women. The settlement house served somewhat the same function for women as the saloon did for men.

Although Packingtown's residents were clearly suspicious of Mary McDowell's motives and aims when she arrived to open the

University of Chicago Settlement House in 1894, she and her as-
sociates worked hard to become an integral part of the community. By meeting the various ethnic groups on their own terms and
coming to appreciate their cultures, by opening the settlement to
various groups in the community, and by actively supporting efforts to improve the quality of life in Packingtown, McDowell and
the settlement came to be well accepted by the early years of this
century.

Since nearly every meeting hall in the neighborhood was
beyond the public sphere of women—either in or directly adjacent to a saloon—the settlement's auditorium was one of the few
places large groups of women could meet. Even more important,
perhaps, were the various social and functional groups McDowell
helped to organize. These provided focal points for socialization
and trained a group of leaders among the community's women.
Located in the heart of Packingtown, the settlement drew women
from many of the community's ethnic enclaves, and thus provided the same sort of common ground that the saloons along
Whiskey Row did for the men. Just as early union organizing
among men took place in saloons, so the earliest spark among
women was struck in the nurturing environment of the settlement
house. McDowell and her staff enthusiastically supported these
efforts from the beginning, and provided the sort of links with
middle-class reformers that were often crucial to the creation of
women's labor organizations. In turn, identification with the settlement lent labor organization an air of respectability in the
metropolitan community.[37]

Our picture of social relations in Packingtown, then, is mixed.
The almost total absence of interethnic marriages and the extended network of ethnic voluntary organizations suggest that sustained social contact across ethnic lines in the neighborhood was
probably unusual, at least among the first generation. There is little indication that the resiliency of the various immigrant cultures
was softening under the rigors of either the extreme poverty and
squalid ecology of the neighborhood or the cultural onslaught of
professional "Americanizers." Indeed, national identification for
the community's dominant groups was probably at its height in
precisely the period under consideration.

Residence patterns and the distribution and functions of

saloons, however, show considerable potential for interethnic contact. Packingtown's families lived in blocks which were quite mixed ethnically. Even at the most microscopic level of analysis—the individual tenement—families of one nationality lived alongside those of others. The importance of saloons, given the exigencies of the labor market, and their location adjacent to the plants facilitated fraternization outside the ethnic divisions of the neighborhood. This is certain: When Pole met Slovak on the tenement front porch or the young Lithuanian shared the bar with the old Irishman, they had at least one thing in common. Above all else, Packingtown was a workers' neighborhood.

Almost 90 percent of family heads in the 1900 census sample were blue-collar workers, and 56.5 percent were unskilled (see table 6). Comparable proportions for Stewart's unsystematic 1905 census are 97 percent and 70 percent. Table 7 provides a detailed occupational classification for all family heads in Stewart's 1905 census. At least 67 percent of the family heads relied on packinghouse work for their livelihood, and the vast majority of these were common laborers. Even these figures probably underestimate the importance of the industry as a source of employment for the neighborhood, since many of the unspecified unemployed (about 10 percent of the total) were probably laid off from jobs in the packing plants. Neither do these figures reflect the employ-

Table 6. Social Structure in Packingtown, 1900–1910

	1900	1905	1909	1910
	(N = 200)	(N = 229)	(N = 1441)	(N = 200)
White-collar	6 (3.0%)	4 (1.7%)	*	17 (8.5%)
Shop-/Saloonkeeper	11 (5.5%)	2 (0.9%)	162 (11.2%)	14 (7.0%)
Skilled	27 (13.5%)	27 (11.8%)	268 (18.6%)	45 (22.5%)
Semiskilled	39 (19.5%)	35 (15.3%)	*	17 (8.5%)
Unskilled	113 (56.5%)	161 (70.3%)	930 (64.5%)	103 (51.5%)
Miscellaneous	4 (2.0%)	*	81 (5.6%)	4 (2.0%)

*No comparable category in data.

Source: Systematic samples, U.S. Bureau of the Census, Manuscript Census of Chicago, 1900, 1910; Stewart Ms. Census, 1905; Edith Abbott and Sophinisba Breckinridge, "Housing Conditions in Chicago, III: Back of the Yards," *American Journal of Sociology* 16 (Jan. 1911): 439.

Table 7. Occupations of Packingtown Male Family Heads, 1905
(N = 254)

		Cumulative Percentage
I. Packinghouse Workers:		
A. Unskilled:		
Common Laborers	119	
By-product Workers	5	
Car-shop Workers	13	
TOTAL	137	53.9
B. Semiskilled:		
Knife Men or		
Machine Operators	21	8.3
C. Skilled:		
Butchers	5	
Auxiliary Trades	7	
TOTAL	12	4.7
ALL PACKINGHOUSE WORKERS	170	66.9
II. Others:		
A. Skilled:		
Bricklayers	1	
Carpenters	6	
Brass Finishers	1	
Lasters	1	
Machinists	3	
Molders	2	
Motormen	1	
Organ Repairmen	1	
Stone Masons	2	
TOTAL	18	7.1
B. Semiskilled:		
Clothing Workers	2	
Factory Workers	2	
Teamsters	5	
TOTAL	9	3.5

(Continued)

Table 7. Occupations of Packingtown Male Family Heads
(continued)

		Cumulative Percentage
C. Unskilled:		
Brickyard Workers	1	
Coalyard Workers	1	
Boiler Firemen	1	
Foundry Workers	4	
Freight Handlers	3	
Lumberyard Workers	3	
Janitors	2	
Railroad Workers	1	
Laborers, Unspecified	19	
TOTAL	35	13.8
D. White-Collar:		
Bookkeepers	1	
Clerks	2	
Switchboard Operators	1	
Horse Traders	1	
Saloonkeepers	1	
TOTAL	6	2.4
E. Miscellaneous:		
Retired	2	
Unemployed	26	
TOTAL	28	11.0

Source: Stewart Ms. Census, 1905.

ment of thousands of boarders living in homes surrounding the stockyards. The University of Chicago's 1909 data, and the 1910 census data, though less dramatic, confirm this image of the neighborhood (see table 6). Of household heads, 83 percent in the 1909 survey and 82.5 percent in the 1910 census sample were blue-collar workers, while most of the rest were saloonkeepers or storekeepers. Over 60 percent worked in meat packing, and most of these were unskilled laborers. Packinghouse employment was thus an experience shared by a large majority of the community's inhabitants. This and the fact that the neighborhood was so close to the yards meant that life in Packingtown was deeply influenced by conditions in the industry.[38]

THE STANDARD OF LIVING AND
THE FAMILY ECONOMY

What standard of living did this employment allow? The question is important not only to gaining a fuller understanding of the lives of packinghouse workers, but also because thousands of other workers shared the kind of working conditions faced by common laborers in packing—irregular employment, low wages, accidents, and industrial disease. The national scope of the labor market in which these workers competed with one another produced a standard common labor rate which varied little from one industry to another. Although there has been some investigation recently of unskilled wages, the standard of living for common laborers remains largely unexplored. An understanding of the economic situation of packinghouse laborers and their families provides a clearer picture of their daily lives and their motivations.[39]

The neighborhood's physical environment provides some indication of living standards, but we must analyze the finances of Packingtown's families in order to understand how work affected family life. The nature of work in the industry, for example, greatly increased the burden of responsibility on married women and mothers by drawing them into the plants. It truncated education and significantly narrowed the future prospects for the community's children. And it tied all into a complicated local economy which allowed the family to survive, while actually subsidizing the industry's employment system and wage structure.

Wages for most male packinghouse workers were extremely low. The common labor rate, the wage earned by at least two-thirds of the labor force, fluctuated between 15 cents and 20 cents per hour from the turn of the century until 1917. Workers won important gains in real wages during the First World War, but these largely disappeared during the postwar depression. Real earnings, moreover, were far lower than these rates suggest, because of the irregularity of employment described earlier. Thousands of laborers in cattle- and hog-slaughtering gangs were laid off for two or three months during the slow summer season and for shorter periods at other points during the year. As the number of cattle fell off, the packers reduced gang size and skilled men often took over common labor jobs at reduced wages. Light cattle shipments at the end of the week also meant that many laborers could not count on more than three days' work each week even during the busier season. Thousands of workers, always more than were needed, milled around the Union Stockyards gates and the employment offices of the various packers. They were called to work only when the killing was about to begin and sent home once it was finished. Some firms made efforts to regularize hours to undercut union agitation over the issue, but seasonal unemployment and erratic scheduling remained problems for many workers throughout the 1920s.[40]

As a result of low wages and high unemployment, the earnings of male family heads in Packingtown came nowhere near meeting their families' minimum budget requirements. A meticulous 1911 study by University of Chicago Settlement House investigators estimated the average weekly wage for laborer husbands at $9.67, while the estimate for minimum weekly expenditures needed to support a family of five (based on family budgets) was $15.40. (In fact, average family size in the community was 5.33.) When *all* sources of income were considered, 30 percent of the 184 families in the study showed budget *deficits*. Estimates did not include such "extraordinary" expenses as weddings, funerals, injuries, or prolonged illness. In a Catholic community with a very high infant mortality rate, such expenses were probably not so extraordinary, and workers often borrowed money to bury their little ones. A wedding, a funeral, or a doctor's bill could present the prospect of stark privation.[41]

How did Packingtown's families survive on a day-to-day basis? The answer, of course, is that family heads' earnings comprised only a portion of family income (54.4 percent in the 1911 University of Chicago study). As in so many other working-class communities of this era, Packingtown's families relied on a complicated local economy aimed at supplementing the insufficient earnings of family heads.[42] Husbands searched for alternative employment in slack periods. Wives took in boarders and sometimes engaged in marginal employment within the home. Children left school early for factory work. Some residents even fell back on the "resources" of the neighborhood, scavenging to make ends meet. Not all families engaged in all of these activities. How a family supplemented the earnings of its head depended upon several factors. But most families who were caught in the web of the common labor market at the yards faced a desperate struggle for survival. [43]

When they could not find work in the industry, some laborers looked elsewhere. They were not alone in their search. Laborers in many other industries relied upon casual hiring practices like those in packing; looking for a job often amounted to walking from the front gate of one factory to another. When the hero of Upton Sinclair's novel *The Jungle* is forced to leave Packingtown in his search for work, he makes the rounds of other seasonal industries. A streetcar ride brings him to the South Chicago steel mills; hopping a freight opens the door to agricultural labor in the rich farmlands west of the city. Although the details of how this and other city labor markets functioned are not clear, Sinclair's fictional description had a firm basis in the reality of industrial employment in early twentieth-century America. There were overlapping citywide, regional, national, and international markets for common labor, and workers often circulated among a number of industries, putting together enough employment to get by.

In her study of immigrant employment agencies, Grace Abbott concluded that the problem of casual employment was especially severe in Chicago. "Chicago is apparently a clearing-house for the seasonal laborers of the country. . . . There are always large numbers of unskilled laborers in the city who in prosperous times keep the price paid this class of laborers in and around Chicago depressed and in times of distress and unemployment become a great burden on Chicago's charitable organizations."[44] The peculiar economic position of Chicago as the hub of a vast railroad network within a highly diversified metropolitan economy encouraged the growth of a casual labor market in the city.

The center of this "seasonal labor exchange" was just west of the Loop, the city's central business district, directly across from the great Union Railroad Station. The market which operated there drew workers from throughout the city and around the world. Here Polish and Lithuanian immigrants mixed with displaced American farm boys and hoboes in employment agencies, saloons, cheap lodging houses, and second-hand clothing stores, each of them waiting for his next job. Casual labor agencies advertised a variety of work, much of it "gang work," which meant hiring on with a group and often traveling a long distance from the city. Sometimes a group of workers from the same ethnic background signed on and traveled together, but more often work gangs were mixed. Many agencies specialized in recruiting recent immigrants for railroad and building construction, ice and lumber cutting, foundry work and, of course, the stockyards. The new immigrants of this era are now well recognized for their mobility in search of industrial work. These sorts of jobs, in the city or away from it, provide part of the answer to the question of how Packingtown's families survived.[45]

But however hard a husband might try, and however far he might travel in his search for alternative work, the family could rarely get by on his earnings alone. The remainder came from a complex local economy involving the boarding system, child labor, and a variety of marginal enterprises based on the peculiar conditions of Packingtown as a community.

Families with teenage children sent them to work in the stockyards or in the surrounding factories and plants. As noted in the earlier sketch of the industry's female labor force, most women packinghouse workers until the First World War were the young, single daughters of butcher workmen. Not only did most of these young women work because of financial necessity, but they were frequently primary breadwinners. The 1906 Illinois Bureau of Labor Statistics Report showed that 55 percent came from families where fathers' earnings were either impaired, because of disease, injury, or some other cause of chronic unemployment, or nonexistent, because of desertion, divorce, or death. These young single women were joined by their brothers. Children contributed significantly to family income throughout the early twentieth century. Two different contemporary studies of family budgets indicate that about 27 percent of the community's families depended upon the earnings of children under the age of sixteen. Naturally, this proportion was higher among older, more established families and lower among immigrant families with younger children.[46]

Of ninety-two children for whom occupational status was enumerated in the 1905 census, at least fifty-four (more than 60 percent) worked in the yards, most as common laborers and machine operators. Many of the eleven unemployed and the fourteen clerks, messengers, and office boys probably also worked for packing companies. The importance of children's contributions to family income varied from one ethnic group to another and was apparently a reflection of the close relationship between family cycle and family economy. The number of children in the industry might have been much higher had it not been for a stringent child labor law, passed under union pressure. The law forbade any child under the age of fourteen to enter paid employment, and it was strictly enforced in the yards. Children who started work under age had to turn to other industries in the area. [47]

The contribution children made to family income was important enough that a large casual child labor market, paralleling that for the adults, grew up in and around the community. Most boys under the age of sixteen worked as messengers or errand boys or as machine tenders. Girls were even more apt to become machine tenders or wrappers, working at piece rates in soap, candy, and cracker factories. Other girls entered the needle trades, and a few took the streetcar downtown to work in offices or department stores. Domestic work, however, was universally despised and rejected by Packingtown's second generation in favor of the "definite duties of the factory." [48]

Like packinghouse work, this juvenile employment tended to be seasonal and irregular, with extremely high turnover and low wages. In 1912, when Louise Montgomery interviewed 258 girls about their jobs, almost 90 percent earned $4.00 per week or less. Upon leaving school at fourteen, or earlier if possible, many of Packingtown's children became locked into an extensive casual labor market, passing quickly from one job to another. When economic conditions improved, turnover skyrocketed. Among messenger boys at Swift, for example, it reached 342 percent during 1918. [49]

When University of Chicago investigators studied school and work opportunities for Packingtown's children in 1910-11, their findings were dismal. A part of the study that focused intensively on an ethnically mixed group of twenty-one sixteen-year-old boys and girls provides some idea of what the second generation had to look forward to upon dropping out of school. The group's mean weekly earnings were $4.13, and the children averaged about six or seven months in a job. As a group, they had been idle more than a third of the time since leaving school. Clearly, one could not sustain an independent existence on these earnings. [50]

But this labor market functioned to supplement the wage of the family head, not to support an independent individual. Boy and girl labor not only kept wages low in the industries that it directly affected, but also subsidized the common labor rate in the packing industry. Packingtown's children were not passive objects in this exploitative system, of course. High turnover, employer complaints about inefficiency, widespread restriction of output, and spontaneous children's strikes all testify to a spirit of restlessness and resistance. Without some lasting form of organization, however, such protests remained largely ineffective; leaving one job did not make conditions any better in the next one. [51]

This integration of children into the family economy was not new to the experience of eastern European immigrants. In the Polish community, for example, a high premium was placed on obedience, love, and respect of one's parents, and contributions to family support represented one way of expressing such familial loyalty. Children had always played an important role in the economic life of Polish peasant society, and in the course of industrialization young Polish migrants frequently contributed their earnings to support parents and siblings back home. [52]

Yet it is probably misleading to describe the family strictly in terms of harmonious familial cooperation based on traditional values. Such an approach obscures the tensions which developed between generations under the wage labor system in American cities. In a fascinating study of working girls in Packingtown, Louise Montgomery documented the persistent conflicts between Chicago-reared "American girls" and their European parents. Such tensions have frequently been analyzed in cultural terms, but Montgomery's study indicates that they often revolved around the issue of wage-earning status and the allocation of scarce resources. Immigrant parents' "effort to sustain a continued sense of national separation is weakened," Montgomery reported, "by the daily recognition of an economic status which, especially among the young, tends to obliterate the rigid old-country standards, prejudices and traditions, and to substitute an unfixed determinant based on changing opportunities."[53]

Once they had experienced wage work, young Polish-American women sometimes resisted the complete control of earnings by their mothers. Very few refused to support their families, but many insisted on keeping a portion of their earnings for fashionable clothes and for recreational activities which their parents considered wasteful. The fancy hat became a symbol on both sides of this generation gap. In eastern Europe no woman below the middle class wore one, but the streets of Packingtown were full of them. To the Slavic mother, the hat represented the corrupting influences of the big-city environment and a threat to traditional values; to her daughter, it was a badge of her status as an American working girl. Montgomery found that many girls clamored to leave school for the packing plant or candy factory, partly to help their families but also to win a measure of the independence which the work symbolized for them. Such evidence suggests that these immigrant families were in a state of flux. While continuing to espouse traditional values, they were forced to adapt to their new environment and the changes in consciousness it produced.[54]

In contrast to those of children, wives' wages for industrial work provided little or no supplement to Packingtown's family income before World War I. In 1905 (even after the entrance of women into several departments during a strike), very few wives worked in the yards or anywhere else outside of the home. Those who did claim earnings tended to be engaged in irregular nonindustrial work of some kind. Out of an entire sample of 280 wives that year, only six reported an income. One was a midwife, two took in washing "occasionally," and two collected firewood. The sixth, clearly the exception, was a newly arrived forty-five-year-old Lithuanian woman who worked in the yards. She had no children and only one boarder and earned a dollar a day making sausage.[55]

Some scholars have explained the failure of certain groups of immigrant women to take up industrial work in terms of the limited employment available to them. Steel mill towns and other heavy industry areas offered few jobs for women. But unlike a steel mill town, Packingtown and the neighborhoods surrounding it offered considerable employment for women from the late nineteenth century on. Others have argued that some immigrant women avoided industrial employment for cultural reasons. Such work would have violated deeply held traditional peasant values regarding the role of women in the family. In Packingtown, however, wives' rejection of wage work crossed all ethnic lines and included Polish women who showed a strong proclivity for industrial work in other communities.[56] Why did so few of Packingtown's wives and mothers choose wage work?

There may, in fact, have been a number of reasons, but the most compelling one was economic. As a money-making proposition, the work which wives did in the home—cooking, washing, and caring for the needs of their boarders—was far more lucrative than employment in the yards, considering the low wages and irregularity of women's work there. In the yards a woman could not expect to earn, on average, more than six or seven dollars a week; she could earn about thirty dollars per week, minus the cost of extra food, by taking in three male lodgers and cooking for them at the prevailing rates.[57]

Descriptions of the family economy also show that the mother occupied the crucial position of managing the family budget, collecting payment from the boarders and the wages of all family members, doling out each person's share, and making do with what was available. This was certainly the case in Packingtown. A mother could make a greater financial contribution to the family's maintenance, while performing what were probably viewed as her family duties of childrearing and caring for the home, by taking in boarders than by going to work in the yards.[58]

Other evidence supports this generalization. Even five of the six wives who did report some kind of income in 1905 were engaged in pursuits which could be integrated into or performed around the domestic work routine. Midwifery, for example, was by its nature irregular work, though vital to the life of the community.[59] Firewood could be collected after domestic chores were finished, and outside washing could be done during the same time as that set aside for the family's and boarders'.

The relative importance of boarding to a family's income was related to a number of factors. One of these was clearly family life cycle. Younger, smaller families relied more on income from boarders, while larger, older families depended more on the earnings of older children. Table 8, which summarizes data on children by ethnic group, demonstrates this relationship between age of children and the family's relative dependence on boarding. Both the mean number and mean age of children for Lithuanians and Slovaks suggest that these were younger families who were forced to take in boarders because their children were not old enough to contribute to the support of the family.

The Poles, who show a slightly higher proportion of working-age children and a relatively high children's contribution to family income, had a mean number of boarders somewhat lower than that for Slovaks and considerably lower than that for Lithuanians, the group most dependent on the system. The most striking contrast can be seen between the Lithuanians' extreme reliance on boarding and the virtual absence of the system among the older, more-established Bohemian families.[60]

The data suggest a function for boarding fundamentally different from that proposed by Hareven and Modell in their work on the system. They concluded that boarding was primarily a method used by older families to make up income lost with the departure of an older child. By taking in a boarder from the same general age group as the departed child, older families were able to offset the decline in earnings due to the advancing age of the family head.[61]

In the case of Packingtown, however, the relationship between

Table 8. Family Economy and Family Cycle: Child Labor and the Boarding System, 1905 (N = 284)

	Total Number of Children	Mean Number of Children	Percentage of Children under Ten Years Old	Mean Age of Children	Percentage of Children Employed	Mean Monthly Children's Earnings	Mean Number of Boarders
Polish	237	1.96	67.1	7.73	14	$21.62	3.12
Lithuanian	126	1.77	88.5	4.59	0	0	4.17
Slovak	50	1.65	77.1	5.26	10	19.80	3.26
Bohemian	126	3.31	41.9	11.40	36	25.26	.13
Irish	40	4.44	30.0	14.15	40	26.56	.22
German	20	2.22	60.0	8.10	10	14.00	.43
Other	12	1.71	50.0	10.33	8	10.50	1.14

Source: Stewart Ms. Census, 1905.

family cycle and boarding seems to have run in the opposite direction: the younger the family, the greater the reliance on boarding. The Bohemian families in the community are precisely the sort of older, larger, more stable families that might be expected to have taken in boarders. Yet boarding was universally shunned among the Bohemians, who had the option of relying instead on the income of children to help fill in holes in the family budget.

Perhaps even more striking than the ethnic and family cycle variations, however, is the extremely high proportion of the total number of families with boarders. Boarding was characteristic, of course, of many early twentieth-century working-class communities. Twenty-four percent of the 25,400 families included in the U.S. Commissioner of Labor's 1901 national survey took in boarders, while totals for several community studies for the period range from 20 to 50 percent.[62] In Packingtown, however, about two-thirds of the families studied had at least one boarder. Many had far more. A 1909 University of Chicago study found the average to be between two and three.[63]

Other factors besides family life cycle were clearly at work. The more recently arrived eastern Europeans, characterized by lower skill levels and wage rates and more erratic employment than the older immigrant groups, hosted far more boarders. These newer immigrant communities also contained larger proportions of the young unmarried males who provided most of the community's boarder population. In a word, the boarding system "fit" both the economic and the demographic situation of the eastern European immigrant families and thus played a vital role in their family economy.

The data suggest the importance of studying boarding as one part of a family economy which was directly related to wage rates, regularity of employment, and other work-specific problems, as well as to family cycle. The relationship between work and the family economy was obviously important for many working-class families, but it was critical in a community like Packingtown, where laborers' families lived on the margin between chronic poverty and utter destitution.

While serving a critical economic function, the much higher incidence of boarding had generally negative consequences for the quality of life among these families. Crowding was worst throughout the early twentieth century in the Lithuanian blocks closest to the yards (see map 2). In one two-bedroom apartment, for example, settlement house investigators found a Lithuanian family of seven sharing the flat with six male lodgers; another family of the same size took in seven. Not surprisingly, these were also the blocks with the highest rates of tuberculosis and infant mortality.[64]

The Packingtown story shows how misleading it can be to think in terms of life choices in trying to understand the plight of people who really had very little choice. Such was the case with Packingtown's young Lithuanian families, who turned to boarding because there was no other way for them to make ends meet.

War changed the economic situation of Packingtown's families in a number of ways. The severe labor shortage and unionization pushed money wages up by 245 percent between 1914 and 1921. Even allowing for rapid inflation (185.3 percent) during these same years, the war brought a significant rise in the standard of living. But even these increases left Packingtown's families far below the Bureau of Labor Statistics' "minimum standard of health and decency." Table 9 compares average yearly wages for unskilled packinghouse workers with the Bureau of Labor Statistics' minimum yearly budget for a family of five.

The table demonstrates two important facts about Packingtown living standards during and immediately after the war. First, while real wages fluctuated with inflation, there was a small but significant rise in the period of union activity, 1917 to 1921. Second, and more important, common laborers could still not earn enough to support their families. Even at their peak, during 1920, average yearly earnings represented less than half of the U.S. Bureau of Labor Statistics' estimated minimum yearly budget for a family of five. An integrated family economy, drawing on the contributions of all members, remained a critical prerequisite for financial stability and an important influence on wage rates.[65]

In fact, Packingtown's intricate family economy, based as much on boarding and children's earnings as on fathers' contributions, faced a crisis during World War I. While rapid wartime inflation placed pressure on family budgets, the boarding system collapsed. Hostilities in Europe and the draft at home cut off the flow of young, unattached immigrants who had provided the bulk

Table 9. Real Wages for Unskilled Packinghouse Workers,
1914–22

	Estimated Average Yearly Wages in Dollars*	U.S.B.L.S. Minimum Budget	Real Wages as a Proportion of Budget*
December 1914	535.56	1405.00	.38
December 1915	535.56	1442.15	.37
December 1916	688.56	1678.93	.41
December 1917	841.56	1992.29	.42
December 1918	1077.12	2418.41	.45
June 1919	1138.32	2451.73	.46
December 1919	1211.76	2818.43	.43
June 1920	1297.44	3015.13	.43
December 1920	1297.44	2715.86	.48
May 1921	1101.60	2506.52	.44

*My calculations.

Source: Butcher Workman 3 (Aug. 1921): 4–5, from U.S. Bureau of Labor
Statistics figures.

of the boarder population. The effects can be seen in demographic changes. Population in a Lithuanian neighborhood just
north of the stockyards, for example, dropped by 1,400 between
1914 and 1924, but the number of families remained about the
same. Before the war there had been 1,555 boarders in an area of
the neighborhood studied at the time; by 1924 the same blocks
contained only 323. Only seventy-six families still kept boarders.
The institution upon which so many families had relied had
nearly vanished. The war itself had contributed to this change,
and then eastern European immigration was virtually cut off by
the 1921 and 1924 immigration laws. This suggests that the decline was probably permanent.[66]

Packingtown's wives and mothers found a new source of family
income in the rapidly expanding wartime market for packinghouse labor. Until the war, the vast majority of the women working in the Chicago plants were single, but as boarding declined as
a viable supplement to family income, more and more married
women sought employment in the yards. With wages rising, meat
packing became an alternative to the declining boarding system.[67]

Table 10. Reasons Given by Packingtown Mothers for Entering
Packinghouse Work, 1918 (N = 590)

	Reasons Suggesting Economic Hardship
Insufficient Income	249 (42.2%)
Widowhood, Desertion, Divorce	116 (19.7%)
Debts Occasioned by Death	6 (1.0%)
Debts Occasioned by Illness	44 (7.5%)
Husband Ill	60 (10.1%)
TOTAL	475 (80.5%)
	Other Reasons
Buying Property	69 (11.7%)
Children's Education	12 (2.0%)
Savings	24 (4.1%)
TOTAL	105 (17.8%)
	No Answer
	10 (1.7%)

Source: Stock Yards Community Clearing House, "Report on the Community
Study, 1918," Mary McDowell Papers, Folder 20, Chicago Historical Society.

The shift of married women into the plants was a matter of
economic imperatives. The vast majority of working mothers did
not *choose* to take up industrial work but rather were forced into it
for financial reasons. Their contributions, now in the form of
wages rather than payments from boarders, remained a crucial
part of the family economy.

Using the packers' own categories and data, table 10 shows that
80.5 percent of working mothers studied left the home for reasons
of financial hardship. This figure corresponds exactly with a 1919
Children's Bureau study of working mothers for the city as a
whole. In this respect, then, married women packinghouse workers were little different from the young single immigrant women
who had preceded them, except that an even higher proportion of
them worked because their contribution, now in the form of
wages, was essential to the family's economic stability.[68]

The entry of married women into the labor force presented the community with another problem. Most of these women had children under school age. Who would care for them? In 1921 the packers opened their own nursery near one of the main entrances to the Yards. A nearby Catholic settlement enrolled another small group, but between them the two institutions could never have cared for more than a tiny fraction of the children of working mothers.[69]

Families dealt with the problem in a variety of ways. In some cases, husband and wife worked different shifts, alternating in the role of primary caretaker. Many women asked for night work so that they could be with their children during the day. But this did not always solve the woman's problem, because most husbands still insisted that their wives do all the normal household chores in addition to working their shift in the slaughterhouse. Most of the forty-six working mothers studied by University of Chicago Settlement residents in 1917 seldom slept more than a couple of hours each night. On Monday and Tuesday, the regular wash days in the community, some did not sleep at all. They returned from their shifts in the boning or canning departments and went right to work on a mountain of dirty clothes. Other families relied on a friend or neighbor to "keep an eye on the kids." Here old-country ties and reconstructed kinship networks may have been important in filling the gap left by the mother's new "career." But often the younger children had to be left in the care of an older brother or sister, and over 40 percent of the children in the packers' own study (including those of school age) received no day care at all—they were simply on their own.[70]

When Judge Louis Alschuler, the government's labor arbitrator for the industry, took a personal tour of a dozen workers' homes in the winter of 1918, he found several in which children had been left unattended. In one, a little Polish girl of eight was caring for six other children, the youngest a baby of fourteen months. The only food in the flat consisted of a kettle of cabbage, a half loaf of stale rye bread and a pot of cold coffee. In the window, a government placard admonished the children: "Don't Waste Food!"[71]

Once again the community underwrote the industry's labor costs; in this case, the introduction of a new group into the labor pool. Packingtown's mothers were forced into the packinghouses through sheer economic necessity and, without the provision of adequate child care services, the children of the community paid the price.

The poorest in Packingtown lived on the edge of absolute destitution and depended on various forms of scavenging to get by. Many families (usually wives and children) combed the railroad sidings for stray coal or searched for wood to sell or use as fuel. The most important asset the community offered the scavengers was the city dump, which attracted not only dozens of women and children but also professionals who did a good business picking through the city's garbage. Here the poorest searched for kindling, old mattresses, and even fragments of edible food. During the 1904 strike immigrant fathers were arrested for violating a city ordinance by searching for food for their children. Normally the authorities were not so vigilant. When William Chenery watched the dump in 1910 as part of yet another University of Chicago study, he commonly found from ten to twenty women and forty to sixty children picking. The dump had one more function which served a broader group and not only the paupers; it provided food for the community's sizable population of domesticated animals and fowl.[72]

In the midst of all this poverty, we find what seems to be a paradox: an unusually large proportion of Packingtown's families owned their own homes. Of the 284 families surveyed in 1905, 64 (22.5 percent) were living in homes which they owned. Home ownership was disproportionately concentrated in those groups

Table 11. Home Ownership in Packingtown, 1905 (N = 284)

	Proportion of Population	Proportion of Homeowners	Proportion of This Group Owning Homes
Bohemian	3.4	28.0	48.6
Polish	42.6	36.0	19.3
Lithuanian	25.0	7.8	7.1
Slovak	10.9	9.4	19.4
Irish	3.2	7.8	55.5
German	2.5	4.7	75.0

Source: Stewart Ms. Census, 1905.

which were more established in the community, included the largest numbers of skilled workers, and showed the greatest amount of savings. The census data show that a majority of the people in the neighborhood financed their homes through savings and loan organizations or personal loans, perhaps from another family or kin-group member. Many families were still paying on their mortgages. [73]

Predictably, the Bohemians included the greatest proportion of homeowners among the more recent immigrants. (See table 11.) They had been in the country much longer than the Poles, Lithuanians, and Slovaks; worked their way into the more skilled jobs; managed to save a certain amount of money; and in many cases had even been able to pay off their mortgages. The Poles, the most established of the recent Slavic immigrants, were slightly underrepresented among home owners, while the Lithuanians were considerably underrepresented.

But the phenomenon of high rates of home ownership extended far below the upper strata of the Packingtown population, and Slavic immigrants showed considerably higher rates than the city population in general. Of sixteen neighborhoods canvassed by University of Chicago investigators in 1914, Packingtown ranked second in home ownership. The home-owning proportion of the neighborhood's population remained much higher than that for the city as a whole throughout the period from 1905 to 1930. By 1920, over 58 percent of the homes in the area "back of the yards" were owned by families who lived in them. Although the foreign-born made up only half of the neighborhood population by this time, they accounted for about 90 percent of home ownership. [74]

Why did immigrants make the enormous sacrifices that were necessary for a common laborer to engage in this sort of investment? One explanation contends that the frame cottage in Packingtown or Gary or any one of a hundred industrial towns reflected the peasant's quest for land which persisted in the mind and soul of the Slovak steelworker or Polish butcher workman or -woman. In this view, home ownership may simply have represented the closest the Slavic immigrant could come to his or her original goal in coming to the United States—to earn enough to return to the land in the old country. [75]

Such considerations undoubtedly influenced some newcomers. But a more practical explanation for the phenomenon of high rates of home ownership emphasizes the immigrant's new role of industrial wage earner over the old one of land-bound peasant. "Home ownership, like multiple family incomes," John Modell argues, "was part of a defensive strategy oriented, as it were, to hoarding resources—saving for a rainy day in the quaint phrase." Owning one's home offered an alternative to high rents, especially when the widespread institution of boarding allowed the owner to make mortgage payments from the contributions of boarders and tenants, while retaining wages for other family expenses.[76]

Home ownership offered working-class families another hedge against the precarious quality of their existence. Evidence for the late nineteenth and early twentieth centuries suggests that while the curve of laborers' earnings dropped considerably as they passed beyond middle age, their chances for illness increased. This change is only logical, but its implications are profound when we consider the predicament of the common laborer. Both of these changes were quite pronounced in an industry like meat packing, which combined a high accident rate and a variety of work-related diseases with an emphasis on strength and speed. For most of the early twentieth century, aging workers could count on neither a pension nor workman's compensation, but decreased earnings were almost a certainty. Facing the likelihood of periodic injury or disease and a real possibility of early death, the common laborer saw home ownership and the opportunity for a sustained income from rent and boarding as a critical resource in the daily struggle for survival.[77]

With this in mind, Packingtown families were willing to make great sacrifices in order to own their homes, bulwarks against an uncertain future. Among those they visited, one home in particular stayed in the minds of University of Chicago researchers. It was a small frame house on Paulina Street containing four apartments and a tiny attic room, and was owned by a Lithuanian stockyards laborer and his family. In order to meet the mortgage payment and still have enough to live on, the man, his wife, and their five children crowded into the attic, which they shared with a "very lively rooster." The four regular apartments were rented. This particular case may have been extreme, but it was common for Slavic families to sacrifice their own comfort in an effort to retain their homes. "Only too often," Abbott and Breckinridge wrote, ". . . ownership is not synonymous with prosperity, but means rather the effort to secure property and future welfare at the cost of present health, comfort and decent living."[78]

The fact that so many immigrants made the sacrifice necessary to buy a home suggests that there was a substantial proportion of families who had made the decision to stay in the United States as early as 1905. This group was certainly augmented by the experience of World War I, which not only cut off the option of remigration but also held out the hope of greater earnings through higher wages and overtime work. There was a growing core of individuals and families who analyzed their economic situation more in terms of the conditions they faced back of the yards and less in terms of what they remembered of life in the Polish mountains or the forests of Lithuania. Some Slavic immigrants were coming to see Packingtown as a permanent home.

Packingtown's complex local economy allowed its families to maintain a precarious existence, but it in no way struck at the root of their poverty. Indeed, boarding, child labor, and other supplementary forms of income helped to subsidize the low wage rates in packing. Each time social workers or social scientists surveyed conditions in the community, they came back to the casual labor system and the common labor rate as the source of its troubles. As long as these conditions remained vital parts of the packinghouse system of production, however, there was no reason to expect changes to come from the packers. For their part, middle-class reformers tended to emphasize either state intervention or employer welfare schemes. But such reforms, if effected, would fail to solve the real problem, which lay in the production process and the labor market. This left one source for social change in the community—the packinghouse workers themselves. To improve conditions in their community, they were forced to organize where their power lay—within the packinghouse.

NOTES

1. Howard Wilson, *Mary McDowell, Neighbor* (Chicago, 1928), 69–70.

2. Wilson, 22–23; Graham Taylor, "Mary McDowell—Citizen," in *Mary McDowell and Municipal Housekeeping*, ed. Caroline Hill (Chicago, 1938), x–xi. On the early philosophy and development of the University of Chicago's famed department of sociology, see Robert E. L. Faris, *Chicago Sociology, 1920–1932* (San Francisco, 1967); Eli Zaretsky, editor's introduction, in William I. Thomas and Florian Znaniecki, *The Polish Peasant in Europe and America*, abridged ed. (Urbana, Ill., 1984), 23–31; Stephen J. Diner. *A City and Its Universities: Public Policy in Chicago, 1892–1919* (Chapel Hill, N.C., 1980).

3. The most important of these studies are Charles J. Bushnell's 1900 Ph.D. dissertation, which was published in four parts in the *American Journal of Sociology* as "Some Social Aspects of the Chicago Stock Yards" (vol. 7, nos. 3, 4, 5, and 6, 1901–1902); a three-part community survey, commissioned by the University of Chicago Settlement, including John C. Kennedy et al., *Wages and Family Budgets in the Chicago Stock Yards District* (Chicago, 1914), Louise Montgomery, *The American Girl in the Chicago Stock Yards District* (Chicago, 1913), and Ernest Talbert, *Opportunities in School and Industry for Children of the Stock Yards District* (Chicago, 1912); and a series of housing surveys directed by Edith Abbott and Sophinisba Breckinridge of the university's School of Civics and Philanthropy, published as "Housing Conditions in Chicago, III: Back of the Yards," *American Journal of Sociology* 16 (Jan. 1911): 435–68 and *The Tenements of Chicago, 1908–1935* (Chicago, 1936). The following profile of the community is also based on a computer-assisted analysis of a special manuscript census conducted in 1905 under the auspices of the United States Commissioner of Labor (hereafter, "Stewart Ms. Census, 1905"). For a description of the data base, see appendix A.

4. Ernest Poole, "The Meat Strike," *Independent* 57 (July 28, 1904): 183.

5. Bushnell, 2: 289.

6. This description is based on the excellent map in Chicago Association of Commerce, *Electrification of Railroads and Smoke Abatement in Chicago* (Chicago, 1915). I would like to thank Steve Sapolsky for this reference.

7. Ibid.; Mary McDowell, "Beginnings," unpub. ms., 2–4, Mary McDowell Papers, Folder 3, Chicago Historical Society (hereafter, "McDowell Papers"). See also the detailed map in Abbott and Breckinridge, "Back of the Yards," and Albert Dilling and Langdon Pearse, *Re-*

port on *Industrial Wastes from the Stockyards and Packingtown in Chicago*, 2 vols. (Chicago, 1921).

8. Bushnell, 2: 296–97, 300; Abbott and Breckinridge, "Back of the Yards," passim; Abbott and Breckinridge, *Tenements of Chicago*, 131–32; Alice Miller, "Rents and Housing Conditions in the Stock Yards District of Chicago, 1923" (M.A. thesis, University of Chicago, 1923), 1–2, 6, 10-12; Mary McDowell, "City Waste," in *Mary McDowell and Municipal Housekeeping*, 1–10.

9. Contagious disease and infant mortality figures for the turn-of-the-century era reflect the rates for the entire Twenty-ninth Ward, which included Bridgeport, to the east of Packingtown. Bushnell, part 1, map 6, 198; Caroline Hedger, M.D., "The Unhealthfulness of Packingtown," *World's Work* 12 (May 1906): 7507; Robert W. DeForest and Lawrence Vieller, *The Tenement House Problem* (New York, 1903), 10; U.S. Commission on Industrial Relations, *Final Report and Testimony*, vol. 4 (Washington, D.C., 1916), 3468–69. See also Caroline Hedger, M.D., "Health—Summer of 1908," McDowell Papers, Folder 13; McDowell, "Beginnings," 36; testimony of Harvey G. Ellerd, arbitration hearing dated Feb. 19, 1918, records of the U.S. Department of Labor, Mediation and Conciliation Service (hereafter RMCS), RG 280, Case 33/864, 3:1848–50, copy in Manuscripts Division, Chicago Historical Society.

10. Stock Yards Community Clearing House, "Report of the 1918 Community Study," McDowell Papers, Folder 20; *Chicago Tribune*, Feb. 23, 1918; *Chicago Record Herald*, Apr. 7, 1901. See also Floyd Bernard, "A Study of the Industrial Diseases of the Stockyards" (M.A. thesis, University of Chicago, 1910); and the arbitration testimony cited in note 9, pp. 1809–11, 1837. The fact that meat packing's accident rate was *lower* than that for steelmaking and railroading suggests just how dangerous the early twentieth-century workplace was.

11. City Homes Association, *Tenement Conditions in Chicago* (Chicago, 1901), 12.

12. "Housing," ms. report, dated 1921, McDowell Papers, Folder 14; Abbott and Breckinridge, *Tenements of Chicago*, 181, 187; Abbott and Breckinridge, "Back of the Yards," 442; Miller, 6–8, 36–37, and the photos of dilapidated housing. For a general discussion of this type of housing and the 1902 reforms, see Thomas Philpott, *The Slum and the Ghetto: Neighborhood Deterioration and Middle-Class Reform, Chicago, 1880–1930* (New York, 1978), chap. 4. The quotation is from the *Chicago Tribune*, Mar. 6, 1918.

13. Average household size is calculated from the Stewart Ms.

Census, 1905. On the relationship among boarding, congestion, and health, see Abbott and Breckinridge, "Back of the Yards," 458 and map; Bushnell, part 2, map 5; Kennedy et al., 70.

14. Stewart Ms. Census, 1905; Abbott and Breckinridge, "Back of the Yards," 456–57. On the proportion of single packinghouse workers, see U.S. Commission on Industrial Relations, *Final Report*, 4:3527; U.S. Immigration Commission, *Reports*, part 11, *Immigrants in Industry*, vol. 13, *Slaughtering and Meat Packing* (Washington, D.C., 1911), 249–51; Kennedy et al., 7.

15. Stewart Ms. Census, 1905. See also the interior photographs of tenements in Abbott and Breckinridge, "Back of the Yards."

16. Stewart Ms. Census, 1905; Breckinridge and Abbott, "Back of the Yards," 438; Kennedy et al., 5; Ernest W. Burgess and Charles Newcomb, eds., *Census Data for the City of Chicago* (Chicago, 1931), 441–53. See also U.S. Immigration Commission, *Reports*, part 11, 13:3471; Carl Thompson, "Labor in the Packing Industry," *Journal of Political Economy* 15 (1907): 89.

17. Kennedy et al., 5; Abbott and Breckinridge, "Back of the Yards," map; Burgess and Newcomb, 443, 445, 452.

18. Stewart Ms. Census, 1905.

19. Montgomery, 9–11; Stock Yards Community Clearing House, "1918 Community Study."

20. *Hull House Maps and Papers* (New York, 1895), 116–28; Alice Masaryk, "The Bohemians in Chicago," *Charities* 13 (Dec. 3, 1904): 206–10; Eugene McCarthy, "The Bohemians in Chicago and Their Benevolent Societies, 1875–1946" (Ph.D. diss., University of Chicago, 1950).

21. William I. Thomas and Florian Znaniecki, *The Polish Peasant in Europe and America* (Boston, 1918), 5:29–92; Edward Kantowicz, "Polish-Chicago: Survival Through Solidarity," in *The Ethnic Frontier: Essays in the History of Group Survival in Chicago and the Midwest*, ed. Peter D'A. Jones and Melvin Holli (Grand Rapids, Mich., 1977), 189–209, and *Polish-American Politics in Chicago, 1888–1940* (Chicago, 1968), chaps. 3 and 4; Dominic A. Pacyga, "Villages of Packinghouses and Steel Mills: The Polish Worker on Chicago's South Side, 1880–1921" (Ph.D. diss., University of Illinois, Chicago, 1981), especially chap. 4; Robert A. Slayton, " 'Our Own Destiny': The Development of Community in Back of the Yards" (Ph.D. diss., Northwestern University, 1982), 159–64; Dominic A. Pacyga, "Crisis and Community: Back of the Yards, 1921," *Chicago History* 6 (Fall 1977): 168, 176; Ethelbert Stewart, "The Influence of Trade Unions on Immigrants," U.S. Bureau of Labor, Bulletin no. 56 (Washington, D.C., 1905), reprinted

in *The Making of America*, vol. 3, *Labor*, ed. Robt. M. LaFollette (Chicago, 1905; reprinted New York, 1969); Victor Greene, *For God and Country: The Rise of Polish and Lithuanian Ethnic Consciousness in America, 1860–1910* (Madison, Wis., 1975), 1–12.

22. Frank Thistelthwaite, "European Migration Overseas in the Nineteenth and Twentieth Centuries," in *Population Movements in Modern European History*, ed. Herbert Moller (New York, 1964), 73–91; "A Century of Immigration," *Monthly Labor Review* 18 (Jan. 1924): 1–19 and especially the table on p. 13; Pacyga, "Villages," 23–24; Thompson, 95. See also Adam Walaszek, *Ze Stanów Zjednoczonych Do Polski Po I Wojnie Swiatowej (1919–1924)* (Warsaw-Cracow, 1983), English summary, 176–80. The Immigration Commission's report contains data on visits home by Packingtown's various ethnic groups. See U.S. Immigration Commission, *Reports*, part 11, 13:253–54; Helene Znaniecki Lopata, "The Polish-American Family," in *Ethnic Families in America*, ed. Charles H. Mindel and Charles H. Habenstein (New York, 1976), 16–17.

23. Greene, chaps. 7–9; Lopata, 20.

24. *Chicago Record Herald*, Oct. 10, 1909; "Citizenship School in the 1908–1909 School Year," McDowell Papers, Folder 11; U.S. Immigration Commission, *Reports*, part 11, 13:258–61; Stock Yards Community Clearing House, "1918 Community Study"; Burgess and Newcomb, 441–52.

25. On Polish-American residential segregation, see Kantowicz, *Polish-American Politics*, 22–23.

26. Philpott, 141; Burgess and Newcomb, 441–52. For clustering around ethnic parishes, see "The Heart of Chicago," map by W. E. McClennan, *Northwestern Christian Advocate*, Apr. 14, 1909.

27. Stewart Ms. Census, 1905.

28. Abbott and Breckinridge, "Back of the Yards," 438.

29. Philpott, 67, 72; Pacyga, "Villages," 79.

30. Bushnell, 2:300; *Chicago Tribune*, Feb. 22, 1918; John M. Kingsdale, "The 'Poor Man's Club': Social Functions of the Urban Working-Class Saloon," in *The American Man*, ed. Elizabeth and Joseph Pleck (Englewood Cliffs, N.J., 1980), 259; McClennan, "Heart of Chicago."

31. Perry Duis, *The Saloon: Public Drinking in Chicago and Boston, 1880–1920* (Urbana, Ill., 1983), 25–26, 34–35, 40–41.

32. Thompson, 107–8; E. C. Moore, "The Social Value of the Saloon," *American Journal of Sociology* 3 (July 1897): 1–12; University of Chicago Settlement, "Prohibition Survey of the Stock Yards Community," 1926, McDowell Papers, Folder 7; Kingsford, 261–67; Duis, 178, 181–82, 185–87; Abbott and Breckinridge, *Tenements of Chicago*, 138–39.

See also the testimony of John Kennedy before Judge Alschuler in the arbitration proceedings cited in note 9 above, pp. 2083–86. For a description of saloon lunches, see John E. George, "The Saloon Question in Chicago," *Economic Studies* 2 (Apr. 1897): 93–94.

33. Abbott and Breckinridge, "Back of the Yards," 464; Hedger, "The Unhealthfulness of Packingtown," 7508–9; Miller, 10; Duis, 178–81; McLennan, "Heart of Chicago."

34. Abbott and Breckinridge, *Tenements of Chicago*, 138–9; Kingsford, 262; Slayton, 168–74.

35. Duis, 152–53, 168–69; Kantowicz, *Polish-American Politics*, 29–30; Slayton, 166–68. Tireless University of Chicago investigators *counted* the number of beer pails crossing Ashland Avenue, tabulating a total of 1,065 in the space of half an hour (see Bushnell, 3:440).

36. Slayton, 166–68; Bushnell, part 2, map 5; Duis, 178–81; Abbott and Breckinridge, "Back of the Yards," map; Kingsford, 268–69.

37. Mary McDowell, "Prejudice" and "Our Proxies in Industry," in *Mary McDowell and Municipal Housekeeping;* Wilson, 95–97; Emily Barrows, "Trade Union Organization Among Women in Chicago" (Ph.D. diss., University of Chicago, 1927), 117; Philip Foner, *Women and the American Labor Movement, from Colonial Times to the Eve of World War One* (New York, 1979), 299, 313. See the following chapter for a discussion of women's unionism.

38. Stewart Ms. Census, 1905; Abbott and Breckinridge, "Back of the Yards," 439. See also U.S. Immigration Commission, *Reports*, part 11, 13:212.

39. Peter R. Shergold, "Wage Differentials Based on Skill in the United States, 1889–1914: A Case Study," *Labor History* 18 (Fall 1977): 485–508; Frank J. Sheridan, "Italian, Slavic and Hungarian Unskilled Immigrant Workers in the U.S.," *Bulletin of the Bureau of Labor*, no. 72 (Washington, D.C., 1907), passim, and for a comparison between wages in packing and several other industries, p. 434. Although a mass of primary sources exists, the only systematic analysis of standard of living is Peter R. Shergold, *Working-Class Life: The "American Standard" in Comparative Perspective, 1899–1913* (Pittsburgh, 1982).

40. Commons, "Labor Conditions," 243–45; U.S. Commission on Industrial Relations, *Final Report*, 4:3467, 3504–5, 3513; Rudolf Clemen, *The American Livestock and Meat Industry* (New York, 1923), 608–9, 707, 710–11; Alma Herbst, *The Negro in the Slaughtering and Meat Packing Industry in Chicago* (Boston, 1932), 111.

41. Estimates of husbands' earnings and minimum family expenditures are from Kennedy et al., 75–76. See also U.S. Commission on In-

dustrial Relations, *Final Report,* 4:3464–67. A proper wedding was estimated to cost about $200, a child's funeral about $35 (Kennedy et al., 80). The 284 families in Stewart's 1905 census averaged about $67 annually in medical expenses. Concerning the deaths of children and what they represented financially as well as emotionally for the families involved, see the testimony of William O'Brien, livestock handler, and Isadore Rubel, machine operator in a butterine department, before Judge Samuel Alschuler, in RMCS, RG 257, Case 33/864, Box 46.

42. Kennedy et al., 169.

43. For relevant analyses of the crucial problem of family economy among working-class families from various racial and ethnic backgrounds, see John Bodnar, *The Transplanted: A History of Immigrants in Urban America* (Bloomington, Ind. 1985), 71–83; John Bodnar, Roger Simon, and Michael Weber, *Lives of Their Own: Blacks, Italians, and Poles in Pittsburgh, 1900–1960* (Urbana, Ill., 1981), 89–112; Elizabeth Pleck, "Two Worlds in One: Work and Family," *Journal of Social History* 10 (1976): 178–95; Tamara K. Hareven, *Family Time and Industrial Time: The Relationship between Family and Work in a New England Industrial Community* (New York and London, 1982), 189–217; and Virginia Yans-McLaughlin, *Family and Community: Italian Immigrants in Buffalo, 1880–1930* (Urbana, Ill., 1981), 159–79. For a comparative analysis of the problem in England and the United States (Birmingham and Pittsburgh), see Shergold, *Working-Class Life,* 64–89, and for a contemporary study, Margaret F. Byington, *Homestead: The Households of a Mill Town,* vol. 5 of *The Pittsburgh Survey* (New York, 1910; reprint, Pittsburgh, 1974), passim. For national data on immigrant families in various industries and communities, see W. Jett Lauck and Edgar Sydenstricker, *Conditions of Labor in American Industry: A Summarization of the Results of Recent Investigations* (New York, 1917), chap. 6.

44. Grace Abbott, "The Chicago Employment Agency and the Immigrant Worker," *American Journal of Sociology* 14 (1908): 293.

45. Abbott, "Chicago Employment Agency," 289–305; U.S. Commission on Industrial Relations, *Final Report,* 4:3512; Carleton Parker, *The Casual Laborer* (New York, 1920), chap. 2; U.S. Immigration Commission, *Reports,* part 22, vol. 18 (Washington, D.C., 1911), 338–40; Papers of the Immigrant Protective League, Folder 53, Urban History Archives, University of Illinois, Chicago. For a brilliant discussion of how the casual labor market functioned in late nineteenth-century London, see Gareth Stedman Jones, *Outcast London: A Study in Class Relations* (Oxford, 1971), part 1.

46. Kennedy et al., 63–68; U.S. Immigration Commission, *Reports,*

part 11, 13:224–27. Children's contributions were, of course, often criti-cal to the economic survival of working-class families. For systematic analysis of the problem, see Bodnar, Simon, and Weber, 89–98.

47. Stewart Ms. Census, 1905; Montgomery, 30; Kennedy et al., 64–67.

48. Montgomery, 52–53; Talbert, 51.

49. Montgomery, 26, 68–70; Talbert, 19–20; Paul H. Douglas, "The Problem of Labor Turnover," *American Economic Review* 7 (1918): 306–16.

50. Talbert, 36.

51. Ibid., 48–51; Montgomery, 25, 28–29.

52. Caroline Golab, "The Impact of the Industrial Experience on the Immigrant Family: The Huddled Masses Reconsidered," in *Immigrants in Industrial America, 1850–1920*, ed. Richard L. Erlich (Charlottesville, Va., 1977), 4–5; Lopata, 22–26. See also Thomas and Znaniecki, 1:93–94.

53. Montgomery, 2.

54. Ibid., especially 1–2, 31–32, 57–61. See also Talbert, 16–19 and 43, and Bodnar, Simon, and Weber, 89–90. Compare the photographs in this volume of young American working women during the 1904 strike and old-country mothers in babushkas.

55. Stewart Ms. Census, 1905. See also U.S. Immigration Commis-sion, *Reports*, part 11, 13:221, 227; Illinois Bureau of Labor Statistics, *Fourteenth Biennial Report* (Springfield, Ill., 1907), 196–98.

56. Susan J. Kleinberg, "Technology and Women's Work: The Lives of Working Women in Pittsburgh, 1870–1900," *Labor History* 17 (Winter 1976): 365–89; Virginia Yans–McLaughlin, "Patterns of Work and Fami-ly Organization: Buffalo's Italians," *Journal of Interdisciplinary History* 2 (Autumn 1971): 299–314; Thomas Kessner and Betty Boyd Caroli, "New Immigrant Women at Work: Italians and Jews in New York City, 1880–1905," *Journal of Ethnic Studies* 5 (Winter 1978): 24–28. For discus-sions of various ethnic groups, see Bodnar, Simon, and Weber, 98–102; Carl Degler, *At Odds: Women and the Family in America from the Revolution to the Present* (New York, 1980), 138–39; and Barbara Klazcynska, "Why Women Work: A Comparison of Various Groups—Philadelphia, 1910–1930," *Labor History* 17 (Winter 1976): 77–84.

57. Stewart Ms. Census, 1905.

58. Commission on Industrial Relations, *Final Report*, 4:3527; Montgomery, 57–59; Lopata, 23–25.

59. As late as 1918, an estimated 74 percent of all children born in Packingtown were delivered by midwives (Stock Yards Community Clearing House, "1918 Community Study").

60. Stewart Ms. Census, 1905. For other data supporting this analysis see Kennedy et al., 66–70; U.S. Immigration Commission, *Reports*, part 11, 13:222–25. The small group of German families in the sample which depart from the pattern described here tended to be younger and more recently arrived than most Germans working in the industry in these years.

61. Tamara K. Hareven and John Modell, "The Malleable Household: Boarding and Lodging in American Families," *Journal of Marriage and the Family* 35 (Aug. 1973): 474–75. See also Ewa Morawska, *For Bread with Butter: The Life-Worlds of East Central Europeans in Johnstown, Pennsylvania, 1890–1940* (London and New York, 1985), 127–29.

62. Martha Fraundorf, "The Labor Force Participation of Turn of the Century Married Women," *Journal of Economic History* 39 (June 1979): 402–3; Stewart Ms. Census, 1905. See also Pleck, 182.

63. The 1905 Stewart manuscript census yielded a proportion of just over 70 percent for all ethnic groups, while a 1910 canvass of Polish households placed the figure at 65 percent. Abbott and Breckinridge estimated that about 53 percent of the families in their sample had boarders, but they strongly suspected underenumeration. Rumors went around the neighborhood that the University of Chicago investigators would report their findings to government officials who would turn the boarders out. Notations on some of the schedules for the Stewart census suggest that enumerators tried to verify the figures provided by respondents (Stewart Ms. Census, 1905; Milton B. Hunt, "The Housing of Non-Family Groups of Men in Chicago," *American Journal of Sociology* 16 [Sept. 1910]: 158; Abbott and Breckinridge, 456).

64. Bushnell, part 2, map 5; U.S. Commission on Industrial Relations, *Final Report*, 4:3468–69; Abbott and Breckinridge, "Back of the Yards," 455–58, map; Kennedy et al., 68–71.

65. Clemen, 712, 720–21; *Butcher Workman* 9 (Apr. 1923): 1–2; *National Provisioner* 59 (Oct. 19, 1918): 131; William Z. Foster, "How Life Has Been Brought into the Stockyards," *Life and Labor* 7 (Apr. 1918): 63–66; *New Majority*, Jan. 1, 1919, 2. See also the compilation of family budgets in the Ernest Burgess Papers, Box 51, Folder 2, Manuscripts Division, Regenstein Library, University of Chicago.

66. Joseph Perry, "Rents and Housing Conditions among the Lithuanians in Chicago" (M.A. thesis, University of Chicago, 1925), 8–16; Miller, 20–21. See also Stock Yards Community Clearing House, "1918 Community Study."

67. U.S. Commission on Industrial Relations, *Final Report*, 4:3527; Stock Yards Community Clearing House, "1918 Community Study"; Perry, 8.

68. Stock Yards Community Clearing House, "1918 Community Study"; Helen Russell Wright, *Children of Wage-Earning Mothers, A Study of a Selected Group in Chicago*, U.S. Department of Labor, Children's Bureau Report no. 102 (Washington, D.C., 1919), 9. One hundred and four of the women in the study's sample of 843 were packinghouse workers. See also Gwendolyn S. Hughes, *Mothers in Industry* (New York, 1925), chap. 2, especially p. 22, which presents very similar data for Philadelphia in the same period.

69. A 1917 University of Chicago Settlement House study found that forty-two working mothers (90 percent) out of a sample of forty-six had children under school age. See Mary McDowell, "Mothers and Night Work," *The Survey* 39 (Dec. 22, 1917): 335. The daycare centers are described in the *Chicago Tribune*, Feb. 21, 1918.

70. Stock Yards Community Clearing House, "1918 Community Study"; McDowell, "Mothers and Night Work," 335–36, and "In the Stockyards District, 1917," McDowell Papers, Folder 15; *Chicago Tribune*, Feb. 21, 1918. See also Wright, 17–26, and Leslie Woodcock Tentler, *Wage-Earning Women: Family and Class in the United States, 1900–1930* (New York, 1979), 153–56.

71. *Chicago Tribune*, Feb. 21, 1918.

72. Abbott and Breckinridge, *The Tenements of Chicago*, 131–32n; City Homes Association, *Tenement Conditions*, 191.

73. Stewart Ms. Census, 1905. Of eighteen families for whom the information was available, ten had financed their homes through savings and loans, four through personal loans, and four through banks. Figures on home ownership in table 11 have been compared with those compiled by U.S. Immigration Commission investigators. The latter figures conform closely to those derived from the 1905 Stewart manuscript census. See U.S. Immigration Commission, *Reports*, part 11, 13:257–58.

74. Stewart Ms. Census, 1905; Abbott and Breckinridge, *Tenements of Chicago*, 363–73; Burgess and Newcomb, 441–52; Dominic Pacyga, "Crisis and Community: The Back of the Yards, 1921," *Chicago History* 6, no. 3 (Fall 1977): 169–70; Greene, 51–55.

75. Greene, chap. 1 and p. 64; Bodnar, Simon, and Weber, 153; Thomas and Znaniecki, 1:162.

76. John Modell, "Changing Risks, Changing Adaptations: American Families in the Nineteenth and Twentieth Centuries," in *Kin and Communities: Families in America*, ed. Alan J. Lichtman and Joan R. Challinor (Washington, D.C., 1979), 128–29; cf. Bodnar, 180–83.

77. Modell, 120–28.

78. Montgomery, 456; Abbott and Breckinridge, *Tenements of Chicago*, 378. On the "defensive" character of Slavic home ownership, see also John Bodnar, "Immigration and Modernization: The Case of Slavic Peasants in Industrial America," *Journal of Social History* 10 (1976): 49–50.

4

Unionization and Americanization, 1900–1904

He never missed a meeting. . . . He had picked up a few words of
English by this time, and friends would help him to understand.
They were often very turbulent meetings, with half a dozen men
declaiming at once, in as many dialects of English, but the speakers were all desperately in earnest, and Jurgis was in earnest too,
for he understood that a fight was on, and that it was his fight. . . .
Their one chance for life was in union, and so the struggle became
a kind of crusade.

Upton Sinclair, *The Jungle*

It is difficult to understand industrial relations in an industry like
meat packing without also analyzing the social relations among
the diverse groups comprised in the industry's work force. The
formation of a working class and the emergence of a labor movement on Chicago's South Side was a continuous historical process
that occurred over several generations. Throughout the late nineteenth century the original generation of Irish and German butchers created their own distinctive culture and built craft organizations to protect their interests. During the labor conflicts of the
1870s, 1880s, and 1890s, this first generation developed a strong
sense of solidarity and a tradition of militancy. Even after their
own union organizations had been destroyed, the Irish and Ger-

man butchers carried this labor ethos with them into the new century.

By the turn of the century such subcultures were increasingly undermined, in Chicago and throughout the country, by the introduction of mass-production technology and the massive influx of new immigrant groups. While the new production methods rendered craft organization much less effective, the creation of new ethnic communities, populated by recent immigrants who shared neither the industrial nor the social and cultural experiences of the earlier generation, threatened the prospects for solidarity and complicated the process of class formation among American workers.[1]

The key to understanding the process of class formation and fragmentation in Chicago and comparable communities in these years lies in the relations between these two generations of industrial workers. The process of unionization in packing was essentially one of socialization through which more experienced, "mature" native-born and old immigrant workers integrated the new generation into the labor movement and the broader working-class community on the city's South Side.[2]

The end result was not assimilation. Polish, Lithuanian, and other new immigrant workers retained a strong sense of ethnic identification and continued to organize much of their social and cultural lives within the boundaries of their ethnic enclaves. But informal contacts across ethnic lines and conscious efforts by union organizers to reach out to the new immigrants resulted in a degree of acculturation. Immigrant workers came to identify the welfare of their own ethnic communities with the strength of an interethnic class organization—the union.

THE NINETEENTH-CENTURY BACKGROUND

Throughout the late nineteenth century packinghouse workers played important roles in the dramatic confrontations between labor and capital which made Chicago famous as a center of class conflict. Indeed, meat packing was the most strike-prone of all U.S. industries in the years between 1881 and 1905.[3] These struggles rested on two overlapping forms of protest—the organ-

ized strike and crowd actions, or "rioting." The skilled butchers
often showed a strong sense of craft identity and at various times
built successful unions and engaged in strikes. The unskilled
were sometimes drawn into these struggles, but remained largely
unorganized for most of the period, while the skilled assumed the
leading role. The neighborhoods surrounding the yards were
often focal points for crowd actions during strikes, and the crowds
themselves were frequently composed of packinghouse workers
and their families. These communities had established traditions
of militancy and solidarity long before the turn of the century,
and for good reason. Because of the increasingly large proportion
of unskilled men and women in the industry and the large pool of
casual labor the packers could draw on in the event of a strike,
the organized strength of packinghouse workers depended ultimately as much on what was happening in the streets outside of
the plants as it did on union organization within their walls.

During July 1877 Chicago, like many other industrial cities
along the country's main rail lines, had been convulsed by a general strike and extensive rioting.[4] In Chicago, most of the action
took place on the South Side and many of those in the crowds
came from Bridgeport, an Irish neighborhood just north and east
of the yards where most packinghouse workers lived at the time.
Yet the packinghouse workers themselves stand out most for the
discipline which they exhibited in the course of the strike and the
rioting. The movement was spread by groups of boys who ran
through the streets, calling workers from the various factories and
lumberyards to join the crowd. The boys were generally successful, and many of the city's industries were shut down in this spontaneous fashion. When the boys reached the packinghouses, however, they were ejected by a group of butchers who held a meeting to discuss grievances and formed their own procession. Gathering workers from each plant as they passed, they demanded a
two-dollar-per-day increase for all workers in the yards. The
butchers, it seems, took great care to distinguish themselves from
the crowds fighting with the police and militia for control of the
streets.

When the butchers did finally take to the streets, they created
quite a spectacle, which conveys something of their stature within
the broader working-class community as well as their own sense of

group indentity. Crowds had tended to gather and disperse spontaneously and were composed in large part of women and children as well as male strikers from the various industries. In contrast, the Irish butchers filed in line, five hundred strong and still wrapped in their bloody aprons, behind a banner which proclaimed "Workingmen's Rights." They marched from Bridgeport down to Halsted Street to meet the police. On their way they forcibly closed down some small rolling mills and the gas works. Many in the crowd held their butcher knives and cleavers aloft, while others carried clubs and stones. The *Chicago Tribune* described them as "men in every sense of the word . . . brave and daring in the extreme." As they marched into Pilsen, where much of the rioting had taken place, a cheer went up from the Bohemian lumber shovers, who were normally at odds with the Irish. At the Halsted Street Bridge, the butchers confronted the Chicago police, who ordered them to disperse and go back to Bridgeport, but they remained in formation and "vowed that they would rather die than return." Many did. A pitched battle for control of the bridge ensued, and the crowd was dispersed only when the police fired repeatedly into its ranks. By the time the fighting in the city had ended, between twenty-eight and thirty-five workers had been killed and over two hundred injured. But the increase had been won. Elected representatives secured signed agreements from each of the packers.[5]

At the time of the 1877 strike, the butchers had no formal organization. The earliest union organization started among cattle butchers about a year after the riots. By the spring of 1879 most of those in the cattle-killing gangs as well as some from other departments in the plants—between five and six thousand—had joined. That summer the union won a twenty-five-cent increase in the daily rate and in the fall demanded a closed shop. A long and bitter strike started on December 18, in spite of the efforts of a neighborhood priest. The militia and police assembled once again, as did the crowd. This time the trouble was restricted to the area immediately around the packing plants, but here the rioting was extensive. Toward the end of the strike, as some butchers began to break ranks and return to work, crowds of men and women actually invaded the plants, beating the scabs on the killing floors and destroying property. By the middle of January, however, the strike was broken. Many of the activists were black-listed, while other butchers returned to work under yellow-dog contracts.[6]

During the early 1880s the Noble and Holy Order of the Knights of Labor, a national labor reform organization, established a tenuous foothold in the industry. The order's strongest assembly in meat packing was among the butcher workmen of Kansas City. By 1881 the Knights had organized butchers, unskilled laborers, skilled auxiliary trades like millwrights and carpenters, and many others into one large Kansas City assembly of over twelve hundred. As was often the case with the Knights, industrial and political organization fused, resulting in a municipal labor administration by 1883. The mayor and "nearly all aldermen were members of the local assembly."[7]

By comparison, Chicago lagged far behind. At least one local assembly was established by 1880 in a small packinghouse on Archer Avenue, and at its height in 1881, this group claimed a membership of over one hundred pork butchers. By 1884, however, it had dwindled to only eighteen men, though it persisted until at least 1887. Another assembly was launched in 1885, but the size and precise composition of its membership are unclear.[8]

The real breakthrough for the Knights came in May 1886, when the great eight-hour movement swept like a prairie fire through the city and its packing plants. The packinghouse workers' response, however, may not have been as spontaneous as it at first appeared. Some trade union organization clearly existed before the strike, though this included no more than about 9 percent of the labor force. More important, migration of cattle butchers between Kansas City and Chicago provided the movement with able leadership. When John T. Joyce, the acknowledged leader of the 1886 strike, came to Chicago in 1884, at the age of twenty-one, he brought with him three years of experience as secretary of the large Kansas City local assembly. Jerry Spellman, another transplanted Kansas City Knight, helped Joyce find work at Swift's, where he met other old friends and also made contact with experienced Chicagoans like George Schick. Personal bonds among the Irish butchers, as well as a shared sense of bitterness left over from an unsuccessful 1884 strike against a wage cut, facilitated the movement.[9]

On May 2 cattle butchers in each of the major plants elected committees to present the eight-hour demand. When the packers refused, Joyce issued the strike call. The butchers cleaned their tools and began to gather for a prearranged mass meeting. The movement spread from one department to another and within an hour most of the butcher workmen and -women, including nearly all of the unskilled laborers and by-product workers, were streaming out of the city's slaughterhouses and packing plants. The strike had hardly begun when the packers capitulated. At least nine Knights of Labor assemblies were organized in the wake of the victory. While the Knights welcomed all manner of worker, ranging from the laborer on the butterine vat to the cattle butcher and from the young women who sewed ham bags to the skilled wool pullers, a clear division along skill lines was enforced. The cattle, hog, and sheep butchers each had their own assembly, while common laborers from the various departments were lumped together into assemblies of "packinghouse employees." Women also had their own small local.[10]

But if the workers remained divided by skill, they shared an enthusiasm for organization. Joyce claimed that the Chicago houses were 100 percent organized by the end of August. This may be an exaggeration, but the strength of the order was demonstrated clearly on Labor Day, when more than thirteen thousand workers marched eight abreast down Halsted Street. Cattle Butchers' Local 7802, the premier organization in the yards, kicked off the procession from the heart of the Irish community at Thirty-fifth Street and Emerald Avenue, marching twelve hundred strong, knives in hand, behind their own fife and drum corps. The line of march was organized by department and trade, designed to show not only the size but also the breadth of the organization. The Knights of Labor's message had swept from the top of the job structure in the yards, represented by the cattle butchers who led the procession, to its depths, represented by the fertilizer workers who closed it. Accompanied by twelve bands and twenty-eight decorated wagons, the parade was as much a spectacle as it was a demonstration of strength.[11]

The packers, however, had been doing some organizing of their own. Over the summer an employers' association was established that included most of the smaller houses and all of the Big Five, except Gustavus Swift, who joined in the fall. The agreement bound all members to act in cooperation on labor matters under penalty of large fines. By the fall the packers were ready to take the offensive.[12]

The impressive organization which had paraded on Labor Day was smashed little more than a month later when the packers launched a counterattack. The defeat tells as much about the organizational weakness of the Knights as it does about the strength of the packers. The conflict that progressed as a strike was, in fact, instigated by the packers. It began on October 8, when notices were posted in most of the city's pork packinghouses declaring the reintroduction of the ten-hour day. A strike started among hog butchers in a small independent plant, who stopped in the middle of their work, leaving slaughtered hogs dangling from the overhead rails. A crowd spread the strike, marching from one plant to another, calling the men from their work. Armour's cattle butchers soon joined. Although the brawny Irish hog butchers threatened to "stick and quarter" the imported Pinkerton guards upon the slightest provocation, the neighborhood remained quiet and peaceful. Most saloonkeepers honored the request of the executive board of Knights District 57 that no liquor be sold during the strike. Community merchants boycotted the Pinkertons and the scabs, who were all housed in the yards for their own protection.[13]

As this point Tom Barry, directing affairs for the order's national leadership, called the strike off despite its obvious strength, citing his inability to control the butcher workmen. "They are a thick-headed, hot-headed mob," Barry said, "and need someone with a rod of iron to rule them for at least three months."[14]

At the beginning of November a second strike broke out among Swift's cattle butchers, nominally over the discharge of a popular Knight. The real issue, however, was the newly reinstituted ten-hour day. The houses emptied quickly. The employers' association led the packers' attack in response, coordinating the hiring of scabs and declaring a lockout. In spite of provocations from five hundred Pinkerton guards hired to protect the scabs, the yards remained peaceful. A police sergeant claimed that there had been fewer arrests during the strike than in normal times. Most observers attributed the calm to union leaders who counseled moderation and patrolled the streets, dispersing crowds.[15]

Just when some union officials thought that the employers' association was in session preparing a compromise, Grand Master Workman Terrence Powderly unilaterally ended the strike. He threatened to revoke the charter of any local which did not comply with his instructions. In a staggering understatement the *Knights of Labor* newspaper concluded, "Evidently, there has been some misapprehension or misunderstanding of the situation." Stunned and confused, the butcher workmen returned to work, expecting to keep their eight-hour day. They were faced instead with what they called the "ironclad" contract that forced them to renounce all unions and authorized the employer to withhold one hundred dollars to be forfeited if the worker quit without two weeks' notice. In one stroke the packers collected about a million dollars, reinstituted the ten-hour day, virtually insured themselves against future strikes, and severely offended the pride of the butchers. When Gustavus Swift confronted his cattle butchers with the contract and gave them three minutes to sign it or get out, Joyce answered, "We don't need the three minutes, we're leaving now." The cattle butchers issued their own strike call and held out for several days, but the movement collapsed quickly, leaving a tremendous sense of bitterness toward the Knights throughout the yards.[16]

Some signs of strain between the butchers and the unskilled had begun to appear in the course of the Knights' organizing. A wage increase negotiated by a committee which included butchers and Knights' officials but no laborers was seen as a sellout by some of the unskilled. Disgusted with Powderly's arbitrary termination of the strike, many of the laborers ignored the butchers' call to continue.[17] When organization reemerged about two years later, however, its strength was among the unskilled and the more recent immigrants rather than the Irish butchers.[18]

At the end of 1889 fifty of Swift's coopers refused to sign the ironclad contract. They called a meeting to organize around the issue and were joined by about two hundred cattle butchers, mostly German, Bohemian, and Polish, calling themselves the Personal Rights League. These groups, together with the United

Brotherhood, composed of remnants of the Knights' locals which had split from the national organization, served as the nucleus for a secret union called the Packinghouse Employees' Union. The new organization set as its goals abolition of the ironclad contract and reintroduction of the eight-hour day. Estimates of the union's strength vary widely. Its organizers' claim that they had the yards better organized than in 1886 was clearly an exaggeration, but there were probably several thousand members by April 1890. This union was more mixed, in terms of both ethnicity and skill, than the Knights had been. While a core of butchers were active, the bulk of the membership consisted of laborers. In a pattern which became common during the early twentieth century, the leadership was Irish, but the membership was drawn from a wide range of ethnic groups, including Germans, Poles, Bohemians, and Scandinavians.

At the end of April the Packinghouse Employees' Union threatened to strike on May Day in support of two demands—a wage increase of two and a half cents per hour and the eight-hour day. The strike never materialized, however, for a number of reasons. By May cattle shipments had fallen off and many laborers were out of work. Apparently, the union worried about sustaining a long strike in the face of growing unemployment. The city's American Federation of Labor leadership also implored the butchers not to strike, because all resources and interest were absorbed by a critical carpenters' strike and lockout. The most important consideration, however, was the failure to organize effectively across skill lines. The bulk of the Irish held aloof from an organization made up largely of unskilled recent immigrants. When a secret gathering of cattle butchers voted to stay at work, three thousand laborers met and abandoned the idea for the strike. By the 1890s, then, skill and ethnic divisions among the butcher workmen remained an impediment to solidarity.[19]

Solidarity among the Irish butchers nevertheless remained strong, in spite of the fact that their unions had been effectively outlawed in the industry. Whatever fleeting strength the organizations of skilled butchers had in the late nineteenth century derived in part from a cohesive Irish-American subculture blending local party politics, Irish nationalism, and various forms of self-help. The Irish butchers' persistent ethnic identification was fueled by the struggle for Irish independence and nationhood. The city's industrial South Side, with its large Irish working-class population, was the focal point for much of the nationalist agitation and organization. Local Land League groups, for example, which mixed broad ideas of social reform with nationalist agitation, were based primarily on stockyard and rolling mill workers. The link between labor and nationalist activity, common to many Irish working-class communities of the late nineteenth century, persisted in Chicago well into the twentieth. [20]

When Knights of Labor Assembly 7802 was crushed in the fall 1886 strike, the cattle butchers formed the Blackthorn Club. The name and the bulk of the membership were Irish, but all cattle butchers were welcomed and the group included Germans and Bohemians. The club successfully ran John F. Kenny, a pro-union Armour foreman, for alderman in 1890, but its interests went beyond politics. It was designed to maintain some of the protection of union organization without formal recognition, and ethnic ties played an important part in its efforts. Sympathetic Irish foremen, for example, helped some of those who had been blacklisted to find work once again in the industry. Where this was not possible, as in the case of Joyce, the political connections helped. After being blacklisted for good in 1890 for refusing to scab during a sheep butchers' strike, Joyce used the club's connections to secure a series of patronage jobs over the next decade. The prominence of others in the movement assured them of customers when they opened saloons or other small businesses in the community. But the community's sanctions could also be turned on those who violated its ethic of solidarity. Those who broke ranks during a strike were remembered as traitors and boycotted. Grudges were held for years. [21]

In the summer of 1894 packinghouse workers were once again at the center of a tremendous labor upheaval when strikers at the Pullman car works several miles south and east of the yards called for help. Workers throughout the city walked off their jobs in sympathy with a general strike of railroad workers across the country. Once again, the skilled butchers relied upon organization based on skill and craft identity, while the laborers and unorgan-

ized workers in the community protested by means of the only
weapon at their disposal. They turned out in large crowds, attacking scabs and railroad property.[22]

On July 13, 1894, at 8:00 A.M., between one and two thousand
cattle butchers left their work, partly in sympathy with the railroad workers but also in support of their own demand for a wage
increase. They marched to a neighborhood hall, where they met
daily during the strike. Shunning the Knights of Labor, the strikers elected their own officers, obtained a charter from the AF of L
to establish the Journeymen Butchers' National Union of America, and sent organizers to Omaha, Kansas City, and East St.
Louis, where the strike soon spread. This conflict was sectional in
nature, however. While the butchers remained quite solid, other
departments took no part in the strike. Once the packers were
able to import a small nucleus of skilled men from out of town,
operations started up again. The conflict dragged on for nine
weeks, at which point it was abandoned. Having beaten the
union, the packers blacklisted men more systematically than they
had in the past. Nelson Morris insisted, "Not a striker will get his
job back in this house."[23] Though decimated, the Journeymen
Butchers' National Union would continue to elect officers and
hold small meetings until the foundation of the Amalgamated
Meat Cutters and Butcher Workmen of North America in 1897.
Once again formal union organization had been smashed, but a
core of activists would remain, and it was upon the remnants of
the old Journeymen Butchers' organization that the new international would build a cattle butchers' local in Chicago in 1900.

The fact that the 1894 call for a general strike caught the packinghouse workers in the slowest month of the slack season during
a severe depression made it practically impossible for common laborers to take part in any organized fashion. The city was flooded
with unemployed, including many "tramps" from out of town.
"No one would suspect a strike was on by the general appearance
of the Yards and packinghouses," the *Tribune* gloated. "Hundreds
of men are hanging about the Yards in search of work." Virtually
all contemporary accounts of the strike suggest that those unemployed packinghouse workers played a major role in the serious rioting that engulfed much of the city's South Side during the Pull-

man Boycott. Most observers insisted that the railroad strikers themselves not only remained peaceful but often tried to stop crowd violence against "scab trains." Some witnesses before the U.S. Strike Commission specifically mentioned packinghouse workers in connection with riots, and both the location of the major crowd actions and the ethnic composition of the crowds suggest that Bridgeport and Packingtown turned out *en masse.* [24]

The most serious trouble spots in the city were all in an area bounded by Thirty-ninth and Fifty-fifth streets on the north and south and by State Street and the city limits on the east and west. Even here there was little serious violence until militia moved into the area; rioting was almost continuous from that point on. Within the four days between July 5 and July 9, hundreds of cars, five shanties, eight railroad towers, and one barn were burned in this region. "The whole section of the city in the vicinity of the Yards is in the possession of a dozen mobs of rioters," the *Tribune* reported. The single most serious fire consumed an estimated one thousand boxcars in the Panhandle freightyards on the northwest border of Packingtown. The bloodiest confrontation, in which four people were killed and seventeen wounded, took place just north of the yards at Forty-ninth and Loomis streets. [25]

Perhaps the most impressive characteristics of the rioting were the size of the crowds and the speed with which they gathered. An estimated ten thousand persons attacked militiamen and police at Forty-ninth and Loomis, for example. Each time the packers tried to move a train loaded with meat, people poured into the streets. On July 4, a locomotive and several cars full of meat pulled up near the great stone gate of the yards on Halsted Street. The *Drovers' Journal* described what happened next: "In less time than it takes to tell about it an immense crowd had gathered about the engine. All the streets leading to the stockyards were black with humanity, and soon 20,000 people were on the scene. News that an attempt was to be made to break the blockade went about with telegraphic speed." [26]

Yet the crowds' motives were clear. Virtually all of the property destroyed was owned by the railroads, which were seen as the prime enemy in the struggle. The crowds were determined that no train should move from the stockyards, and between June 29 and July 8 the blockade remained solid. At that point it became a question of the army's superior firepower, and the trains began to roll once again.[27]

The composition of the crowds was comparable to that of those which had taken part in the 1877 riots except that in 1894 they tended to be quite mixed ethnically, reflecting the growing diversity of the population in the neighborhoods surrounding the yards. "In the mob the jargon of foreign tongues was conspicuous," the *Drovers' Journal* noted, "and the latent hatred of capital found full effervescence." While newspaper reporters and other observers thought that most of those in the crowds were Polish, Bohemian, and German, Bridgeport's Irish still figured prominently. Women and children also once again made up a large proportion of the crowd. The *Tribune* found the neighborhood children "steeped in the spirit of insurrection."[28]

In all, thirteen people were killed, fifty-three injured, and more than eighty million dollars' worth of property destroyed. Yet the most important effects of the strike may have been psychological. Among middle-class Chicagoans, the rioting contributed to a growing conception of Packingtown as a place full of dangerous foreigners, better segregated from the more respectable neighborhoods of the city. Hyde Park residents watched in fear each night as the light from burning railroad cars illuminated the sky to the northwest. Each Illinois Central commuter train which ventured downtown in early July carried its own armed guards, and passengers sometimes had to fall to the floor to avoid snipers' bullets. The strike and rioting even affected residential architecture in the community. Several houses in the adjacent Kenwood area were built with a special family security room on the third floor where the residents could sit out a labor siege, safe behind metal-reinforced doors.[29]

Among the workers themselves, however, the experience left a legacy of despondency and fear. In its wake, the packers instituted an efficient blacklist designed to rid their labor force of agitators. Spies gathered information about workers suspected of union sympathies, and each attempt at organization was quickly crushed. By the end of the nineteenth century, David Brody concludes, "meat packing was virtually unorganized."[30] The butcher workmen seemed to be defeated; yet grievances remained. In the next round of organization, the workers would not be divided along skill and ethnic lines. Those union activists who remained carried the lessons of the nineteenth century into the twentieth and brought a new generation of packinghouse workers into the movement with them.

UNIONIZATION

As in previous periods of union activity, skilled butchers provided much of the early personnel and initiative for organization in the 1900–1904 era. But the spread of unionization through the yards in these years, into the unskilled occupations dominated by recent immigrants and young women workers, suggests not only that the concept of unionization was changing but also that these newcomers clearly and quickly grasped its importance. The key to understanding the unionization process in packing lies in the relations between these two generations.

A new union led the national campaign to organize packinghouse workers. The Amalgamated Meat Cutters and Butcher Workmen of North America was founded in the back room of a Cincinnati Odd Fellows Hall by four men—Homer D. Call, a meat cutter from Syracuse; George Byer, a sheep butcher from Kansas City; John F. Hart, a butcher workman from Utica, New York; and John F. O'Sullivan, a Boston union official assigned by the AFL leadership to advise the group. The new international union was officially chartered in January 1897 with jurisdiction over both retail butchers and packinghouse workers.

Early growth was particularly slow among packinghouse workers until the election in December 1898 of Michael Donnelly, a South Omaha sheep butcher, as president of the Amalgamated. Deeply devoted to his cause, Donnelly proved to be a gifted organizer. By the middle of 1900 the Amalgamated had a membership of four thousand, and Donnelly set out for Chicago's Union Stockyards.[31]

In Chicago the earliest action came not from the cattle butchers, with their strong union traditions, but rather from young women workers in the canning department. In early 1900, without any formal organization, a small group of young Irish-American women led a revolt against a succession of piece-rate cuts. The packers brought foreign-born women in to break the strike and then blacklisted its leaders. The women sued, but the court found that their employers had the right to discriminate against them. Several of the strike leaders remained in contact with their workmates, however, and eventually helped to organize a union. The women's struggle, together with the Amalgamated's decision to extend their organizing to packinghouse workers, helped to spark a major unionization drive in Chicago within a few months of this minor defeat.[32]

When Michael Donnelly arrived on Chicago's South Side in the spring of 1900, he faced some formidable obstacles. The blacklist and an extensive network of informers were known quantities, and the packers were adamant. The lesson they had drawn from the history of labor relations in the meat industry was simple: "It was cheaper to fight than to appease."[33]

The packers fired anyone seen talking to Donnelly, and the terror campaign had its desired effect. He repeatedly failed to make any lasting contacts. Acknowledging the depth of fear among the workers, he approached George Schick and eleven other veterans of labor activism individually and arranged a secret meeting in one of their homes. These men formed the core of the union over the next few months, while the existence of the organization remained a well-guarded secret. Within a year Donnelly had organized about 95 percent of the cattle butchers, and six other unions were also in place.[34]

The process of unionization generally descended the job structure as it worked its way through the various plants. The cattle, hog, and sheep butchers, all skilled knife men, formed the first three locals, building once again on neighborhood and kinship ties. The twelve charter members of Hog Butchers' Local 116, for example, held their meeting in the home of a neighborhood cattle butcher and union activist. Nine of the twelve were Irish, and two were brothers. When Patrick Coakley, who became the union's business agent, arrived for the meeting, he found that most of the others were former classmates who knew one another from the parish school.[35]

After the skilled butchers came the beef luggers and shipping department employees. These men were in close contact during the workday with those in the killing gangs, who had been among the first to organize. They were a skilled and cohesive group and responded quickly to the union's call. Although there were some Poles among the skilled in the killing gangs, the union encountered its first large group of Slavic immigrants among the beef cutters and boners. There was nothing in this local's experience, however, to suggest that the new immigrants presented any particular obstacle. Beef Cutters and Boners' Local 135 started in June 1901 with seventy-four charter members, and within a year four hundred workers had signed up. [36]

For the first year or so, the Amalgamated followed the nineteenth-century organizational pattern. Skilled butchers organized on their own, leaving the unskilled to fend for themselves. But the craft model no longer fit the reality of packinghouse work. Extreme division of labor had not only reduced the bargaining power of the few highly skilled specialists; it also left them vulnerable to replacement by less skilled knife men whose own jobs could often be done by common laborers. "Today it is impossible," the union's journal concluded, "to draw the line where the skilled man leaves off and the unskilled man begins." As a result, the union's leadership soon rejected the strict craft model. "Experience has taught us that this latter class in their unorganized condition are a menace to those who are members of Union Labor," explained Michael Donnelly. ". . . It is our duty to educate them in the labor movement."[37] And he reiterated in early 1901, "There must be no aristocracy in the labor movement. I have worked at the highest wages paid in the packing plants, but I cannot forget that the man who washed the floor while I worked at the tables is entitled to the same consideration I am. I cannot forget that he is a human being, and that he has a family. It should be our purpose to make the injury of the common laborers the concern of the skilled workman."[38] By the end of that year the union was aggressively wooing the unskilled.

Adopting a departmental structure, the Amalgamated established a local union for each of the departments in the modern packinghouse. Every worker engaged in the killing of cattle in Chicago, for instance, belonged to Cattle Butchers' Local 87, regardless of whether he was a splitter at Swift's or a common laborer at Armour's. Other locals were set up for soap and butterine workers, beef and hog casing workers, livestock handlers and sausage makers, even the stockyards police force. Eventually, twenty-one locals covered every production worker in the indus- try.[39] The fact that such departmental locals mixed workers from the various houses facilitated identification on the basis of occupa- tion rather than plant.

As David Brody has observed, however, "The inclusive mem- bership policy did not turn the Amalgamated into an industrial union." Not only were the Chicago locals organized on a depart- mental rather than a plant basis, but the Amalgamated also respected the jurisdictional claims of other international unions. The skilled auxiliary tradespeople—coopers, steamfitters, station- ary engineers and firemen, carpenters, and others—were parceled out to locals of their respective craft unions. This sectionalism of key auxiliary workers was inherent in adapting a craft model to an integrated mass-production industry like packing, and in the long run this structural weakness proved crucial to the union's de- mise.[40]

To view the Amalgamated's efforts solely from the perspective of modern industrial unionism, however, is essentially ahistorical. If one compares the Amalgamated's structure to that of a nineteenth-century craft union as well as to the CIO industrial union which emerged in packing more than three decades later, it is clear that the butcher workmen's early twentieth-century union was a transitional form embodying elements of both kinds of or- ganization. Unlike a nineteenth-century craft union, the Amal- gamated set out to organize all production workers, regardless of skill, gender, or race, and, like later industrial unions, the Amal- gamated was forced to develop new organizing strategies in order to integrate workers from widely variant social backgrounds into locals based on the workplace. Department locals were nominally based on "trades," but this was more a matter of convenience than an affirmation of the craft principle. Certainly the soap work- ers' local, for example, composed of laborers who carted fat and tended vats, had little in common with a traditional craft union. The cattle butchers' local included not only the aristocratic splitters and floormen but also the common laborers who mopped blood. Indeed, laborers comprised a majority of the local's membership. What is most striking, then, about the early twentieth-century butchers' unionism is not that they failed to develop a full-blown industrial organization but rather that, in experimenting with new forms, they were clearly headed in that direction.

The creation of a Packing Trades Council with delegates from each local in the stockyards was another step toward greater amalgamation. The council facilitated united planning and action and provided the natural leadership for a general strike in the industry. The trade council concept for a time also allowed for a degree of unity with the auxiliary tradesmen who were members of various AFL craft unions rather than the Amalgamated. Eight of twenty-seven local unions affiliated with the Chicago council in July 1903 were constituents of other international unions. By helping with organizing, handling major grievances, mediating jurisdictional and other disputes between locals, and doing central planning, the council provided a critical link among all workers in the industry.[41]

In the spring of 1904 Amalgamated delegates voted to restrict the membership in the packing trades councils to their own locals. Apparently the move was prompted by a fear that the actions of the Allied Trades locals, which were beyond the Amalgamated's control, might draw the butcher workmen into damaging sympathy strikes. In retrospect it is difficult to see how the separation could do anything but weaken the Amalgamated in the event of a major confrontation with the packers. The skills of some tradesmen, notably the stationary engineers who maintained refrigeration units, were essential to the operation of the plants. Their support in a long strike could be crucial to its success. Yet the decision was made, and the tradesmen withdrew in June 1904 to form their own council.[42]

The only local which deviated from the departmental structure was 183, one of the largest in the union, which organized all women in the yards. With a separate organization, the women were assured of their own representation on the Packing Trades Council and at the international convention. Had they been integrated into departmental locals with men, they could easily have been outvoted, and problems peculiar to the situation of women workers might have been ignored. Also, the character of women's work at the turn of the century meant that they were still often segregated into separate departments.

Local 183 originated with a social group of second-generation Irish women which coalesced around the University of Chicago Settlement House. Reflecting the values of their community, as well as some of their own, they named their club for a contemporary Irish radical nationalist, Maude Gonne.[43] Many of those active in the club and the union local which grew from it were veterans of the spontaneous piece-rate strike in the spring of 1900. The sixteen charter members were all discharged, but within six months five hundred had been organized and by November 1903 the local had grown to almost two thousand—probably more than 80 percent of the women in the industry. While the union was at first stronger among the young Irish women than among their Slavic sisters, it eventually comprised virtually all of the ethnic groups represented in the yards, including blacks.[44]

Some butcher workmen actively opposed women's employment and organization. The sausagemakers, for example, lost a 1903 strike partly as a result of women strikebreakers, and John Floersch pressed the sausagemakers' case at the union's 1904 convention. He offered a resolution charging that the introduction of women downgraded men's work and calling on the union to expel women from all sausage departments and ban their introduction into any job involving the use of the knife. Molly Daly, who had been organizing the women whom Floersch now sought to drive from the industry, took the floor. She argued forcefully against the resolution and for the principle of equal pay for equal work.[45]

Most of the butcher workmen took a position closer to that of the union's conservative secretary-treasurer, Homer Call. Call argued, correctly, that most women worked because of economic necessity and that they should be organized, if only to protect men's wages. Significantly, Molly Daly was supported by several male speakers at the 1904 convention, one of whom noted the importance of unionization to women who were frequently primary breadwinners. "It would be unfair now," he argued, "to discourage their organization, as many of them have families to support." Most delegates apparently agreed. The sausagemakers' resolution was defeated by a wide margin and replaced with a compromise resolution calling for *both* confinement of women to jobs which were not "brutalizing" *and* equal pay for equal work in departments where women were already doing work comparable to men's. Acknowledging the unusually low income of women, the Amalgamated also remitted the per capita tax for Local 183, at first in order to attract members and later to pay for two full-time women organizers.[46]

Michael Donnelly, the Amalgamated's president, was particularly supportive of women's unionization. Working closely with Mary McDowell, Donnelly helped to build Local 183 and to develop the Chicago branch of the Women's Trade Union League.[47]

For their part the women tried to protect men's wages by fighting first in those departments where they worked alongside men. They were able to increase both piece rates and weekly wages, though their progress was slower than that for men. The women took as their organizing call to all female packinghouse workers the message, "Organize for your own protection and because it will be an education—it will change your life."[48]

Why did the Amalgamated's position on women's organization contrast so sharply with the more typical trade union demand of this era for their total exclusion from union and shop?[49] The key seems to lie in the packing industry's production process and labor market. Few if any turn-of-the-century industries could match packing in extreme division of labor and assembly-line organization of work. By subdividing tasks and grossly reducing the degree of skill, and in some cases strength, required for most jobs, the packers made it acceptable for women to do all but the heaviest slaughtering and hauling work. The consistent expansion of the proportion of women to total labor force reflects these changes in production technology. (See table 4.) As it became increasingly difficult to exclude "cheap female labor" from most departments in a modern packinghouse, so it became necessary to raise women's wages in order to protect men's. It was not surprising that highly skilled craftsmen or unskilled laborers engaged in heavy work were able to exclude women from unions; it was more difficult to do so in a mass-production industry where women already made up an important part of the labor force.

Americanization from the Bottom Up

Even more significant than those of gender, nationality divisions among the packinghouse workers posed a potential obstacle to unionization. Such divisions comprised more than language difficulties. Packinghouse workers came to the stockyards with widely divergent cultural perspectives. In packing, as in many other industries, the fact that recent immigrants settled into the least skilled positions meant that such cultural differences might be reinforced by skill divisions. Any ideological common ground among these diverse groups of workers had to be created by the workers themselves. For unionization to succeed, it was essential that the older, more experienced generation of packinghouse workers reach out to the newcomers.

Historians have frequently viewed the acculturation of immigrant workers primarily as a top-down process of socialization. Personnel managers, evening school teachers, and settlement house workers employed "Americanization" programs as instruments of social control aimed at producing not only responsible citizens but also obedient, efficient workers.[50] Such efforts certainly represented one element in the immigrant worker's process of adjustment, but their influence has been exaggerated. As noted earlier, formal "Americanization"—through citizenship classes and government naturalization procedures, for example—proceeded very slowly in Packingtown.

Yet this does not mean that immigrant workers failed to come to terms with their new lives. There were simply alternative conceptions of Americanism to those of management. Historians have often overlooked the acculturation of immigrants as it took place informally among workers from diverse backgrounds and through the efforts of unions and other working-class institutions.[51] In packing, union militants made an informal but conscious push to integrate new groups into the broader working-class community and the labor movement. The union's efforts to reach the immigrants suggest a new way of looking at the acculturation of immigrant workers, an "Americanization from the bottom up."

The notion of the union as an independent force in the acculturation of immigrants was first noted by U.S. Commissioner of Labor Ethelbert Stewart. Studying the problem in Packingtown in 1904, Stewart found that ethnic hostilities had been rife before unionization. Communities tended to be dominated by charismatic "clan leaders" who often viewed the union as a threat to their own prestige and influence. Union activists fought a running battle with these men and steadfastly opposed their demands for organization along ethnic lines.[52] In a world organized largely on the basis of nationality, Stewart argued, the union represented "the first, and for a time the only, point at which [the immigrant] touches any influence outside of his clan. . . . The Slav mixes with the Lithuanian, the German, and the Irishman—and this is the only place they do mix until, by virtue of this intercourse and this mixing, clannishness is to a degree destroyed, and a social mixing along other lines comes into play."[53]

Mary McDowell saw the process in similar terms from her vantage point at the University of Chicago Settlement. "The labor union has been the only institution that has brought the immigrant in touch with English-speaking men for a common purpose and in preparation for self-government."[54] An immigrant's introduction to the workings of the American political and economic system frequently came through conversations with fellow workers, discussion and debate at union meetings, and labor movement publications. The union's conception of Americanism tended to emphasize the free expression of one's opinions and standing up with fellow workers to demand one's rights.

A Polish or Lithuanian laborer's first contact with the union was likely to be in the person of an Irish business agent for one of the locals. If the immigrant worked in one of the by-product rooms, for example, he or she might be confronted by John Mahony of the Hide Cellar Men, or Denny O'Donnell of the Lard Room Employees, or Barney McKevett of the Soap Workers. It was the business agent's job to organize, and in order to do this he had to explain to the immigrant just what this union business was all about. Alone among the institutions at the immigrants' disposal, the union could promise to improve their material conditions and those of their families. The union's growth and its progress from one department to another suggests that its message was reaching the newcomers.

During the 1900–1904 union campaign the Irish played the role of "Americanizers." In each department, even in the by-product works, with their heavy concentrations of recent immigrants, it was the older immigrant groups and particularly the Irish who took the initiative in organizing and who ended up being elected local union officers (see table 12). These Irish-American activists quickly and successfully integrated the various other ethnic groups into their organizing.[55]

Local unions made their bridges to immigrant communities in several ways. The use of interpreters at local union meetings encouraged participation by even the most recent immigrants. Many of the Polish workers and a large minority of Slovaks and Lithuanians spoke at least some English, and these individuals may have served as linguistic links between old-immigrant activists and those who spoke no English at all. Hog Butchers' Local 116 provided simultaneous translations into five languages; the more ethnically diverse sheep butchers required seven, "thereby giving every member equal rights." Integration of Slavic organizers and officers often facilitated breakthroughs. Frank Klawikowski's election as vice president of the hog butchers' local provided a crucial link between the union's Irish-American officers and its Slavic members. The original organizers in the canning department, like those in most others, were Irish. Faced with a

Table 12. Local Union Officials, Classified by Nationality, 1904

Nationality	Number of Officers	Percent of Officers	Percent of Nationality in Labor Force, 1904
Irish	64	57	25
German	21	19	15
Bohemian	8	7	20
Polish, Slovak, or Lithuanian	8	7	38
Unclassified	11	10	2*
TOTAL	112	100	100

*American and Scottish

Sources: Amalgamated Meat Cutters and Butcher Workmen, *Official Journal* 5 (Mar. 1904); Ethelbert Stewart, "The Influence of Trade Unions on Immigrants," U.S. Bureau of Labor Statistics, Bulletin no. 56 (Washington, D.C., 1905).

serious language barrier, the group made little headway for three months. Then they managed to convince a few people representing the various ethnic groups in the department to act as shop stewards. This group took up the organizing, and within three months the local had seven hundred members. The Irish corresponding secretary found his new Slavic brothers "the very best union men we have got."[56]

A young Lithuanian laborer on the cattle-killing floor described his own experience with the union to a journalist in 1904.

> It has given me more time to learn to read and speak and enjoy life like an American. . . . It is combining all the nationalities. The night I joined the Cattle Butchers' Union I was led into the room by a negro member. With me were Bohemians, Germans and Poles, and Mike Donnelly, the President, is an Irishman. He spoke to us in English and then three interpreters told us what he said. We swore to be loyal to our union above everything else except the country, the city and the State—to be faithful to each other—to protect the women workers—to do our best to understand the history of the labor movement, and to do all we could to help it on. Since then I have gone there every two weeks and I help the movement by being an interpreter for the other Lithuanians who come in. That is why I have learned to speak and write good English. The others do not need me long. They soon learn English, too, and when they have done that they are quickly becoming Americans.[57]

Mary McDowell observed the process in action when she visited a meeting of the women's local. When the Irish chairwoman called for any outstanding grievances, a young black woman rose to accuse a Polish member of insulting her. The chairwoman asked both to come forward.

> Now what did yez call each other?
> She called me a nigger.
> She called me a Pollock first.
> Both of yez oughta be ashamed of yourselves. You're both to blame. But don't you know that this question in our ritual don't mean that kind of griev-e-ances, but griev-e-ances of the whole bunch of us?[58]

The episode suggests that racial and nationality differences could indeed bring conflict. But it also shows a conscious effort to discourage such thinking and to encourage concentration on common interests and problems.

The structure of the local unions themselves encouraged this identification on the basis of work, rather than race or nationality, and facilitated the process of acculturation. The city-wide department or "trade" locals maximized contact and solidarity across nationality lines and provided the institutional context for Americanization from the bottom up.[59] Each local union became an instrument of education, reflecting the values of the labor movement and the broader working-class community and imparting these to the immigrants.

The American Standard

The immigrant packinghouse workers who responded so positively to the unionization drive lived in a city which was the home of one of the most highly organized and militant labor movements of the early twentieth century. In an era characterized by growing union organization, Chicago was clearly a pacesetter. The rise of the packinghouse workers' own organization came as part of a massive upsurge of the city's labor movement during 1903. Union membership doubled; 251 strikes were launched; and a general campaign for shorter hours brought the nine-hour day to several industries. By the end of the year the Chicago Federation of Labor (CFL) had a membership of more than 245,000—over half of the city's labor force. The CFL also led the way in the organization of women workers, having drawn more than 35,000 from twenty-six different occupations into the fold by 1903. Even more impressive than its size was the *scope* of the movement. It included not only unions of building trades workers, machinists, and factory operatives, but also organizations of teachers, scrubwomen, and waitresses. Federation leaders claimed that their town was the "best-organized city in the world." Chicago was one of those places where it was easier to be a union member than to be nonunion. "The city could possibly challenge London," David Montgomery writes, "for the title, trade union capital of the world."[60]

A workingman or -woman in Chicago in 1904, then, was surrounded by a *labor ethos*. His or her neighbors were union people, and the values of the labor movement—class solidarity, industrial militancy, and a certain pride in being a part of the movement—were important influences in daily life. These values were not necessarily counterposed to more traditional ones associated with religious and ethnic identification. Much of Packingtown's cultural life continued to flow along well-worn ethnic channels. Yet the Amalgamated managed to organize effectively across ethnic lines and to socialize the new immigrants within a distinctly working-class worldview.

The union's role of Americanizer consisted of more than simply mixing the recent immigrants with the older English-speaking groups in a common organization directed to class interests. Many contemporaries saw in the union an important source of stability in an otherwise chaotic and dangerous social environment. Mary McDowell and others associated with the University of Chicago Settlement were among those taking this broader view. Their support for unionization went beyond moral pronouncements in the press. McDowell herself was involved in the formation of the women's union and later became a leading figure in the Women's Trade Union League. Part of the reason for the settlement staff's support derived from the fact that they had succeeded in becoming a part of the neighborhood and could appreciate some of the adverse social implications of the casual labor system in the yards. They also admired the union for its ability to break down the ethnic barriers which they saw as obstacles to citizenship.

Interwoven with these accomplishments was the gradual establishment of what Mary McDowell and later the union called the "American Standard of Living." By raising the living standards of the neighborhood's families, McDowell argued, the union was helping to create a more stable population and to defuse a social time bomb. McDowell and others in the community noted a significant rise in the level of home ownership following the advent of the union, which was also reflected in Ethelbert Stewart's 1905 census of the neighborhood. A banker noted that the period immediately following unionization saw an unprecedented burst of home buying among the most recent arrivals, especially the Lithuanians and Slovaks. He attributed the trend to a new sense of security which the immigrant had found in the union's efforts to maximize employment.[61] McDowell argued that once the prospect of home ownership became a viable alternative to reemigration, the population of the neighborhood had stabilized somewhat.[62]

Some observers saw a dramatic decline in the neighborhood's crime rate as another product of unionization. A sergeant in the Stockyards Precinct station told Commissioner Stewart that since the coming of the union, Packingtown had seen "less disorder, better living, more intelligence, and more understanding of American institutions and laws." The precinct, which had long had more policemen than any other, actually reduced the size of its force after unionization. There may have been other reasons for the decline in crime reflected in arrest statistics, but some observers saw this as another indication that the union was fulfilling a positive role in Packingtown.[63]

Figures provided by the Chicago Bureau of Charities, Relief and Aid Societies suggest that unionization also reduced pauperism in the community. These show a distinct drop in applications for the period of the union's ascendancy, though prosperity certainly accounted for part of this improvement. The records indicate that during the years 1897–98 20 percent of Packingtown's population was receiving charity on a regular basis. The bureau reported in 1904 that since unionization had begun only one in every one hundred families receiving aid was headed by a union man or woman.[64]

The social balance sheet of the meat-packing industry in Chicago—its social implications weighed against its importance to the metropolitan economy—was not read in the same way by all of the city's residents. The industry's area of operations and the residential neighborhood adjacent to it were increasingly seen as sources of serious social problems. The neighborhood had been swept by epidemics more than once, and its health and sanitary conditions indicated that the same thing might happen again. Since no adequate public relief system existed, Packingtown's chronic mendicancy had to be underwritten by the more prosperous communities in the city (or, of course, ignored). The experience of 1894 had demonstrated that when the poverty-stricken community did rise in protest, the result could be costly in human lives and property. For Hyde Parkers, Packingtown was coming to be seen as more than a place to dump their garbage or to send sociology students; it was also a threat to their comfortable existence. These social costs of the meat-packing industry convinced settlement house workers and some others that the union's stabilizing effects in Packingtown should be welcomed in the interests of the community at large.

Mary McDowell's conception of an "American Standard of Living" became important in the union's efforts to socialize new immigrants. If the frame of reference that an immigrant used to judge living and working conditions remained that of the Lithuanian forest, then there was little reason for him or her to oppose conditions in any American industrial environment, even the notorious Chicago packinghouses. Commissioner Stewart explained the union's efforts to argue for a *new* standard.

> The union gets him to compare himself not with what he was in Lithuania, but with some German or Irish family, and then stings him with the assertion that he has as much right to live that way as anybody. . . . The union's point of view is that for a Lithuanian peasant to be contented, satisfied and happy with the Lithuanian standard of living in America is a crime, a crime not only against himself but against America and everyone who wishes to make individual and social development in America. [65]

The union's efforts to convey this new standard to the immigrants met with considerable success. Mary McDowell recalled years later, "I heard in Bohemian, Slavish and Lithuanian languages the same opinion expressed as that of a Polish worker, who spoke with the calmness of a firm conviction, as he said: 'We cannot bring up our children as Americans on 15 and a half cents an hour and 40 hours a week. We cannot live decently. Our wives, our children, our homes demand better wages.' "[66]

How successful was the Amalgamated in raising Packingtown to the American standard? What effect did unionization have on the quality of life? The preceding figures on charity and home ownership in the community and table 13 provide a partial answer. The table shows the proportion of one large packing company's labor force paid at the various wage levels before, during, and after unionization. These figures do not take into account the effect of

Table 13. Movement of Wages for Employees at One Chicago
Packinghouse, 1896–1910

Cents per Hour	October 18–31, 1896 Proportion of Those Employed	October 11–22, 1903 Proportion of Those Employed	October 9–22, 1910 Proportion of Those Employed
16½ or less	61.10	19.93	45.24
17 to 17½	9.80	18.59	20.24
18 to 20	13.62	39.96	13.72
21 to 27½	12.96	17.07	14.11
28 to 35	1.84	3.53	4.97
36 or more	.68	.92	1.72

Source: Adapted from John C. Kennedy et al., *Wages and Family Budgets in the Chicago Stockyards District* (Chicago: Univ. of Chicago Press, 1914), 20.

inflation on real wages in the period following the union's demise. But since the figures show a *decline* in money wages for those at the lower end of the pay scale, and government figures for the same years (1903–10) show an *increase* of 1.5 percent in prices, there was clearly a deterioration in the standard of living, as measured by real wages, following the destruction of the union.[67] Table 13 indicates a general increase in wages for all grades of labor as well as a relative upgrading of common labor during the union era. But it also demonstrates a decline in the wages for the majority of packinghouse workers in the years following the Amalgamated's decline.

Even in its short lifetime, then, the union managed not only to integrate and acculturate the newcomers but also to make some headway in its effort to establish an American Standard of Living in Packingtown. Since the sources of the community's poverty lay in the organization of the meat-packing industry itself—the seasonal nature of the work year, the irregular hours of the workday, low wages, the unregulated fluctuations in the common labor market, and the injuries and exhaustion produced by intense speed—the attainment of this higher standard of living depended directly on the ability of the workers to impose some order on the work process through organization at the point of production. The living standards of Packingtown's families depended on the efforts of the workers themselves to "rationalize" packinghouse work.

NOTES

1. Mike Davis, "Why the U.S. Working Class Is Different," *New Left Review*, no. 123 (1980): 3–44; David Brody, *Steelworkers in America: The Non-Union Era* (New York, 1969); Richard Oestreicher, "Solidarity and Fragmentation: Working People and Class Consciousness in Detroit, 1877–1895" (Ph.D. diss., Michigan State University, 1979), chap. 8; John Bodnar, *Immigration and Industrialization: Ethnicity in an American Mill Town* (Pittsburgh, 1977), chaps. 1 and 2; Gabriel Kolko, *Main Currents in Modern American History* (New York, 1976), chap. 3. The following analysis is based in part on James R. Barrett, "Unity and Fragmentation: Class, Race, and Ethnicity on Chicago's South Side, 1900–1922," *Journal of Social History* 18 (1984): 37–55, reprinted in *"Struggle a Hard Battle": Essays on Working-Class Immigrants*, ed. Dirk Hoerder (De Kalb, Ill., 1986), 229–53.

2. Alan B. Spitzer, "The Historical Problem of Generations," *American Historical Review* 78 (Dec. 1973): 1353–85. On the problem of sociological generations within the American working-class population, see Herbert Gutman, "Work, Culture and Society in Industrializing America, 1815–1919" in his *Work, Culture and Society in Industrializing America* (New York, 1976); David Montgomery, "Workers' Control of Machine Production in the Nineteenth Century" in his *Workers' Control in America* (New York and London, 1979), 9–31, and "Gutman's Nineteenth Century," *Labor History* 19 (1978): 420; John Bodnar, *The Transplanted: A History of Immigrants in Urban America* (Bloomington, Ind., 1985), 85–93; Leopold Haimson, "The Russian Workers' Movement on the Eve of the First World War" (Paper presented at the American Historical Association Convention, 1972); and E. J. Hobsbawm, "Custom, Wages and Workload in the Nineteenth Century" in his *Labouring Men* (London, 1964), 344–70.

3. See David Montgomery, "Strikes in Nineteenth Century America," *Social Science History* 4 (1980), 90–91.

4. The most recent national account of the strikes is Philip Foner, *The Great Labor Uprising of 1877* (New York, 1977). A description of the strike and crowd actions at Chicago is provided in chapter 8. My description is based largely on Richard Schneirov, "Chicago's Great Upheaval of 1877," *Chicago History* 9 (Spring 1977): 3–17. See also Kenneth Kann, "The Big City Riot: Chicago, Illinois" (Paper presented at

the American Historical Association Convention, December 28, 1976); Louise Carroll Wade, *Chicago's Pride: The Stockyards, Packingtown, and Environs in the Nineteenth Century* (Urbana, Ill., 1987), 117–19.

5. Foner, 153–54.

6. *Chicago Tribune*, Dec. 16, 1879–Jan. 17, 1880; *Daily Drovers' Journal*, Dec. 15, 1879; Chicago *Inter Ocean*, Dec. 29, 30, 1879, *Chicago Daily News*, Oct. 20, 1886, clipping in Chicago Citizens' Association Scrapbooks, vol. 43, Chicago Historical Society; Harper Leech and John C. Carroll, *Armour and His Times* (New York, 1938), 226. See also Wade, 122–26.

7. For recent treatments of the Knights, see Leon Fink, *Workingmen's Democracy: The Knights of Labor and American Politics* (Urbana, Ill., 1983); Bryan Palmer and Gregory Kealey, *Dreaming of What Might Be: The Knights of Labor in Ontario* (New York and London, 1981); and Susan Levine, *Labor's True Woman: Carpet Weavers, Industrialization, and Labor Reform in the Gilded Age* (Philadelphia, 1984). On the Kansas City assembly, see *Butcher Workman* 18 (Feb. 1932): 2; and Fink, chap. 5.

8. Jonathan Garlock and N. C. Bilder, *Directory of the Local Assemblies of the Knights of Labor* (Westport, Conn., 1982), 65, 68, 614–15.

9. The *Butcher Workman's* account is based on Joyce's own recollections of the movement. See *Butcher Workman* 18 (Feb. 1932): 2. On the Great Upheaval of 1886 in Chicago, see Richard Schneirov, "The Knights of Labor in the Chicago Labor Movement and in Municipal Politics, 1877–1887" (Ph.D. diss., Northern Illinois University, 1984), chap. 8.

10. John R. Commons et al., *A History of Labor in the United States* (New York, 1918), 2:381–82; Alma Herbst, *The Negro in the Slaughtering and Meat Packing Industry in Chicago* (Boston, 1932), 14–16; *Butcher Workman* 18 (Feb. 1932): 2, and (Mar. 1932): 3; Edna Clark, "A History of Labor Controversies in the Slaughtering and Meat Packing Industry in Chicago" (M.A. thesis, University of Chicago, 1922), chap. 1.

11. Clark, chap. 1; Garlock and Bilder, 71–74; *Butcher Workman* 18 (Apr. 1932): 3. On skill divisions, see David Brody, *The Butcher Workmen: A Study of Unionization* (Cambridge, Mass., 1964), 15–16.

12. *Butcher Workman* 18 (Aug. 1932): 2; Clark, chap. 1; Howard B. Meyer, "The Policing of Labor Disputes in Chicago: A Study" (Ph.D. diss., University of Chicago, 1929), chap. 3; Wade, 246.

13. Wade, 246–49; Clark, chap. 1; Meyer, chap. 3; Commons et al., 2:418–20.

14. Clark, 63; quotation in Commons et al., 2:419.

15. Meyer, chap. 3; Wade, 250–54.

16. Clark, chap. 1; Meyer, chap. 3; *Butcher Workman* 18 (Nov. 1932): 2. Powderly's decision to abandon the strike has loomed large in explanations of the order's decline. For varying interpretations, see Norman Ware, *The Labor Movement in the United States, 1860–1895* (New York, 1929), 152–54; Terrence Powderly, *The Path I Trod: The Autobiography of Terrence V. Powderly* (New York, 1940), 140–62; Joseph Buchanan, *The Story of a Labor Agitator* (New York, 1903), 316–21; Philip Foner, *History of the Labor Movement in the United States*, vol. 2 (New York, 1955), 86–88; and Commons et al., 1:419–20. For a recent analysis of the strike, see Schneirov, "Knights of Labor in Chicago," 504–14.

17. Brody, *Butcher Workmen*, 16–17; *Butcher Workman* 18 (Aug. 1932): 2.

18. *Butcher Workman* 18 (Apr. 1932): 2.

19. Chicago *Times*, Jan. 6, 1890, and Apr. 17, 1890; Chicago *Inter Ocean*, Mar. 29 and 31, 1890; *Chicago Daily News*, Apr. 25, 29, and 30, 1890; Chicago *Record Herald*, Apr. 28, 1890; *Chicago Tribune*, Apr. 29, 1890; Chicago Citizens' Association Scrapbooks, vol. 43, Chicago Historical Society.

20. Schneirov, "Knights of Labor in Chicago," chap. 4; Michael Funchion, *Chicago's Irish Nationalists, 1881–1890* (New York, 1976); Wade, 293–95. For the relationship between working-class organization and Irish nationalism, see also Eric Foner, "Class, Ethnicity and Radicalism in the Gilded Age: The Land League and Irish America," *Marxist Perspectives* 1 (Summer 1978): 22 and passim; John Bennett, "The Iron Workers of Wood Run and Johnstown: The Union Era" (Ph.D. diss., University of Pittsburgh, 1977), chap. 7; cf. Victor Walsh, " 'A Fanatic Heart': The Cause of Irish-American Nationalism during the Gilded Age," *Journal of Social History* 15 (1981):187–204.

21. *Butcher Workman* 18 (Nov. 1932): 2; 18 (Dec. 1932): 2.

22. For general descriptions of the Pullman Strike, see Almont Lindsey, *The Pullman Strike* (Chicago, 1942); Foner, *History of the Labor Movement*, 2:261–78; and Jeremy Brecher, *Strike!* (San Francisco, 1972), chap. 3.

23. *Butcher Workman* 19 (Feb. 1932): 2; Clark, 80–81; Chicago *Daily Drovers' Journal*, July 1, 16, 24, and 26, 1894. Small labor disturbances among the skilled men persisted through the 1890s and suggest a continuing sense of grievance. (See Brody, *Butcher Workmen*, 14.)

24. United States Strike Commission, *Report*, S. Doc. 7, 53d Cong., 3d sess., testimony of Harold I. Cleveland, Victor Harding, William Shade, and Benjamin Atwell, reporters, 370–83, 396–99; *Chicago Tribune*, July 13, 14, 19, 22, and 25, 1894.

25. U.S. Strike Commission, *Report,* testimony of John Fitzgerald, battalion chief, Chicago Fire Department, 390–92, and Herbert F. Miller and Victor Harding, reporters, 402–8; *Chicago Tribune,* July 13, 1894.

26. *Daily Drovers' Journal,* July 5, 1894.

27. Ibid.; Meyer, chap. 3.

28. U.S. Strike Commission, *Report,* 370–74; *Chicago Tribune,* July 9 and 10, 1894.

29. Meyer, chap. 3; Jean F. Block, *Hyde Park Houses: An Informal History* (Chicago, 1978), 65. My thanks to Steven Sapolsky for this reference.

30. Brody, *Butcher Workmen,* 18. See Mary McDowell's vivid first impressions of the community just after the 1894 strike: *Mary McDowell and Municipal Housekeeping,* ed. Caroline Hill (Chicago, 1938), 25; *Chicago Tribune,* July 13, 1904.

31. For an overview of these early years, see Brody, *Butcher Workmen,* 21–33. Little is known about Donnelly, despite his importance to the union. For a brief biographical sketch, see *Biographical Dictionary of American Labor,* ed. Gary M. Fink (Westport, Conn., 1984), 190–91.

32. Howard E. Wilson, *Mary McDowell, Neighbor* (Chicago, 1928), 86–90; John R. Commons, "Labor Conditions in Slaughtering and Meatpacking," in *Trade Unionism and Labor Problems,* ed. John R. Commons (Boston, 1905), 238–39.

33. Brody, *Butcher Workmen,* 17.

34. Amalgamated Meat Cutters and Butcher Workmen of North America, *Official Journal* 3 (Aug. 1902): 71; *American Federationist* 8 (Sept. 1901): 383; 8 (May 1901): 173.

35. *Official Journal* 3 (Sept. 1902): 1, 44.

36. *Official Journal* 5 (May 1904): 99; 3 (Aug. 1902): 72.

37. *Official Journal* 6 (Nov. 1904): 11; 2 (Mar. 1901): 1.

38. *Official Journal* 5 (Sept. 1904): 7.

39. Rudolf Clemen, *The American Livestock and Meat Industry* (New York, 1923), 696; Theodore Glocker, *The Government of American Trade Unions* (Baltimore, 1913), 19–20; Commons, "Labor Conditions," 222–23.

40. Brody, *Butcher Workmen,* 42; Philip S. Foner, *History of the Labor Movement in the United States,* vol. 3 (New York, 1964), 192–93.

41. Brody, *Butcher Workmen,* 43–44, 49; Commons, "Labor Conditions," 223.

42. *Official Journal* 5 (July 1904): 15, 19; Amalgamated Meat Cutters and Butcher Workmen of North America, *Proceedings of the Fifth General Convention, 1904* (Syracuse, N.Y., 1904), 69, 72–73.

43. Wilson, 95–97. Maude Gonne was active in the Home Rule

Movement, the Land League, and James Connolly's Socialist Republican Party. During the Boer War, she established *Inghinidbe na h'Eireann*, a women's nationalist organization. See C. Desmond Greaves, *The Life and Times of James Connolly* (New York, 1961), 81, 88–89, 116; Maude Gonne (Mrs. Maude MacBride), *Servant of the Queen* (London, 1938); Nancy Cardozo, *Lucky Eyes and a High Heart* (New York, 1978), 127–30, 188–93.

44. Alice Henry, *The Trade Union Woman* (New York, 1905), 52–58; Wilson, 85–90, 95–97; Commons, "Labor Conditions," 239–40; *Official Journal* 2 (Nov. 1903): 1–4; 2 (Feb. 1903): 39; Emily Barrows, "Trade Union Organization among Women in Chicago" (Ph.D. diss., University of Chicago, 1927), 117.

45. Amalgamated Meat Cutters and Butcher Workmen of North America, *Proceedings, 1904*, 51–52. On the sausagemakers' strike, see Illinois State Board of Arbitration, *Report, 1904* (Springfield, 1905), 34 (from notes in the Bessie Louise Pierce Papers, Box 86A, Chicago Historical Society).

46. *Official Journal* 4 (Feb. 1903): 20–21; Amalgamated Meat Cutters and Butcher Workmen of North America, *Proceedings of the Fourth General Convention, 1902* (Syracuse, N.Y., 1902), 23, and *Proceedings, 1904*, 51–52; Philip S. Foner, *Women and the American Labor Movement, from Colonial Times to the Eve of World War One* (New York, 1979), 320; Commons, "Labor Conditions," 239–40.

47. Foner, *Women and the American Labor Movement*, 299, 313.

48. *Official Journal* 4 (Dec. 1902): 16–17; 3 (Mar. 1902): 39; 4 (Oct. 1902): 28–29.

49. For numerous examples of exclusion, particularly by AFL craft organizations, see Alice Kessler-Harris, *Out to Work: A History of Wage-Earning Women in the United States* (New York, 1982), 153–59, and "Where Are the Organized Women Workers?" *Feminist Studies* 3 (1975): 92–110; Foner, *Women and the American Labor Movement*, 250–52. Carl Degler argues that the decision of whether or not to include women in a union often turned on the question of whether or not they represented a serious threat to men's wages if they remained unorganized. Maurine Greenwald's case studies of telephone operators, railroad workers, and streetcar conductors during World War I seem to support this generalization. See Carl Degler, *At Odds: Women and the Family in America from the Revolution to the Present* (New York, 1981), 395–96, 397–400; and Maurine W. Greenwald, *Women, War, and Work: The Impact of World War One on Women Workers in the United States* (Westport, Conn., 1980).

50. Edward G. Hartman, *The Movement to Americanize the Immigrant* (New York, 1948). For the efforts of managers and middle-class reform-

ers to use Americanization programs as a means of social control, see Gerd Korman, "Americanization at the Factory Gate," *Industrial and Labor Relations Review* 18 (1965): 396–419; Daniel Nelson, *Managers and Workers: Origins of the New Factory System in the United States, 1880–1920* (Madison, Wis., 1975), 144–45; Brody, *Steelworkers in America*, 189–97; Stephen Meyer, "Adapting the Immigrant to the Line: Americanization in the Ford Factory, 1914–1921," *Journal of Social History* 14 (1980): 67–82. Herbert Gutman's "Work, Culture and Society in Industrializing America, 1815–1919," in his collection of essays under the same title, remains the most subtle analysis of this theme.

51. For brief, perceptive comments on informal socialization of immigrants at work, see Montgomery, *Workers' Control in America*, 42–43; and for a treatment which considers the efforts of both management and unions to "Americanize" Slavic immigrants, see Neil Betten, "Polish-American Steelworkers: Americanization through Industry and Labor," *Polish-American Studies* 33 (1976): 31–42.

52. Ethelbert Stewart, "The Influence of Trade Unions on Immigrants," U.S. Bureau of Labor Statistics, Bulletin no. 56 (Washington, D.C., 1905), reprinted in *The Making of America*, vol. 3, *Labor*, ed. Robert M. LaFollette (Chicago, 1905; reprinted, New York, 1969), 230. See also Wilson, 98–100.

53. Stewart, 226, 230.

54. Quoted in Wilson, 99.

55. Commons, "Labor Conditions," 246. The preponderance of Irish-Americans in the national leadership of the labor movement is, of course, well established. Between 1900 and 1910 nearly half of the AFL's one hundred constituent unions had Irish-American presidents. Irish influence in shaping *local* labor movements may have been even more significant in the long run. It was at this level that the acculturation and integration of new ethnic groups occurred. The definitive study of this process remains to be done. For a brief overview, see David Montgomery, "The Irish and the American Labor Movement" in *America and Ireland, 1776–1976*, ed. David N. Doyle and Owen D. Edwards (Westport, Conn., 1976).

56. Stewart, 229–31; *Official Journal* 2 (July 1901); 3 (May 1902): 26; 4 (Nov. 1902): 20; 4 (Mar. 1903). See also Brody, *Butcher Workmen*, 40–41; Commons, "Labor Conditions," 247–48. For figures on English speakers among the new immigrant groups, see U.S. Immigration Commission, *Reports*, part 11, *Immigrants in Industry*, vol. 13, *Slaughtering and Meat Packing* (Washington, D.C., 1911), 260.

57. Antanas Kaztauskis, "From Lithuania to the Chicago Stockyards—An Autobiography" in *Plain Folk: Life Histories of Undistinguished*

Americans, ed. David M. Katzman and William M. Tuttle, Jr. (Urbana, Ill., 1982), 112–13. See chap. 1, n. 44.

58. Quoted in Wilson, 100. See also Henry, 56.

59. Glocker, 19–20, 28; Stewart, passim; Commons, "Labor Conditions," 233.

60. *Chicago Record Herald,* Mar. 26, 1903, 2; Dec. 27, 1903, 6; *The Economist,* Sept. 5, 1903, 299, from notes, Pierce Papers, Box 86A, Chicago Historical Society; Steven Sapolsky, "Class-Conscious Belligerents: The Teamsters and the Class Struggle in Chicago, 1901–1905" (University of Pittsburgh, 1974, typescript), 1–2; Glocker, 24; Dorothy Richardson, *The Long Day: The Story of an American Working Girl* (New York, 1905), 283, and "Trade Unions in Petticoats," *Leslie's Monthly Magazine* 57 (Mar. 1904): 489–500; Luke Grant, "Women in Trade Unions," *American Federationist* 10 (Aug. 1903): 655; Montgomery, *Workers' Control in America,* 57–58.

61. Stewart, 234–35; Mary McDowell, "The Struggle for an American Standard of Living," in *Mary McDowell and Municipal Housekeeping,* 62–66.

62. Wilson, 93; Mary McDowell, "American Standard of Living," 62–66.

63. Stewart, 235. See also Meyer, chap. 9; Harry Rosenberg, "The Great Strike," Mary McDowell Papers, Folder 15, Chicago Historical Society.

64. *Official Journal* 5 (Aug. 1904): 16. See also Wilson, 78.

65. Stewart, 234. For the union's argument that it was raising the immigrants to an American standard, see *Official Journal* 5 (Aug. 1904): 13–16.

66. McDowell, "American Standard of Living," 66.

67. Kennedy et al., *Wages and Family Budgets in the Chicago Stockyards District* (Chicago, 1914), 22–23.

5

Work Rationalization and the Struggle for Control, 1900–1904

> The sense of class solidarity began to appear. It extended across all lines of race and nationality and sex. . . . So the strike was on. With a unanimity and solidarity that surprised even the workers themselves, the slaves of the slaughter pens laid down their work.
>
> Algie Simons, *Chicago Socialist*,
> August 6, 1904

Management's crucial role in the transformation of packinghouse work is clear. In their drive for productivity, the packers took the initiative by subdividing the butcher's craft, cultivating a new, more specialized type of skill, mechanizing some tasks, and generally expanding their control over the production process.[1] But what role did the butcher workmen and -women play in all of this rationalization?

Recently several scholars have considered this issue of control and the part labor played in the evolution of mass-production work. These studies have focused primarily on the early introduction of new technology and management reforms, on craftsmen's defense of their own prerogatives, and on their resistance to skill dilution.[2] Yet the transformation of factory work was an ongoing process which continued after the introduction of early assembly-line methods, and workers' own ideas and behavior remained an integral part of work rationalization. The story of how this occurred in meat packing is fascinating because here shop-floor organization and conflict emerged during the early twentieth century after the battle to maintain craft traditions and control had clearly been lost. Skilled butchers, machine tenders, and common laborers all joined together to develop new strategies and forms of organization in the struggle for control.[3] Their motivation for all of this is not difficult to understand if we view the new system of production from the shop floor.

The same work situation which represented such a high degree of rationalization from the packers' perspective brought chaos to the lives of their employees. Not only was their work year rent by a long slack season, but they could not depend on anything like regular hours during the rest of the year. From day to day, their livelihood depended on the number of cattle coming through the gates of the Union Stockyards. Though the killing day started as late as ten or eleven in the morning, they had to be standing before the gates by seven; otherwise, they lost their chance for work. Even the skilled had to expect to work fourteen hours at a grueling pace one day and go without work the next. If a machine or the overhead conveyor broke, the worker lost the repair time. With management in control of the production process and the labor market, the lives of the packinghouse workers and their families were shaped in large part by exigencies of the markets for livestock and dressed meats. The process and practice of unionization was aimed at the heart of this management control. The ways in which early mass-production workers went about their own process of work rationalization reflected earlier strategies but also foreshadowed those which would be employed by industrial unionists in later years.

WORKERS' RATIONALIZATION

Most changes in the character of work arose, not from formal negotiations, but rather from a decentralized, informal bargaining process in the plants. The keys to this system were unofficial shop-floor organizations called house committees. Since union locals were based on trades, each one established a house committee in the city's various plants. Committees consisted of three production workers elected semiannually, and care was taken to represent a variety of jobs and skill levels in each department.

Committee members were frequently reelected, a fact that may suggest that rank-and-file workers had a great deal of confidence in them.[4] The official purpose of the committees was to hear grievances from management as well as from the workers and to try to settle them at the workplace. In practice, committees interpreted the term "grievance" very broadly, and it was through the committees that workers temporarily shifted the balance of power in the packinghouses and began to reshape their work environments.

The *range* of workers' demands is impressive. Committees in various departments pressed successfully for regular hours, restriction of output, higher wages, layoff and recall by seniority, and increases in the size of work groups. They also fought and sometimes reversed disciplinary measures. Most rationalization initiatives originated with workers' discussing problems at union meetings and formulating resolutions aimed at solving them. Often ideas trickled down from those groups, particularly the cattle butchers, who had organized earlier and had stronger shop-floor organizations. Resolutions were voted on by the local membership as a whole at well-attended meetings, and this high degree of democracy explains the broad base of support for the house committees. They were simply delivering to management the demands of the rank and file in the various plants.

One of the first problems to which many house committees turned was regularization of employment and control of the casual labor market. Most committees established regular work hours and an overtime differential designed to discourage foremen from keeping workers after the regular quitting time. It is clear from local reports and the way the rule was enforced that the object was to abolish overtime rather than to increase earnings. The shift to a regular workday came first among the cattle butchers, who often initiated such campaigns. Before unionization it was common for butchers to work from 7:00 A.M. to 10:00 P.M. one day, 11:00 A.M. to 9:30 P.M. the next, and perhaps not at all on the third day. By the summer of 1902, a guaranteed ten-hour day was in effect. If a foreman wanted his gang to work overtime, he had to guarantee a full day's work for the following day. The rule provided regular work hours and reduced the length of the workday.[5] The new system spread through the plants. E. G. Purcell, an officer of Beef Boners' Local 135, explained how the system worked in his shop: "Our working hours before we organized were from three, four, five, and six o'clock in the A.M. to all hours in the evening. We have since adopted resolutions regulating our hours of labor, also specifying that work done before 7 o'clock A.M. and after 5:30 o'clock P.M. be considered overtime to be paid at the rate of time and a half, and it has been the means of doing away with a great deal of unnecessary overtime."[6]

The committees also tried to regularize the workyear and stabilize employment. All workers lost under the packers' normal practice of simply discharging about one-third of the labor force during the slack season and spreading the remainder over the entire job structure. The skilled were forced to perform low-paying and disagreeable tasks in order to remain employed, while many of the common laborers were simply thrown out of work. In both instances the fate of the more skilled workers was linked to that of the common laborers. The unemployed represented a threat to the butchers, who watched with trepidation as the crowd outside the stockyards gates and employment offices grew during the slack season. The union argued that wages were determined more by those at the gate than by those on the floor; the more unemployed, the greater the downward pressure on wages.[7]

The committees demanded that all workers in a department be retained during slack season, even if this meant part-time work for the gang. Although this demand had some success in the killing gangs, which included a large number of casual laborers, employment had certainly not been regularized in all departments by 1904. But even if the union had not reached its goal of a stable, unionized labor force and regular employment by this point, its strength represented a threat to the whole system of casual labor, which the industry's seasonality and volatile cattle market seemed to dictate.[8]

The shop-floor organizations also enforced seniority systems in the departments where they were strongest. The system in cattle killing amounted to promotion on the basis of time on the job. In hog killing, where seasonal layoffs remained a problem even with the union, workers enforced the last-hired-first-fired concept. As the volume of work picked up once again, they insisted that those who had been with the house longest should be hired first. This erosion of the foreman's control over employment represented not only an affront to his authority but also the loss of a lucrative source of supplementary income. In the past, workers had paid for the chance to work as well as for promotions. The foremen bitterly resented this infringement on their prerogatives, but the practice continued to spread.[9]

Certainly the most controversial strategy to regularize work was restriction of output, and this was the one which irritated the packers most. First in the cattle- and sheep-killing gangs and eventually in most other departments, house committees drew up what workers felt were fair scales of work and wages and presented them to the plant superintendents. The effect of the slow-down on the killing beds was felt throughout the plants, and management sources complained that output had been cut by 30 to 50 percent. Although this figure is probably an exaggeration, there is little doubt that union control over the pace of work hurt the packers. John R. Commons estimated in 1904 that the cut in production ranged from 16 to 25 percent, depending on the plant.[10] But more important than any immediate financial cost, especially since this was probably passed on to the consumer, was the demonstration of collective strength that the tactic represented. Now the packers' own division of labor was turned against them. Workers at strategic points in the flow of production were given scales of work which were disproportionately low, necessitating the employment of more people throughout the line. Floormen, for example, who had the delicate task of separating the hide from the carcass, handled only fifteen head per hour, while splitters handled twenty-five. A foreman had the option of either hiring two floormen for every splitter or allowing his one splitter to kill time while the floorman caught up.[11]

This restriction aimed not only to slow down the pace of work but also to dry up the labor pool. A member of the Beef Luggers' local explained how the process had improved conditions in his department: "We used to load 60 to 70 cars of beef with 5 or 6 men, and this was certainly slavery, as anyone who understands the work will admit. This was the first thing we changed, and now we load 60 cars a day with 8 men, thereby putting more carriers to work; and where we had only 37 carriers before we organized, we now have 53, and they do no more loading than the 37 used to do."[12]

The restriction was very important to skilled workers, but it offered something to the casual laborer as well. In addition to slowing the speed of work, which had reached a deadly pace by the time of unionization, it also produced more jobs. One indication of the effectiveness of the restriction was the demise of the pacesetters—those well-paid workers placed at strategic spots in the production line who drove others around them to keep up the pace. By vigorously enforcing their scales, the house committees became the new pacesetters.[13]

How did the house committees acquire so much control? The adjustments they made in working hours, wages, advancement, and employment were bound to receive widespread support among workers; but how were they won, and how were they enforced? Aided by relative prosperity and high employment between 1901 and 1904, much of the workers' success was a result of their readiness to engage in short, unofficial strikes around specific issues. These were control strikes, used as levers in the struggle with management to change aspects of the production system. A few examples, drawn from various departments, suggest how they were used to increase workers' power at the point of production.

Strikes sometimes were used to enforce new wage scales. Shortly after organizing, pork casing workers devised a wage scale which amounted to a twenty-five-cent-per-day increase and submitted it to management. When the raise was not immediately forthcoming, a one-day strike brought the concession.[14]

Once the process of unionization was well advanced in a department, a strike or the threat of one could also be used to establish a *de facto* closed shop. By 1903, numerous locals, including those of unskilled workers in a number of by-product departments, were reporting that they allowed only union men and women to work with them. A system of color-coded monthly dues buttons clearly indicated those who were fully paid-up members and those who were not. A confrontation in the wool-working department suggests an early racial conflict as well as the pervasiveness of this closed shop drive: "One of the large packers during the slack season of 1902 started to discriminate by discharging union men or laying them off and putting colored men in their places, who were not union men, and as the union men were idle we refused to let these men work until our men were reinstated, which the firm refused to do. We went on strike and remained out for one week to uphold the principle, and won out."[15]

Strikes were also used to enforce traditional work rules regarding size of work gangs, for example, or to establish new ones. The regularization of the workyear and the workday described above were also introduced into cattle gangs under threat of a strike.[16]

Typically, these unofficial strikes were spontaneous and limited to one department. There was always the possibility, however, that a strike which started in this manner would spread, with workers in other departments or even other houses coming out in sympathy or seizing the opportunity to redress their own grievances. Such a strike occurred in early 1903 when a Swift foreman laid off part of a beef-killing gang in spite of an earlier verbal agreement to keep the whole gang. Killing in every Swift plant in the country stopped at 9:30 the next morning. The Amalgamated's president was called in immediately to accept the company's concession. "Chicago," the *National Provisioner* complained at the end of 1903, "is always in the face of strikes . . . in a state of siege all the time."[17]

During the two years between the summer of 1900 and the summer of 1902, the union tabulated only five strikes and lockouts. At the union's 1902 convention, delegates passed a resolution authorizing local unions to dispense strike benefits to members involved in small-scale, spontaneous strikes when quick action was needed. In the following year unionization spread through the Chicago plants and in other stockyard centers, and the strength of shop-floor organization grew. Between May 1903 and May 1904, the union counted a total of thirty-six strikes. Unofficial strikes were also increasing in frequency by the spring of 1904. Part of the explanation for the spread of this system is contained in the strike figures themselves, as well as in local union reports. Of those which had been brought to some sort of conclusion by May 1904, the workers had won nineteen and the employers five.[18]

Clearly, the strikes were successful. The figures for both

periods are certainly underestimates, with many short strikes going unreported. But even these rough estimates tell us something about the nature of the strike in packinghouse work during these years. The figures, together with local union reports detailing the causes of conflict, suggest that strikes were used in lieu of what we now recognize as the "normal" procedure of collective bargaining and negotiation. Conditions were changed in the packinghouses through unilateral action on the part of workers. Issues were discussed; resolutions were passed and presented to the superintendent by the house committee. The superintendent's only choices were to accept the demand or to face a strike.

To appreciate the significance of this decentralized workers' rationalization process from management's view, we need only put ourselves in the place of the superintendent at one of the largest plants, who had to deal with over one hundred of these house committees.[19] Now it was the packers who saw chaos in the ever-changing work environment. They complained that union officials could not follow through on agreements, since the house committees could always disregard them and call a strike. So long as the bargaining procedure remained decentralized, with the house committees responsible for establishing minimum wages and conditions and restricting output, the trend toward higher wages, lower productivity, and greater worker initiative continued. In this sense, a national contract signed by the packers in 1903 brought some degree of stability to labor relations in the industry. But the agreement covered only skilled butchers, and even among them, grievances remained. As long as conditions were fluid, i.e., not written into a contract, the committees were free to implement any decision which they had the power to enforce. Both the union officials and the packers may have desired an agreement which would provide greater stability, but pressure for change continued to emerge from below. The chronic struggle on the shop floor propelled the two parties in opposite directions and led ultimately to a bitter strike in 1904.

THE LIMITS OF CORPORATE LIBERALISM

Conflicts over control in the workplace and their results in the 1904 strike have direct implications for the view that a significant shift in the nature of class relations took place during the early twentieth century. Several historians have argued that business and labor leaders reached an ideological consensus that embodied a new attitude toward labor relations in these years. The more enlightened employers, usually representing the largest corporate oligopolies, accepted the fact that some form of workers' representation was both inevitable and desirable. Their goal was to foster the development of more responsible labor leaders who were willing to talk out problems rather than resort to strikes. Many trade union officials, the argument contends, agreed that the strike should be scrapped in favor of a system of collective bargaining and arbitration which would place them at the center of the emerging corporate order. The organizational manifestation of this new, more rational form of class relations was the National Civic Federation (NCF) and particularly its industrial department, which included representatives from capital and labor. Thus, historians of corporate liberalism argue, American workers were integrated, ideologically and structurally, into the political economy of monopoly capital in its earliest stages.[20]

On the surface, this analysis seems to describe the situation in meat packing admirably. The major packing companies supported the NCF and its program. Indeed, the packers were just the sort of large-scale, highly rationalized firms which have been described as the mainstays of the new corporate liberal movement. J. Ogden Armour and Louis F. Swift, representing the second generation of leadership in the industry's two largest corporations, were both prominent NCF members. And these giant corporations clearly set the tone for industrial relations in packing.[21]

While Amalgamated officials did not see themselves as corporate liberals, their view of labor relations resembled that of the NCF. Homer Call, the union's treasurer and the editor of its journal, was a great admirer of the Federation's "calm, cool-headed businesslike approach" to industrial relations and a foe of what he called "hasty strikes." Call believed that the packers had accepted the Amalgamated as a "business institution in every sense that the word implies." Noting a series of wage increases and other improvements, he argued that these concessions were won through responsibility and conservatism, not strikes.[22]

Call suggested how to ensure continued good relations. Workers should avoid all hasty action; a longstanding grievance could wait a little longer rather than imperil the organization as a whole. When parts of an agreement worked against the interests of union members, their duty was clear. They must wait until the expiration of the contract and then try to renegotiate the trouble areas. The packers, Call concluded, were businessmen and could be relied upon to act honorably. [23]

Michael Donnelly, the Amalgamated's president, devoted considerable time to traveling around the various packing centers settling unofficial strikes. A veteran packinghouse worker, Donnelly was clearly more tolerant of these initiatives than was Call, a meat cutter, but Donnelly, too, in trying to negotiate a national contract with the packers, worried about the union's image and the trouble such strikes caused. [24]

Yet pronouncements of the Amalgamated's leadership about the conservative nature of their organization and their desire to run the union on "sound business principles" stood in stark contrast to what was happening on the killing floors and in the packing rooms of the industry. Here, butcher workmen and -women carried on a continual conflict with management over the issue of control.

Throughout the period 1902–4 negotiations and bargaining took place in two fairly distinct but related arenas—at the plant level, between house committees and superintendents, and at the national level, between corporate and union executives. Both spheres of activity were important. Where shop-floor organization was strongest, as among sheep and cattle butchers for example, major changes could be accomplished through plant-level bargaining. In addition, such shop-floor strength could be translated into pressure for a national contract. National contracts were won for both these groups in October 1903. Pay scales, setting standard rates for various "trades," and work scales, which formalized restriction of output, were incorporated into both contracts. The extension of such standards to all union members, however, though essential, was quite difficult to achieve, particularly in those departments with few skilled workers. That the union's move for national standards came in the spring of 1904, in the midst of a trade depression and heavy unemployment, made the venture even more perilous. While national officials tried to stem the tide of local initiatives and strikes, delegates arrived at the union's 1904 Cincinnati convention ready to move. Representatives from each of the various trades met and developed industry-wide standards. These were adopted, over official opposition, as the basis for contract bargaining. [25]

Perhaps the most vital standard of all was a fixed rate of twenty cents per hour for common labor throughout the industry. This was a particularly ambitious demand and yet one which packinghouse workers believed was essential to their employment security and the stability of the union itself. Whatever its formal philosophy, the union as an organization had to assert some degree of control over this part of the labor market. "The union had to organize the casuals at the gates," economist Carleton Parker wrote, "or give up." The Amalgamated tried to do this by writing a minimum common labor rate into their contract proposals, thereby placing the wages of the industry's least skilled workers beyond the play of market forces. The decision to press for this demand during the 1904 depression may have been a mistake, but delegates seemed to feel there was little choice. Without asserting this kind of control over the price of common labor, the union was living on borrowed time. The packers were prepared from the outset to sign an agreement covering the skilled workers, but the maintenance of a large, tractable pool of unskilled labor was crucial from their perspective. Common labor wages, Edward Tilden of Libby, McNeill and Libby later explained, "naturally are regulated by supply and demand and ought not be regulated, arbitrarily, by a joint agreement." Both sides recognized the importance of the demand, and the result of its refusal by the packers was a bitter strike. [26]

By integrating the common labor rate into its industry-wide wage scale and setting an absolute minimum, the union served notice of its intention to exert some control over the casual labor market in the yards. Most striking was the fact that the more skilled, old-immigrant men, recognizing the importance of this control, were prepared to risk their own standards in order to enforce the demand. As John R. Commons later wrote, "Perhaps the fact of greatest social significance is that the strike of 1904 was not merely a strike of skilled labor for the unskilled, but was a strike of Americanized Irish, Germans, and Bohemians in behalf of Slovaks, Poles, Lithuanians, and negroes." When a referendum of local unions rejected a compromise offer of sixteen and a half cents, Donnelly ordered his members to prepare for a general strike. The packers changed their minds at the last minute and agreed to arbitration, but the momentum had carried too far. The strike was on.[27]

While the common labor rate was crucial in the 1904 strike, the packers were also animated by a more general irritation with the daily problems of having to deal with union organization in their plants. During the strike, a spokesman for the packers explained the forces behind their decision to resist the union. By 1904 it had come down to a question of who was running the packinghouses, management or the house committees.

> The domination of the packing plants by the union gradually had become unbearable. The proprietor of an establishment had forty stewards to deal with and nothing that failed to suit them could be done . . . the packer could not run his own plant. It was run by the stewards. Discipline grew lax and the men did not attend to their work as they should have done. . . . As sure as either employer or worker gets control of an industry like meat packing a conflict such as that [which is] now on seems inevitable. The side having the power abuses it and domineers over the other.[28]

Whether or not its policies were domineering, it is clear that from 1901 to 1904 the union, operating through the house committees, was the "side having the power." When the union sought to extend its control still further by winning a minimum wage for all common laborers, the packers decided to make their stand. Encouraged by mounting unemployment in the city and a unity of purpose, they dug in for what proved to be a long, bitter strike which they perceived as a just struggle to maintain control over their industry.

THE 1904 STRIKE

Throughout the late nineteenth century packinghouse strikes had been characterized by two related forms of protest—disciplined walkouts, usually by the skilled butchers, and large-scale crowd actions which drew in many of the laborers beyond the reach of the craft unions. An example of the latter form of protest, the 1894 conflict had in fact developed more as a riot than as a strike. With the advent of the 1904 struggle, Chicagoans feared another round of massive violence and destruction of property. As the hour of the strike approached, many Packingtown residents grew apprehensive. They remembered the rampaging crowds and the burning boxcars; the fusillade at the corner of Forty-seventh Street and Ashland Avenue; and the militia tents and cannon at "Whiskey Point."[29]

What happened instead was a well-organized, disciplined, and relatively peaceful struggle. Precisely at noon on July 12, twenty-eight thousand packinghouse workers finished the killing which they had in hand, wrapped up their tools, cleaned their work-places, and marched out of the plants. Thousands of others in packing centers throughout the country joined them. Even the packers were impressed by the spectacle and the high degree of organization and planning involved.[30] Like the 1894 strike, this one was as much a demonstration of discontent as a test of strength over specific issues, but the widespread rioting of 1894 was replaced by giant parades and rallies planned and directed by the union and the Socialist Party.

The behavior and mentality of thousands of individuals is more complicated, of course, than a simple distinction between "modern" and "premodern" protest will allow.[31] Indeed, one might have expected Packingtown's 1904 protest to be every bit as "traditional" and violent as that which had taken place in 1894, because the social composition of the community had been transformed since then by a massive influx of eastern European peasants. But the transformation of the packinghouse workers' protest from spontaneous and often riotous to more organized behavior under the direction of a national union is consistent with the general evolution of strike activity across the nation during the late nineteenth and early twentieth centuries.[32] The nineteenth-century pattern reemerged sporadically during the 1904 strike, with large crowds attacking scabs, but it is the discipline and or-ganization exhibited by large numbers of "premodern" people—the recently arrived Slavic immigrants—which is most striking. If the shop-floor struggles may be seen as part of a search for new strategies to rationalize working conditions within the plants, then workers' behavior during the strike may be seen as an attempt to adopt new forms of mass action to defend and advance their control over the work process and labor market.

The contrast between the 1894 and 1904 strikes is explained in part by the character of the union itself and its strategy. For the first time, skilled and unskilled—virtually all of the production workers in the yards—were organized together across racial and ethnic lines. Unlike the Knights, the Amalgamated consciously mixed workers from various skill levels and social backgrounds in the same local unions. The organizers had carefully integrated the new generation of Slavic immigrants into the unions and, in the process, won the support of various organizations and leaders in the neighborhoods around the yards.

Another major factor affecting the character of the 1904 strike was the general context of industrial relations in Chicago during these years. From the workers' perspective, their close relationship with the powerful Chicago Federation of Labor provided invaluable financial, strategic, and moral support. But this very strength and militancy was perceived as an affront by the packers and other Chicago employers. For them the packinghouse conflict was the focus of a more general struggle against "tyrannical" labor unions. This broader context helps to explain the bitterness of the strike and the determination displayed on both sides.

Notwithstanding the strike's auspicious beginning, the long-range prospects for a union victory were not bright. Because of high unemployment, the packers were able to recruit strikebreakers from outside the city for the unskilled work, while they filled the skilled jobs with a combination of salaried employees and a small number of nonunion butchers from smaller packing centers. Because the strike originated in a struggle between the packers and the Amalgamated, the mechanical and maintenance unions of the Allied Trades Council honored their own contracts and remained at work. Production levels certainly fell, however, and both parties may have been looking for a way out when events took a new course.[33]

On July 20 officials of the Allied Trades Council warned that the strike might spread to their own members unless resolved soon; they demanded a conference. The resulting agreement offered no improvement in conditions, but it did provide for a guarantee against discrimination in the reemployment of union members. Union officials reluctantly agreed, and the strike ended on July 21.[34] The agreement began to unravel, however, as soon as butcher workmen and -women gathered at the plants on the morning of July 22. Foremen and superintendents, encouraged apparently by what they took to be a sign of union weakness, adopted a belligerent attitude and discriminated against union members. At Armour, the superintendent told the crowd of strikers, "You went out like cattle; we'll take you back in the same way." Ernest Poole described the scene at another plant: "On Friday morning the great mass of men and women, most of them Poles, Lithuanians, and Slovaks, poured into the Yards. Foreman Penson came out to a large crowd of men and women at the door, and speaking to them there, he used the vilest epithet that can be applied to a woman. The effect on the crowd was instantaneous. The report spread, was translated in language after language. . . . "[35] Outraged workers besieged their union halls, demanding some response. With tremendous pressure being generated from below, Donnelly saw little option but to declare the strike on again.

The Union

The union maintained strict discipline throughout the strike. Signs printed in six languages, plastered to walls and trees throughout the neighborhood, exhorted workers to remain peaceful and warned that the union would not support members engaged in violence.

> We can win, if we stand by the union, if we obey the union's rules to molest no person or property and abide strictly by the laws of the country. All men on strike should retire to their homes and attend their various union meetings for all information. If you follow the above instructions, you will be of great assistance in helping to win this strike. Your organization will not assist you if you get into unlawful trouble.[36]

When fighting did occur between strikebreakers and union members, union officials were frequently called in by police to quell the disturbance.

Daily union meetings not only maintained solidarity in the face of a long strike, but also minimized crowd activity. Packingtown's streets emptied at the beginning of the strike as thousands of workers sat in mass meetings of the twenty-six local unions in the yards. Beyond these regular meetings, the union used several other measures to maintain discipline and solidarity. Relief stations which dispensed meat, vegetables, bread, and other items were established at various points throughout the neighborhood. On July 13, 655 families were served. The Amalgamated dispensed seven thousand pounds of meat at one station, six thousand pounds at another, and eventually ran out of food. In order to maintain the greatest possible hold on its membership, the union made relief services and admission to meetings conditional upon possession of a new union card which was punched daily at the worker's union hall.[37]

The Amalgamated's most dramatic effort to demonstrate its members' solidarity was a giant parade held on August 7, after most of the workers had been on strike for nearly a month. There had been spontaneous parades in 1894, but this time the marchers were in close formation behind an American flag. An estimated twenty thousand men, women, and children lined up in Ashland Avenue for ten blocks between Forty-fifth and Fifty-fifth streets, with the leaders of the Chicago Federation of Labor and the Packing Trades Council at the front. Behind the leaders marched the skilled auxiliary trades—steamfitters, carpenters, and others—who had now come out in sympathy with the Amalgamated. The butcher workmen themselves were organized into three divisions and followed by a contingent of four hundred neighborhood children, the little girls dressed in white and carrying white banners. Three thousand women workers marched at the rear with flags and banners, and both marchers and onlookers who lined the parade route chanted, "We will win!" The line of march was accompanied by several bands and ended at Oswald's Grove, just south of the yards, where a picnic and meat-dressing contests were held. In spite of the taunts from scabs on the roofs of the packing plants, the march was exceptionally well ordered. Even the *Chicago Tribune*, always on the alert for labor violence, could not find any disturbances.[38]

The Amalgamated's leaders appealed for public support by identifying the union with the effort to bring Packingtown up to an "American standard of living" and to minimize its threat to the city as a whole. Chicago, they argued, could not afford the social overhead which the casual labor system in the yards entailed. Nor could it afford a return to the days of rampant disease and high infant mortality, with thousands of its people on charity and its streets filled with crime. This, according to the Amalgamated, was what the conflict was all about. "Are the profits of the trust to be the one supreme consideration?" the Amalgamated's official journal asked. ". . . We submit that it is not right. We have built their industry and we demand to be treated like fellow workers—not mere items of expense. . . . If these 40,000 unskilled workers are reduced to $5.50 per week, what effect will it have on the community?" The editorial described the filth, disease, overcrowding, high mortality, and poverty in the community as it existed on the current $6.50 per week and suggested that these conditions would worsen if the packers prevailed.[39] Other editorials painted the packers as the enemy of the entire community, mentioning high meat prices, pollution of air and water, and the theft of millions of gallons of water by means of pipes connected illegally to the city's supply.

Such appeals were part of a union strategy to maximize public support for the strikers. Organization, union leaders argued, meant not only a decent standard of living for the people of Packingtown but also a solution to some of the social problems that had grown up along with the industry. More than one middle-class observer noted that it might indeed be safer to have an organized union which negotiated contracts, agreed to arbitration, and tried to discourage violence than the spontaneous and destructive rioting that the community had known in the past. The union, it seemed, offered something to Hyde Park as well as to Packingtown.

With its large constituency of unskilled immigrants, the Amalgamated had to wage the 1904 strike differently than a typical AFL craft union might have done. Living standards in the community were so low that a long strike raised the specter of bitter suffering and starvation. More than most unions in the city, the butchers were dependent on the labor movement at large, and with its financial support they launched an elaborate relief program. Along with the problem of physical privation came the danger of despair, and to counter this the union organized parades, picnics, rallies, and frequent meetings to sustain a high level of morale and solidarity. Although small numbers of skilled workers were beginning to drift back to the plants by the end of the strike, the workers' spirits seem never to have broken.

The Community

Notwithstanding the union's efforts to keep a tight rein on the strikers, however, a certain amount of crowd activity was almost inevitable, for two reasons. The union's leadership was not blind to the importance of aggressive picketing in an industry so dependent on unskilled labor. Having to conduct the strike during a depression in Chicago, temporary home for thousands of transient unemployed, could only have underscored the point. But crowd violence was also a product to some extent of the ecology of Packingtown as a neighborhood. The yards were the natural focal point of the community—physically, of course, but also economically and socially. The most important institutions in the community, aside from its churches, were the saloons. These, together with a few stores, constituted the community's only commercial areas, concentrated on either side of the yards, along Ashland Avenue and Halsted Street near the main gates. It was therefore difficult for scabs to enter or leave the yards without being the center of attention, and many of the crowds which attacked strikebreakers emerged from saloons, especially along Halsted, which bordered the old Irish neighborhood of Bridgeport. Finally, those residential blocks closest to the yards were the most densely populated in the neighborhood. Here, a great deal of normal community activity occurred in the streets.

Disturbances were concentrated heavily along Halsted Street. Of eighteen documented crowd actions, fifteen occurred on the east side of the yards, closest to Bridgeport. Although the crowds were ethnically mixed and included Slavic workers, a disproportionate number of those involved were Irish. Part of the explanation for this concentration undoubtedly had to do with the position of the main gate at Thirty-ninth and Halsted streets, directly across from the old Irish neighborhood. There were other entrances, however, along Ashland Avenue, on the west side, and there were fewer attacks in that area. Bridgeport had already established its reputation for militancy and solidarity, and it provided many of the professional and amateur "labor sluggers" during strikes.[40]

The strikebreakers, the objects of all these attacks, deserve some attention as well. William Tuttle, for example, has argued that the role of black strikebreakers in the 1904 conflict contributed to the image of blacks as a "scab race" and more generally to racial hostility within the Chicago working-class community.[41] This problem is an extremely important one in understanding the subsequent development of workers' consciousness and race relations in the city. It is difficult to draw firm conclusions on the basis of crowd behavior, however, and observations must remain speculative.

There were certainly violent attacks on black strikebreakers, some of whom defended themselves with arms. Black workers who attempted to commute from their homes in the Black Belt about one mile east of the yards were especially vulnerable, and they were frequently attacked while trying to board streetcars.[42] In one of the most serious of such incidents, a group of strikebreakers guarded by a small detachment of police was attacked by a crowd of five thousand. One streetcar after another passed the group without stopping. Teamsters backed their wagons onto the tracks to ensure that the cars could not move even if they did stop for the blacks, and the word was passed north along Halsted all the way to Twelfth Street (a distance of about four miles). Those blacks who made it that far were pursued by strike sympathizers as they disembarked and headed for the black neighborhood. In at least one other case an effigy was lynched, bearing the epithet "nigger scab."[43]

Yet these attacks on blacks blend in with a general pattern of intimidation of strikebreakers. Any person who decided to work during the strike did so in the face of overwhelming community hostility. Pressure was exerted in a number of ways. A scab was apt not only to be shunned, but also hooted at and physically abused in the street. Ritualized lynching was a common means of showing contempt for those who acted against the interests of the community. Bessie Undreshek claimed that she had been forced to remain at work when she returned to the canning room to get her personal belongings. She was greeted by neighborhood women with cries of "traitor," and an effigy bearing the caption, "Bessie, the traitor," was hung from a post before her home. Another ritualized lynching took place near the home of Michael Flynn at Thirty-seventh Street and Emerald Avenue, in the heart of the Irish neighborhood. This effigy bore the title "Flynn, the traitor sausage maker." The tactic was so common that Mary McDowell walked the streets asking that the effigies be taken down for the sake of the neighborhood's reputation.[44]

While many crowds were made up of men emerging from saloons along Ashland and Halsted, the community at large took a hand in the action. Photos of crowds show many women and children. In fact, one pattern in the crowd's behavior was the tendency for different segments of the community to take responsibility for punishing "their own." Joseph Patritza, for example, a Lithuanian sausagemaker who had quit the union and returned to work, was attacked by a group of fifteen men in the Lithuanian neighborhood at Forty-fifth and Paulina. But Josephine Romisky, aged sixteen, who had returned to work at Armour's, was chased by a crowd of one thousand girls and boys who threw mud and stones and shouted epithets. Four young women strikebreakers were set upon by a large group of their peers who pulled their hair and taunted them.[45] Apparently, each of the various groups involved focused its rage on its own peers.

But the vast majority of strikebreakers came from outside Packingtown, many having traveled from other cities. The few skilled men came from as far away as Cleveland, and even many of the common laborers were brought into the yards by train. In at least one case, a large group of immigrants was brought to the Union Stockyards directly from Ellis Island. The pay was $2.15 per day plus food and lodging, considerably more than the normal common labor rate.[46] Contemporary accounts tended to focus on the introduction of blacks, but as a group the scabs were quite mixed ethnically, the largest groups being Italian, Greek, and black.[47]

The labor movement promulgated an image of wild depravity within the strikebreakers' living quarters and suggested that their ranks were riddled with criminals and prostitutes.[48] But descriptions of the strikebreakers as an undifferentiated mass of criminals are probably misleading. While the union worked to retain the loyalty of the strikers, the packers were having their own dif-

ficulties with the new workers. One serious problem was turnover. On August 4 the packers managed to put another 432 scabs
to work, but this did not even replace a total of 545 who had recently left. A week earlier 100 blacks had marched in a body to an
employment agency and shipped out for railroad work in the
West. Two days later another group of 300 organized a meeting,
elected a committee to negotiate with the union for safe conduct,
and then marched out of Packingtown amid the cheers of the
strikers. A group of 70 Italian laborers at Armour refused to work
when they learned of the strike. In another incident, 250 recruits
climbed onto a train in Cleveland. When the cars were opened at
Chicago, only 75 were left. The others had taken the free ride
and dropped off along the way. Of the 75 who completed the
journey, 50 quit immediately. Perhaps the cruelest blow of all to
the packers was a strikebreakers' strike at Hammond, Indiana,
which resulted in a large raise.[49]

Resistance during the strike owed a great deal to the role
played by important community institutions. Among those with
influence, the churches were paramount, and they strongly supported the strike. Father Max Kotechi, pastor of Packingtown's
largest Polish parish, SS. Peter and Paul, with one thousand families, preached restraint but urged his flock to support the strike.
He took one man to the union office personally to ensure his enrollment. Another Polish pastor in the community was equally
supportive. Reverend Thomas Hayes of Saint Rose of Lima at
Forty-seventh Street and Ashland Avenue admired the degree of
perseverance and planning demonstrated by his people. "Personally, I do not believe in strikes," he said. "But I realize that the
men must keep together to maintain the principles of their
union." Father Hayes believed that much of the bitterness toward the packers was due to a widespread belief in their determination to destroy the union. Another Irish priest simply believed
in "lending the arm of the Church to what we believe is a righte-
ous cause. It is natural that our sympathy is with the men." Some
priests felt that it would be wrong for them to speak out publicly,
but they confided that their prayers were with the workers. Only
Father Thomas Bobal of SS. Cyril and Methodius, the Bohemian
church at Fiftieth and Paulina, spoke openly against the strike,
and there is no evidence that his efforts met with much success.[50]

Packingtown's skyline, circa 1910–15, viewed from Ashland Avenue, looking east across a vacant lot. Smoke belches from the stacks of a packing plant. (Courtesy of the Chicago Historical Society, ICHi-01869)

Children scavenging on one of the city dumps "back of the yards," circa 1910. (Courtesy of the Chicago Historical Society, ICHi-18555)

Old-country mothers in babushkas on the streets of Packingtown, 1904. (Courtesy of the Chicago Historical Society, DN-960)

Young American working women in Packingtown during the 1904 strike. (Courtesy of the Chicago Historical Society, DN-984)

Children of Packingtown, 1904. (Courtesy of the Chicago Historical Society, DN-967)

Michael Donnelly, president of the Amalgamated Meat Cutters and Butcher Workmen of North America, 1897–1907, organizer of the Chicago packinghouse workers, and leader of the 1904 strike. (Courtesy of the Chicago Historical Society, ICHi-15016)

A giant parade near the corner of Forty-seventh Street and Ashland Avenue, in the heart of Packingtown, during the 1904 strike. (Courtesy of the Chicago Historical Society, DN-883)

One of several union relief stations that distributed food to strikers' families during the 1904 conflict. (Courtesy of the Chicago Historical Society, DN-933)

Policemen escort a racially mixed group of strikebreakers into the stockyards during the 1904 strike. (Courtesy of the Chicago Historical Society, DN-884)

Black strikebreakers at work, Swift and Company, during the 1904 strike. (Courtesy of the Chicago Historical Society, DN-989)

A policeman holds back a crowd of children in the street near the stockyards during the 1904 strike. One of the boys in the front row is wearing a union button. (Courtesy of the Chicago Historical Society, DN-940)

John Fitzpatrick, president of the Chicago Federation of Labor (1901 and 1906–46), addresses a large crowd of packinghouse workers in Davis Park, across from the packing plants, during the World War I organizing drive. (Courtesy of the Chicago Historical Society, ICHi-10294)

Policemen drag a strike sympathizer down the steps of a wooden tenement "back of the yards" during the 1921–22 strike. (Courtesy of the Chicago Historical Society, DN-73, 753)

Mounted policemen patrol the streets of Packingtown during the 1921–22 strike. (Courtesy of the Chicago Historical Society, DN-73, 749)

The next generation: a young boy wearing a union button near the stockyards in Packingtown, 1904. (Courtesy of the Chicago Historical Society, DN-1019)

Packingtown's small businesspeople generally supported the strike. The Businessmen's Stock Yards Aid Society, formed to lend financial help, made an initial contribution of $1,250 and set a goal of $100,000. In order to increase support for its canvass of the neighborhood's businesses, the organization drafted a letter explaining the issues involved in the strike. The Association of Bohemian Businessmen similarly resolved "to appeal to everyone who can contribute, no matter how little, because in many families misery, a cruel guest, is beginning to appear." The association reminded its constituents that the ranks of the strikers included a large number of their countrypeople. Presumably, much of this small business support was based on a genuine identification with the workers' cause, but there were also practical considerations involved. A boycott awaited any business breaking the bond of solidarity. One saloonkeeper went so far as to appeal for a trial before an impartial third party (Mary McDowell) in order to clear his name of the crippling libel that he had served scabs. Strikebreakers often could not cash their checks because saloonkeepers, out of sympathy with the strikers or sheer self-interest, refused even to speak to them.[51]

The experience of workers accused of strike violence suggests community support of another kind. At this point in the city's history, prosecution for lesser offenses occurred at a local level, in the precinct police court. Here, Justice Fitzgerald of the Stock Yards Police Court strongly sympathized with the workers. Fitzgerald dismissed twenty of twenty-three complaints brought against strikers on one day, and twenty-one of twenty-four on another. In all, he dismissed from 80 to 85 percent of the strike-related cases brought him, while in most of the other cases he either granted continuances or remitted the fines of those who had been sentenced. His record brought bitter protests from police officials in charge of the strike detail at the yards, and eventually all cases involving strike action were transferred to the Hyde Park Police Court, where Justice Quinn tipped the scales of justice back in the packers' favor with vigorous prosecutions. Now the union protested, but with no results.[52]

The families of Packingtown took measures of their own to make it through the crisis. Some had seen it coming and were prepared for the worst. *Tribune* reporters found the cellars of some

Polish and Lithuanian families stocked with huge caches of food.[53] Some of those who were not so well prepared simply returned to the old country. The trek home was, of course, a well-established tradition in the community by this time, but the pace picked up considerably. During the first two weeks of the strike 150 people left. The steamship agent at the Stock Yards Bank did a brisk business.[54] For some, the struggle for life in "the Jungle" was over; others probably went home until the trouble ended, hoping to return to Chicago and its packinghouses. The cultural and social life of the community also adjusted itself to the exigencies of the strike. The "Bride's Dance" and other Polish wedding customs were transformed by some newlyweds into fund-raising affairs. The money pinned to the bride's dress by those wishing to dance was turned over to the union's strike fund. A similar Lithuanian custom served the same function.[55]

Packingtown's wives and mothers played an extremely important role in holding the strike together. When the packers launched their own propaganda drive to counter the union's, they aimed their leaflets at the community's women, asking wives to encourage their men to return to work for the sake of their families. Yet halfway through August a settlement house worker still saw no weakening among the women. "I have yet to find a woman who will admit that the strike is lost," she said. "They will be the last to give up." Many wives took jobs outside of the home for the first time, some going out into the country to work on farms.[56] Above all others in the community, these women realized what was at stake.

The Labor Movement

The packinghouse strike was part of a great wave of industrial unrest which hit Chicago in the summer of 1904. During the first nine months of the year, the city experienced ninety-two strikes, involving almost seventy-seven thousand workers. By the end of July, there were more than a thousand policemen on strike duty throughout the city. Among those employers affected were Link Belt Corporation, National Box, a bakery, three cigar factories, dozens of cloak and machine shops, and the Illinois Steel Works.[57] All of the striking unions, along with the Amalgamated, were members of the Chicago Federation of Labor and depended upon one another for support.

Of the support which the people of Packingtown derived from their relationship with the broader Chicago labor movement, the most direct came in the form of strikes. Sympathetic strikes were enjoying a resurgence throughout the nation during 1904, and Chicago was convulsed with such activity.[58] When the strike started up again on July 22, the beleaguered butchers were quickly joined by thousands of other working men and women. First, on July 24, ten thousand workers from the allied trades—carpenters, painters, carworkers, electricians, and others—walked out. Only the stationary firemen and engineers crossed the picket lines, refusing to abrogate their own recent contracts with the packers. This gap in the line of defense was crucial because it allowed the packers to operate and maintain their refrigeration equipment. It would have been practically impossible to run the industry in the middle of a Chicago summer without refrigeration. Yet the defection of the firemen and engineers should not obscure the solidarity demonstrated by most maintenance and auxiliary tradespeople.[59]

The teamsters were the linchpins of the sympathetic strike strategy in Chicago. They always seemed prepared to use their own very considerable bargaining power—the ability to tie up traffic along congested commercial streets—to help other groups of workers.[60] The packinghouse teamsters, drawn heavily from the Bridgeport neighborhood just east of the yards, had been waiting for an opportunity to walk out in sympathy with their butcher neighbors. G. F. Golden, head of the teamsters' packinghouse local, ignored his rank and file's call for a sympathetic walkout, fearing that such an action would complicate his own negotiations with the packers. But his membership called a meeting themselves and walked out in defiance of orders from the international union. The entrance of the teamsters distressed city authorities as well as the packers. The companies announced that they would not attempt to move meat with nonunion drivers, and Mayor Carter Harrison feared that the relatively peaceful strike would now become a "street strike." The term described labor conflicts characterized by widespread rioting and "slugging" of strikebreakers. Both the packinghouse teamsters' own 1902 strike and a recent walkout by streetcar men had been violent. The rising of the teamsters, well-known for their aggressive "picketing," introduced the prospect of strike violence spreading throughout the city as roving bands of teamsters stopped meat deliveries to retail depots in various neighborhoods.[61]

Dramatic strikes like those of the teamsters and allied trades were only part of a general pattern of solidarity displayed throughout the strike. Toward the end of July, Swift decided to serve strikebreakers in the firm's dining hall, which had never before served production workers. When waitresses saw to whom they were to serve food, however, they walked out. The company asked its stenographers to fill in, but fifty of them followed the waitresses.[62] The incident is suggestive of the widespread moral support given the butcher workmen and -women by other groups of workers in the city. Streetcar drivers often refused to stop for strikebreakers at all. Teamsters used their wagons to block the entrance of police vehicles into the neighborhood.[63] Support during this strike probably surpassed that in others precisely because it was against the "Meat Trust," which was hated nowhere more than in its hometown.

The leadership of the Chicago Federation of Labor feared that the entrance of the allied trades and teamsters would spread the strike to others in these occupations whose work was not in any way connected with the packinghouses. Then the struggle might escalate into a general strike. Many of the city's workers were, in fact, already engaged in their own disputes. In the end, however, most unions settled for contributing financial support, which was crucial to sustaining the strike. Two weeks before it started, the union had only $25,451.61 in its national treasury, about 50 cents per member.[64] The Chicago labor movement's response was impressive. The Federation pledged $4,700 per week, and many individual unions, including some with quite conservative reputations, subscribed amounts beyond this. The streetcar men, for example, who had just finished their own long and bitter strike, pledged a dollar per member, and the painters voted a day's wage for each member, a total of $12,000. The actors' union offered its members' services for fund-raisers hosted by other unions and announced its own plans for a "monster benefit."[65]

Socialist organizing also bolstered neighborhood resistance during the strike. The Party held an average of thirty to forty outside rallies each week at various points in the neighborhood and especially at the corner of Forty-seventh and Halsted. These meetings sometimes lasted for hours and drew crowds of several hundred. During the course of the strike activists distributed twenty thousand pieces of literature in various languages throughout Packingtown.[66] Noting the rise of socialist sentiment in the neighborhood, the *Chicago Socialist* concluded, "No place in the country offers greater promise for the future of Socialism than Packingtown. There capitalism is exhibiting its ripest fruit. The seeds of Socialism find its [*sic*] most congenial soil."[67]

In retrospect it is plain that the paper had certainly exaggerated the prospects for a mass socialist movement in Packingtown. Yet there *was* an increase in the party's strength in the neighborhood. That fall Packingtown sent Socialist James Ambrose to Springfield as its state senator, while the Twenty-ninth Ward recorded the city's second highest total for the Socialist presidential ticket. Ethnic-based radical groups like the Lithuanian Socialist Alliance grew in the community over the next decade and joined the Socialist Party as language federations, providing a link between Packingtown's newer ethnic communities and the city's long-standing tradition of labor radicalism.[68]

Yet time was on the packers' side. More scabs entered the city daily, and production climbed slowly toward normal output. Intent on total victory, the packers refused to negotiate, until the Packing Trades Council called a boycott of all meat and spread the strike to the smaller independent packers and the Union Stockyards and Transit Company. This made the movement of meat much more difficult and may have influenced the packers to approach the union. On September 5, they proposed that the union call off the strike. In return they would reemploy as many workers as possible immediately and thereafter give preference to strikers as more workers were needed. Skilled wage levels were to remain stable, but no mention was made of the common labor rate. In effect, this meant that the wages of unskilled laborers would once more be abandoned to market forces. When union officials submitted the agreement to a referendum, the rank and file, having been on strike for two months, rejected it overwhelmingly. The allied trades, who had jeopardized their own agree-

ments in order to support the butcher workmen, were particularly
anxious to see the strike through to a successful conclusion.[69] But
the position had become untenable. After securing from the packers a statement promising that strikers would be treated "fairly"
and that an attempt would be made to regularize employment,
Donnelly abruptly called off the strike. Workers drifted back to
the plants over the next couple of weeks.[70]

Predictably, the results of all this for the union were disastrous.
Despite the packers' promises, activists, including Donnelly,
were blacklisted and driven out of the industry. "A certain proportion who made trouble," a plant superintendent confided,
"will never get back." Factionalism, which had surfaced before
the strike, spread in its wake. Within one year the number of locals in the yards fell from twenty-one to six and then, during the
1908 recession, to only one. Amalgamated membership dropped
from 34,000 to 6,200. The few remaining packinghouse locals
around the country were small and concentrated among the
skilled butchers.[71]

The disruption and decline of the Amalgamated was person-
ified in the tragedy of President Michael Donnelly's subsequent
career. Some activists who had pressed for a continuation of the
strike accused him of a sellout. Whatever his other faults, however, Donnelly was scrupulously honest. In fact, he had been sav-
agely beaten by sluggers on two occasions for his leading role in
the Chicago Federation of Labor's reform caucus. It is unclear
whether Donnelly's later difficulties had more to do with the lasting effects of these beatings or with alcoholism, but his health
and emotional problems persisted. Passing through a succession
of demeaning jobs, Donnelly resurfaced briefly in Fort Worth,
Texas, in 1916. He was organizing packinghouse laborers once
again and asked for support. The AFL agreed to appoint him as
an organizer, but he dropped out of sight once again, this time for
good.[72]

As organization went into eclipse, shop-floor conditions reverted to the pre-union situation. Seniority in hiring and advancement was replaced by the old system based on kinship, favoritism, and bribery. Speeding was reinstituted, and the foreman's
control over production reasserted. As the "unnatural" pressure of
unionization was broken, the common labor rate was once again

left to the forces of supply and demand. Under recession conditions, it fell to sixteen cents per hour, with the inevitable effects on living standards. The people of Packingtown were caught up once again in a vicious cycle of irregular employment, low wages, and chronic poverty for more than a decade.[73]

Between 1900 and 1904, the packinghouse workers had built up a strong movement representing virtually all of the wage earners in the industry. Common work problems, a core of experienced trade unionists, and a particularly supportive metropolitan working-class community offered optimal conditions for organization. Newcomers in the labor force were acculturated and integrated into the movement. The departmental unions brought skilled and unskilled, new immigrant and old, together, while shop-floor organization provided a powerful weapon in the struggle to improve working conditions in the plants and the quality of life in the community.

Despite all these accomplishments, the workers' movement in the stockyards collapsed. Why? Concrete factors such as economic conditions and the union structure provide part of the answer. Union strength was greatest during the boom just after the turn of the century; it was weakest in the midst of high unemployment during the 1904 recession. Because of the large proportion of unskilled in packing, the Amalgamated was particularly vulnerable during such downturns. The packers had little difficulty in recruiting strikebreakers outside the immediate community. The division between production and maintenance workers also certainly weakened the effect of the strike. Both in terms of the strike's timing, then, and also in terms of its organization, the union's strategy and structure had as much to do with its demise as the packers' own clear determination to rid themselves of all union interference.

Less tangible perhaps but also important was the general atmosphere in which the strike took place. The fragmentation of the movement in the stockyards was only one part of a general decline of the labor movement in Chicago and throughout the country. Most strikes which engulfed the nation during 1904, like the butchers' own, were defensive actions in which workers fought to save their unions. In Chicago the labor ethos which had nurtured the movement in the yards was under siege.[74] In packing, the disastrous defeat of the strike and the introduction of the blacklist crushed any immediate prospects for union activity.

Yet some people in Packingtown seem never to have accepted the 1904 defeat as a final verdict. A meeting of fifty Polish and Lithuanian laborers in the midst of the 1908 recession seems only a pathetic remnant of the union spirit, but it is significant that the lessons of those years persisted among the new immigrants. (The packers recognized the importance of the little meeting; they sent a spy.)[75] The strength of the union, and the changes it had wrought in Packingtown's standard of living and in the self-image of its people, were not quickly forgotten. When economic conditions allowed for it during World War I, packinghouse workers once again streamed into the union, organized on the shop floor, and fought to improve the quality of life in their community. It was upon the dreams and dedication of Slavic laborers like those who attended the pathetic little meeting in 1908 that these and later struggles were built.

NOTES

1. For discussions of early mass-production work which emphasize new technology and management ideas, see David Landes, *The Unbound Prometheus: Technological Change and Industrial Revolution in Western Europe* (New York and London, 1969), 290–326; and Daniel Nelson, *Managers and Workers: Origins of the New Factory System in the United States, 1880–1920* (Madison, Wis., 1975), 3–23. For an alternative view, see David Noble, *America by Design: Science, Technology, and the Rise of Corporate Capitalism* (New York, 1977).

2. Among the scholars of job control are Harry Braverman, *Labor and Monopoly Capital: The Degradation of Work in the Twentieth Century* (New York, 1974); Richard Edwards, *Contested Terrain: The Transformation of the Workplace in the Twentieth Century* (New York, 1977); David Montgomery, *Workers' Control in America: Studies in the History of Work, Technology, and Labor Struggles* (New York and London, 1979). Montgomery, Carter Goodrich, and James Hinton have studied skilled workers' self-defense, in particular. See Montgomery, *Workers' Control in America;* Carter Goodrich, *The Frontier of Control* (London, 1975); and James Hinton, *The First Shop Stewards' Movement* (London, 1973).

3. This analysis is based in part on James R. Barrett, "Immigrant

Workers in Early Mass Production Industry: Work Rationalization and Job Control Conflicts in Chicago's Packing Houses, 1900–1904," in *German Workers in Industrial Chicago, 1850–1910: A Comparative Perspective,* ed. Hartmut Keil and John Jentz (De Kalb, Ill., 1983).

4. On the structure and function of the house committees, see Carl Thompson, "Labor in the Packing Industry," *Journal of Political Economy* 15 (Feb. 1906): 100. See also John R. Commons, "Labor Conditions in Slaughtering and Meat Packing," in *Trade Unionism and Labor Problems,* ed. John R. Commons (Boston, 1905), 249.

5. For a cattle butcher's description of these changes, see George Schick's letter in the Amalgamated Meat Cutters and Butcher Workmen of North America's *Official Journal* 3 (Aug. 1902): 71.

6. *Official Journal* 4 (Dec. 1902): 7.

7. Commons, "Labor Conditions," 231–32.

8. Ibid., 230; *Official Journal* 5 (May 1904); Thompson, 103–4.

9. Commons, "Labor Conditions," 233–35. See also Rudolf Clemen, *The American Livestock and Meat Industry* (New York, 1923), 689; and Thompson, 103.

10. U.S. Commissioner of Labor, *Eleventh Special Report, Regulation and Restriction of Output* (Washington, D.C., 1904), 711; Commons, "Labor Conditions," 228; *Chicago Inter Ocean,* Sept. 28, 1904.

11. U.S. Commissioner of Labor, *Regulation and Restriction,* 711–16; Commons, "Labor Conditions," 228.

12. *Official Journal* 4 (Mar. 1903); 4 (Nov. 1902): 30, 32.

13. Commons, "Labor Conditions," 227–29.

14. *Official Journal* 4 (Mar. 1903).

15. Ibid.

16. Commons, "Labor Conditions," 228, 230, 233.

17. *National Provisioner,* Nov. 28, 1903, 14; Amalgamated Meat Cutters and Butcher Workmen of North America, *Proceedings of the Fifth General Convention, 1904* (Syracuse, N.Y., 1904), 36–37.

18. Ibid., 16, 75; Amalgamated Meat Cutters and Butcher Workmen of North America, *Proceedings of the Fourth General Convention, 1902* (Syracuse, N.Y., 1902), 17.

19. Commons, "Labor Conditions," 249. See also Harry Rosenberg, "The Great Strike," in the Mary McDowell Papers, Folder 15, Chicago Historical Society.

20. For relevant analyses of corporate liberalism and its influence on labor relations in this era, see James Weinstein, *The Corporate Ideal in the Liberal State* (Boston, 1968); "The IWW and American Socialism," *Socialist Revolution* 1 (1970): 3–24; Ronald Radosh, "The Corporate Ideology of American Labor Leaders from Gompers to Hillman," *Studies on*

the Left 6 (Nov.—Dec. 1966): 66–67, and "Labor in the American Economy: The 1922 Railroad Shop Crafts Strike and the 'B & O Plan,' " in *Building the Organizational Society: Essays in Associational Activities,* ed. Jerry Israel (New York, 1972); Gabriel Kolko, *Main Currents in Modern American History* (New York, 1976), 177. For an alternative analysis which has influenced my own, see Montgomery, 48–90.

21. Philip Foner, *History of the Labor Movement in the United States,* vol. 3 (New York, 1964), 64, and "Comment," *Studies on the Left* 6 (Nov.–Dec. 1966): 91.

22. *Official Journal* 4 (Oct. 1902): 14–16. See also *Official Journal* 3 (Sept. 1902): 14, 16.

23. *Official Journal* 5 (Feb. 1904): 14–16. For Call's contrast between the NCF's "calm, cool-headed businesslike" approach to industrial relations and the National Association of Manufacturers' open-shop mentality, see *Official Journal* 3 (Sept. 1903): 10–11.

24. *Official Journal* 2 (Jan. 1902): 30–31. On unofficial strikes as an organizational problem, see also Amalgamated, *Proceedings of the Fifth General Convention; Official Journal* 5 (Oct. 1903): 23–24; David Brody, *The Butcher Workmen: A Study of Unionization* (Cambridge, Mass., 1964), 37, 47–49.

25. Commons, "Labor Conditions," 235, 243–45. See also U.S. Commissioner of Labor, *Regulation and Restriction,* 716; Brody, 46–47, 50.

26. Carleton Parker, "The Labor Policy of the American Trusts," *Atlantic Monthly,* Feb. 1920, 229; *National Provisioner,* Aug. 6, 1904, 14, quoted in Brody, 51.

27. Commons, "Labor Conditions," 243–45; Brody, 51–52.

28. *Chicago Tribune,* Aug. 2, 1904.

29. Caroline Hill, ed., *Mary McDowell and Municipal Housekeeping* (Chicago, 1938), 25.

30. *Chicago Tribune,* July 13, 1904; *Chicago Daily News,* July 13, 1904. On the relatively peaceful character of the strike in contrast with others during this era, see Sidney L. Harring, *Policing a Class Society: the Experience of American Cities, 1865–1915* (New Brunswick, N. J., 1983), 121–27.

31. Charles Tilly, "The Changing Place of Collective Violence," in *Social Theory and Social History,* ed. M. Richter (Cambridge, Mass., 1975); Herbert Gutman, *Work, Culture and Society in Industrializing America: Essays in Working Class and Social History* (New York, 1976), chap. 1.

32. David Montgomery, "Strikes in Nineteenth-Century America," *Social Science History* 4 (1980): 81–102; J. Amsden and S. Brier, "Coal Miners on Strike: The Transformation of Strike Demands and the For-

mation of a National Union," *Journal of Interdisciplinary History* 7 (1977): 583–616.

33. John R. Commons et al., *History of Labor in the United States* (1918; reprint, New York, 1935), 4:118; Brody, 53–54.

34. Brody, 52–53; Commons, "Labor Conditions," 245.

35. Ernest Poole, "The Great Meat Strike," *The Independent* 57 (July 28, 1904), quoted in Howard Wilson, *Mary McDowell, Neighbor* (Chicago, 1928), 107. See also Howard B. Meyer, "The Policing of Labor Disputes in Chicago: A Study" (Ph.D. diss., University of Chicago, 1929), chap. 9.

36. Quoted in Wilson, 105.

37. *Chicago Tribune*, July 31, 1904.

38. *Chicago Tribune*, Aug. 7, 1904. This issue of the *Tribune* and the *Daily News* for the same date contain good photographs of the parade.

39. *Official Journal* 5 (Aug. 1904): 24.

40. Bridgeport had erupted once again in 1902 during a strike of packinghouse teamsters, many of whom lived in the neighborhood. During a citywide teamsters' strike in 1905, much of the violence was concentrated in or around Bridgeport. See Steve Sapolsky, "Between Class-Conscious Belligerents: The Teamsters and the Class Struggle in Chicago, 1901–1905" (University of Pittsburgh, typescript, 1974); William J. Tuttle, *Race Riot: Chicago in the Red Summer of 1919* (New York, 1970), 121–22; Graham Taylor, *Chicago Commons through Forty Years* (Chicago, 1936), 118. For a teamster's own account of the strike, see "The Chicago Strike: A Teamster" in *Plain Folk: The Life Stories of Undistinguished Americans,* ed. David M. Katzman and William M. Tuttle, Jr. (Urbana, Ill., 1982), 119–23.

41. Tuttle, 117–20.

42. *Chicago Tribune*, July 20, 1904; Tuttle, 119; Alma Herbst, *The Negro in the Slaughtering and Meat Packing Industry in Chicago* (Boston, 1932), 24–25.

43. *Chicago Tribune*, July 17, 1904.

44. *Chicago Tribune*, July 29, 31, and Aug. 8, 1904; Wilson, 111; Harry Rosenberg, "The Great Strike," McDowell Papers.

45. *Chicago Tribune*, July 23, 26, 1904.

46. *Chicago Tribune*, July 26, 1904; *Chicago Daily News*, Aug. 4, 9, 16, 1904.

47. Commons, "Labor Conditions," 247; Herbst, 23–25; cf. Tuttle, 117–20; *Chicago Daily News*, Aug. 2, 1904.

48. *Chicago Socialist*, Aug. 20, 27, 1904; *American Federationist* 13 (Aug. 1906): 354.

49. *Chicago Tribune*, July 20, 29, 30, and Aug. 5, 1904; *Chicago Daily*

News, Aug. 13, 1904.

50. *Chicago Tribune*, July 24, Aug. 8, 1904. See also Dominic Pacyga, "Villages of Packinghouses and Steel Mills: The Polish Worker on Chicago's South Side, 1880–1921" (Ph.D. diss., University of Illinois, Chicago, 1981), chap. 4.

51. *Chicago Tribune*, Aug. 5, 1904; *Denni Hlasatel*, Sept. 4, 1904, Chicago Foreign Language Press Survey, microfilm copy, Chicago Historical Society (hereafter CFLPS); Wilson, 110–11.

52. Meyer, chap. 9; *Chicago Tribune*, Aug. 14, 1904.

53. *Chicago Tribune*, July 24, 1904.

54. Ibid., July 31, 1904; July 20, 24, 1904.

55. Ibid., Aug. 14, 1904.

56. Ibid., July 24, Aug. 11, 14, 1904.

57. Ibid., July 31, 1904; Bessie Louise Pierce Papers, Chicago Historical Society, Box 86A.

58. Montgomery, "Strikes in Nineteenth Century America," and *Workers' Control in America*, table 2, p. 92.

59. Foner, *History of the Labor Movement*, 3: 193; Brody, 55–56.

60. Commons, "The Teamsters of Chicago," in *Trade Unionism and Labor Problems*, 36–64; Sapolsky.

61. *Chicago Tribune*, July 28, 29, 30, 1904. On the 1902 strike, see Steven L. Piott, "The Chicago Teamsters' Strike of 1902: A Community Confronts the Beef Trust," *Labor History* 26 (1985): 250–67.

62. *Chicago Tribune*, July 27, 1904.

63. Ibid., Aug. 4, 1904.

64. Amalgamated Meat Cutters and Butcher Workmen of North America, *Proceedings of the Seventh General Convention, 1906* (Syracuse, N.Y., 1906), 12.

65. Chicago Federation of Labor minutes, Aug. 21, 1904, microfilm copy, Chicago Historical Society; *Chicago Tribune*, Aug. 8, 1904. See also *Denni Hlasatel*, Sept. 9, 1904, CFLPS, for information on contributions from Bohemian unions.

66. *Chicago Socialist*, July 16, 23, Sept. 3, 10, 1904.

67. *Chicago Socialist*, Sept. 10, 1904.

68. Rosenberg; *Chicago Daily News Almanac, 1905* (Chicago, 1906), 345–53.

69. Meyer, chap. 4.

70. Brody, 57–58; *Chicago Record Herald*, Sept. 7, 1904; *Chicago Tribune*, Sept. 9, 1904; Commons et al., *History of Labor in the United States*, 4:122–23.

71. On factionalism, see Homer D. Call to Frank Morrison, Apr. 21 and 30, 1908, *American Federation of Labor Records: The Samuel Gompers*

Era (Sanford, N.C., 1979, microfilm), National and International Union File, Reel 39. On blacklisting, see Edna Clark, "A History of the Labor Controversies in the Slaughtering and Meat Packing Industry in Chicago" (M.A. thesis, University of Chicago, 1922), 139–40; U.S. Commission on Industrial Relations, *Final Report and Testimony*, vol. 4 (Washington, D.C., 1916) 17–18. For a full discussion of the Amalgamated's decline in the wake of the strike, see Brody, 59–69. See also *American Federationist* 12 (May 1905): 300, and 12 (Aug. 1905): 530.

72. Gary M. Fink, ed., *Biographical Dictionary of American Labor* (Westport, Conn., 1974), 190–91; and E. N. Nockels to Samuel Gompers, Feb. 18, 1906, H. D. Call to Frank Morrison, Feb. 15, 1906, H. D. Call to Gompers, Feb. 20, 1906, Michael Donnelly to John P. Hart, Apr. 3, 1916, Hart to Gompers, Apr. 7, 1916, and Gompers to Hart, Apr. 14, 1916, all in *American Federation of Labor Records: The Samuel Gompers Era*, Reel 39; H. D. Call to Mary McDowell, Feb. 5, 1908, McDowell Papers, Folder 15. See also *Chicago Record Herald*, Jan. 30, 1905.

73. Thompson, 89–90; Commons, "Labor Conditions," 149; Parker, 230.

74. On the national strike trend and the employers' offensive, see Commons et al., *History of Labor in the United States*, 4:129–37; Montgomery, *Workers' Control in America*, 57–63, 92. On the decline of the movement in Chicago, see *Chicago Socialist*, May 1, 1904; *Chicago Record Herald*, Sept. 3, 1905, from notes in the Pierce Papers, Box 4, Folder 86A.

75. Mary McDowell to Homer Call, Feb. 21, 1908, McDowell Papers, Folder 15A.

6

Class, Race, and Ethnicity, 1917–21

I am going to help out unionism. I have been in a union since I was fourteen years old. . . . I stay with my fellow workmen.
> Frank Guzior, Polish-American unionist, June 1919[1]

You are nothin' but a lot of white folks' niggers or you wouldn't be wearing that button.
> Nonunion Black worker, June 1919[2]

Some of the most dramatic struggles of the First World War era were waged not in the trenches of France but in the factories and neighborhoods of American cities. In meat packing the war brought changes in all those factors most directly affecting the prospects for organization—the social composition of the work force, the strategy and structure of the unions involved, and the broader social, economic, and political context. The severe wartime labor shortage and the need for war supplies brought highly favorable organizing conditions and government arbitration, but they also posed the danger that the workers' movement would fragment along racial, ethnic, and skill lines. While organizers and many rank-and-file workers tried to overcome these barriers, the packers developed personnel policies designed to accentuate them.

As the economy declined and political reaction set in during 1919–21, the danger of fragmentation was heightened.

Again Chicago's South Side became a focal point for the most vital questions facing the labor movement in this era: What form of labor organization might successfully challenge the open shop in basic industry? Was it possible to create mass interracial unions? What role would the state play in this confrontation between labor and capital?

THE WARTIME CONTEXT

The Allies' World War I campaign depended directly on workers in the munitions plants of Bridgeport, the steel mills of Pittsburgh, and the packinghouses of Kansas City and Chicago. Production levels in packing and other industries shot up dramatically. Average monthly beef exports, which ran just over one million pounds during the three years before the war, exceeded ninety-two million pounds in June 1918. Struggling to keep up with the demand for meat, especially after American entry into the war, the packers aimed to slaughter 100,000 head of cattle per week. A new record was set in October 1917, when 415,456 head entered the yards. The increase in profits was equally steep. The four largest firms, which had shown an aggregate profit of nineteen million dollars for 1912–14, registered forty-six million dollars for 1916 and sixty-eight million dollars for the following year. This upsurge of war production had a striking effect on the size of the labor force. The number of workers in one of Chicago's largest houses rose from eight thousand to seventeen thousand in the course of the conflict, and such growth was typical of the industry. By 1919 there were forty-five thousand people working in the Chicago plants.[3]

The kind of labor recruitment demanded by this growth would have been a difficult problem in the best of times, but the war aggravated the situation. The draft and enlistment took over four million young men off the nation's farms and out of its industrial cities, depositing many of them on the battlefields of Europe. At the same time, hostilities on land and sea cut the packers off from their traditional source of common labor. Between 1914 and 1918 immigration dropped by 80 percent, falling in the latter year to less than 113,000.[4] Caught between a dramatic rise in demand and a severe constriction of the labor supply, the packers turned to new sources for their workers.

Married immigrant women, for example, entered the packinghouses in large numbers for the first time during World War I. Packingtown's families were struggling to keep up with inflation. At the same time that rapidly rising consumer prices and the decline of the boarding system created a need for more income, increases in unskilled wage levels made meat-packing work more attractive. A more important labor source was found on the farms and in the small towns of the Deep South. Thousands of black migrants streamed into the Union Stockyards to take up unskilled positions on the killing floors and in other departments throughout the plants. By 1917 about ten to twelve thousand blacks had entered the yards in Chicago, representing a fourth of the industry's labor force.[5]

The increases in production generated by war orders, the accompanying profits, and the serious labor shortage facing the packers offered an excellent situation for workers' organization. But if the war brought the opportunity for labor action, it also forcefully introduced the issue of race. In the early twentieth century, organizers had successfully confronted the problem of ethnic fragmentation through a careful process of socialization and integration of new immigrants into the union. The World War I organizational campaign faced the danger of division and hostility between white immigrants and black migrants.[6]

The packinghouse workers' movement that emerged in the course of the First World War contrasted sharply with that of the early twentieth century in terms of organization and strategy. The shift toward an industrial form of organization advanced with the development of the Stockyards Labor Council, which not only coordinated the activities of the various international unions in the yards but also financed and directed organizing and represented the workers in negotiations.

Strategically, the leaders of the movement were faced with the options of building up their strength on the shop floor through the kind of organization which had characterized the earlier period, or relying heavily on a system of arbitration introduced during the

war by the federal government. The labor leaders threw themselves into arbitration with an enthusiasm which in the long run
proved misplaced. The federal government retreated from the
arena of labor relations precisely at the moment when workers' organization reached a low point, and the movement proved fatally
vulnerable.

The disintegration of the stockyards labor movement in the
postwar period was not the inevitable consequence of divisions
among the workers themselves but rather the product of a
number of factors, including the structure and strategy of the
unions, violence between white street gangs and Black Belt
residents, factional conflicts among labor leaders, and the packers'
efforts to break down organization by exploiting the racially tense
atmosphere of Chicago in the tragic summer of 1919.

THE STOCKYARDS LABOR COUNCIL

The Chicago labor movement of the World War I years was, according to journalist Ray Stannard Baker, "more closely organized, more self-conscious, more advanced in its views" than any
other in the United States.[7] Chicago workers stood out in part because of the sheer size of their movement, but also for two other
related reasons. The Chicago movement was the heart and brain
of the two great World War I drives to organize mass-production
workers in the steel and meat-packing industries. In the process,
Chicago labor activists confronted the problem of building mass
interracial unions. William Z. Foster, who played an important
role in both organizing campaigns, noted that the whole labor
movement was "looking to us in Chicago to take the lead."[8] As in
the early twentieth century, packinghouse workers received crucial support from the broader labor movement. During the wartime agitation the city's labor federation was even more directly
involved in financing and directing the campaign than it had been
in the 1900–1904 period.

The Stockyards Labor Council (SLC), which led the drive to
organize the packinghouses, was the creation of the Chicago
Federation of Labor (CFL), which Foster called "the most progressive labor council in the United States at that time." John
Fitzpatrick was the spirit behind the federation. Born in Athlone,

Ireland, in 1871, Fitzpatrick came to Chicago's South Side at the age of eleven. He worked briefly on a killing floor in the stockyards before taking up the horseshoer's trade. Fitzpatrick was active in the labor movement from his earliest days in the city and lived in the same Irish neighborhood near the stockyards throughout his tenure as president of the CFL (1899–1901; 1906–46). An ardent Irish nationalist and teetotaler, he refused to attend any union meeting held in a saloon. Fitzpatrick's scrupulous honesty and total dedication to labor's cause infused the movement with a strong sense of purpose. He was the embodiment of the city's militant labor traditions.[9]

Fitzpatrick gathered around him a group of mainstream activists and radicals who shared his dedication to strengthening the city's labor movement. The progressives included Edward Nockels, a steamfitter and the CFL's secretary; Margaret Haley and Lillian Herstein of the Chicago Teachers' Federation; the socialist carpenters Tom Slater and Anton Johannsen; and Robert M. Buck, editor of the CFL's brilliant newspaper, the *New Majority*. The most cohesive group of radicals was composed of syndicalists, including William Z. Foster and Jack Johnstone, both of whom became SLC leaders. Many of these radicals from various unions had founded the International Trade Union Education League (ITUEL). Although the ITUEL had disintegrated by 1917, many of its members remained delegates to the CFL. This progressive alliance fought another faction composed of grafting business agents, "sluggers," and labor bosses. The campaign to organize the packinghouses was one part of a broad CFL program in the 1917-19 period that also included national leadership of the movement to free Tom Mooney, a Chicago Railway Council to link all locals of railroad workers, an independent labor party, and the great steel campaign and strike of 1919.[10]

The Amalgamated Meat Cutters and Butcher Workmen's strength in the packinghouses had not disintegrated entirely during the decade before 1917. In addition to numerous meat cutters' locals in towns throughout the country, the union also retained a few small butcher workmen's locals. With the onset of war, the Amalgamated once again moved to build a base in the large packing centers. By early 1917 four organizers were working in the field, joining five others who had been commissioned by the AFL. Yet little lasting organization had been achieved as late as the summer of 1917, and the movement in Chicago was still quite weak.[11]

The earliest signs of movement among Chicago's packinghouse workers came long before any major organizing drive. As unemployment fell and the labor shortage became severe, many workers took advantage of the situation by simply moving from one job to another. When the Department of Labor investigated turnover in ten Chicago industries between June 1, 1917, and June 1, 1918, meat packing topped the list with an annual turnover rate of 334 percent. In order to maintain a combined average labor force of 5,219, the three plants studied hired a total of 17,418 workers in the course of the year.[12] There were also strikes. During 1916 and 1917 a series of unorganized strikes by unskilled workers forced the common labor rate up several times. Mary McDowell observed that "when the workers, mostly Poles, Slovaks and Lithuanians, became conscious of the undersupply of labor they grew restless. In separate departments there were constantly sporadic, unorganized strikes. This general unrest was somewhat allayed by a universal raise of wages throughout the various plants." At the same time, the skilled men began returning in small numbers to the few remaining Amalgamated locals in the yards. Chicago, it seemed, was ripe for organization. By the time the SLC came into being, the unionization process had already begun informally on the shop floor.[13]

At the July 15, 1917, Chicago Federation of Labor meeting, William Z. Foster and Robert McQueen of the Railway Carmen and Dennis Lane and Joe O'Kane of Cattle Butchers' Local 87 presented a motion that interested unions should meet to plan an all-out organizing campaign in Chicago's stockyards. The federation's delegates adopted the resolution unanimously, and the Stockyards Labor Council was established on July 23 with Martin Murphy, a hog butcher, as president and Foster as secretary.[14]

The new body was composed of representatives from twelve international unions but represented another halting move in the direction of industrial unionism. It was modeled on the systems federation movement among railroad workers which Foster had helped to create. He explained the concept in his autobiography. "We decided to move towards industrial unionism by setting up

Blacks' segregated or excluded

an industrial federation and by locking the various component craft unions so firmly together under one Council, one Executive Board, one set of Business Agents, etc. as to create a firm front in the whole of the industry."[15]

Still, the new structure failed to unify the labor force. Many of the problems which led to the eventual destruction of the council were related to a complicated organizational form that actually reinforced divisions among the workers. Skilled auxiliary workers, like machinists, stationary firemen, and structural ironworkers, had their own locals affiliated with both the international craft unions and the SLC. Most skilled packinghouse workers, regardless of ethnicity, joined the various departmental locals of the Amalgamated. But the great mass of common laborers in the industry entered the Amalgamated's community-based locals. In effect, this structure not only divided skilled from unskilled; it also created organizations based as much on ethnic as on occupational identification. Separate ethnic locals also were established for women. In the case of both men and women, the largest of these by far were those composed of Polish and Lithuanian laborers.[16]

This question of organizational structure was especially complicated in the case of black workers. Many of the craft unions drew the color line quite rigidly, excluding blacks through clauses in their constitutions. Others were more subtle in their racism, but the effect was the same. William Tuttle estimates that at least thirty-seven of one hundred Chicago AFL affiliates either excluded black workers entirely or segregated them into separate locals. The SLC's solution was a weak compromise. The Labor Council persuaded the AFL to charter special federal labor unions for groups of black tradesmen excluded from their respective craft unions. Because of the numbers involved, the question of where to put black butcher workmen was even more serious. At the start of the campaign, black workers joined mass laborers' locals along with whites from various ethnic groups, but there was concern in the black community that this would leave the black workers a small minority without adequate representation. Then a separate all-black local was set up, but this exposed the SLC to charges of Jim Crowism. The idea of neighborhood-based locals, theoretically open to any worker, developed as a solution. Organizers set up union headquarters in the various neighborhoods where packinghouse workers lived. In effect, Local 651, with its headquarters in the heart of the Black Belt, became a primarily black local just as other unions became primarily Polish and Lithuanian. Black women joined local 213, while two other locals organized Polish and Lithuanian and English-speaking women. [17]

Since crushing the union in 1904, the packers had ruled with an iron hand, and organization was slow at first. The CFL financed the Labor Council's first mass meeting and also helped to line up early organizers. From that point on, the SLC was on its own. The first street meeting attracted a large crowd of about ten thousand workers, but an appeal for the audience to sign union cards brought only a "dull silence for a moment—then many of those in attendance began to slip away." The disappointing response probably was due more to a healthy fear of the packers' intelligence network than to lack of conviction. Two of three Polish and Lithuanian organizers, for example, were dismissed by the SLC after admitting that they had been planted by the packers. Mid-November, however, brought a mass influx sparked by submission of a list of demands, including substantial wage increases, equal pay for women doing the same work as men, and the eight-hour day. [18]

The response foreshadowed what would become the movement's sources of strength and weakness. Unskilled workers came in more quickly at first than the skilled, though most of the skilled workers had joined by the end of 1917. Amalgamated organizers found the foreign-born much easier to organize than the native-born, and Slavic workers more enthusiastic than the older immigrant groups. Most responsive were those Slavic immigrants who had been in the industry several years, presumably those who had experienced the last period of union strength. By far the best union men and women were the Poles, the largest foreign-born group in the labor force. Union organizers were struck by the loyalty of the Polish workers. One noted that "the union became a household word among these workers." The largest Chicago laborers' local recruited ten thousand Polish and Lithuanian workers within a month. The recent immigrants not only joined but also participated enthusiastically. In January 1918 the same local held a membership meeting attended by twelve thousand workers, an attendance rate of about 75 percent. While enthusiasm was probably at its height in these months and in the spring of 1918, Polish workers remained union stalwarts to the bitter end. By the end of World War I more than twenty thousand Slavic workers, including four thousand women, had poured into the unions.[19]

This pattern of organization held true for women as well as men. The foreign-born and particularly the Polish women joined in large numbers, while many of the English-speaking women held back. Ominously, progress was slowest among black workers. While the organizing campaign progressed, the number of black workers continued to rise; nevertheless, although by the end of the year the total proportion of the labor force in unions was estimated by the President's Mediation Commission to be between 25 and 50 percent and growing,[20] the number of black unionists remained small.

Much of the Council's success in the Polish community may be explained by the fact that it fastened itself to deep roots there. To direct the work among Poles and Lithuanians, the AFL chose John Kikulski, an indigenous ethnic leader who had been active in both fraternal and labor organizations since at least 1904. An activist in the Polish National Alliance and a former president of the Polish Falcons, Kikulski was a charismatic figure in Chicago *Polonia* and a brilliant orator in Polish and Lithuanian as well as in English. During the organizing drive Kikulski started publishing his own paper, *Glose Rabotnica*, or *Labor's Voice*. He established five immigrant laborers' locals, which provided the bulk of the Amalgamated's membership in the Chicago plants. Kikulski was elected president of Local 554, the largest in the union, which by January 1918 had a membership of almost sixteen thousand. Large crowds gathered at regular mass meetings to hear Kikulski berate the packers, and he became a symbol of the tremendous pride which the Polish community felt for the immigrant locals. The packinghouse workers were rising and with them Polonia.[21]

The packers responded to the severe labor shortage and the success of the council's organizing drive by repeatedly raising the common labor rate and expanding their welfare activities. Each time management sensed a restiveness among the workers, they hiked the rate another two and a half cents. In March 1916, wages for all common labor except women reached a uniform twenty cents per hour. By September 1917 three more increases had raised the rate to twenty-seven and a half cents, while piece rates and women's hourly wages were raised proportionally. In one last-ditch effort the packers offered a 5 percent increase in September 1917, just as the SLC's drive was getting off the ground. They withdrew the offer when they recognized that it would not stop the campaign.[22]

The other half of the packers' strategy was embodied in the welfare plans of the various firms and a more comprehensive personnel policy for the industry as a whole. Several of the larger corporations, like Armour and Swift, which had established welfare programs after the last round of organization, expanded them considerably as a result of wartime labor problems. Other firms, like Wilson, established programs for the first time in the fall of 1917 to undercut the union drive. Another product of unionization was the Stockyards Community Clearing House, set up in October 1917 to coordinate welfare activities and provide a greater presence for the packers in the community. Each corporation contributed to the organization in proportion to its share of the market. The clearinghouse was intended to "foster communication between industrial, civic, social and religious organizations" and help to meet the welfare needs of Packingtown. Following the conventional wisdom of "scientific charity," the clearinghouse staff undertook a careful survey of the community and sponsored a variety of activities—including athletic and social events for the community's children and a small nursery for working mothers—designed to meet the community's needs and those of the industry. To the extent that it was specifically planned to undercut the union campaign, however, the welfare strategy failed—at least in the short term.[23]

Where private capital proved unable to maintain stability in the labor relations of the industry, state intervention, in the form of the President's Mediation Commission, succeeded. As workers poured into the unions, pressure mounted for a strike, and the packers forced the issue at the end of November 1917. In the middle of the month a committee representing the various unions was politely dismissed when it met with the packers to submit the workers' list of demands. Within a few days union activists were fired at Libby, McNeill and Libby, a Swift subsidiary, and the day before Thanksgiving mass meetings of butcher workmen in all the major packing centers voted overwhelmingly to sanction a strike. A federal conciliator succeeded in getting the unionists reinstated, but the packers refused to meet with union representatives or to consider their demands. [24]

As more accusations of discrimination against union members rolled in, Foster and other SLC leaders pressed for strike action, but most of the local AFL leaders with interests in the organizing pinned their hopes on the federal government. A committee representing the CFL, the SLC, and various international unions got the President's Mediation Commission to set up a system of binding arbitration in exchange for a no-strike pledge. When the packers balked, the unions argued for government seizure of the plants. Already under pressure from the wartime Federal Trade Commission investigation and public hostility over charges of profiteering, the packers gave in. Many of the unions' demands were settled in direct, government-sponsored negotiations. Others, largely involving matters of wages and hours, were submitted to Judge Samuel B. Alschuler of Illinois, the federal administrator appointed to oversee disputes in the industry. [25]

Wartime arbitration in packing was a trade-off for all concerned. Workers won important improvements in conditions and made limited progress in terms of their living standards; while the national increase in hourly wages for the year following December 1917 ranged between 20 percent and 27 percent and the cost of living rose 31 percent, packinghouse wages jumped by 42.5 percent. [26] For their part, union leaders gained a vital measure of acceptance as workers' representatives and occupied a central position in the system. Protected against the threat of major strikes, employers maximized production, then passed on increased labor costs to the government and consumers, realizing huge profits. The government was able to supply its own troops and those of its allies without having to contend with disruptive strikes. Yet government arbitration was only a temporary solution. Sooner or later there would be a confrontation over union recognition.

Focusing a spotlight on the depths of poverty in Packingtown, the mediation sessions held in February 1918 amounted to something like a public trial of the packers' labor policies. Large crowds of packinghouse laborers, social workers, and other interested observers thronged to the Federal Building each day. Consumptive Polish housewives, normally isolated from the more "respectable" elements of the city's population by the anonymity of the slum, were suddenly thrust into the public limelight and encouraged to testify about the misery and insecurity of their lives. Management lawyers and witnesses argued that living standards were relatively high by introducing evidence on the increase in savings deposits in neighborhood banks. The large number of saloons in Packingtown suggested to them that much of the squalor was due to mismanagement of family budgets and dissipation, not low wages. In response, the people of Packingtown spoke of decaying houses, disease, and dying children.[27]

"It was," wrote William Z. Foster, "as if the characters in *The Jungle*, quickened to life, had come to tell their story from the witness chair." Union lawyers put the packers themselves on the stand to testify about exactly what they meant by a "decent standard of living." They quizzed Armour and Morris about their food, shoes, socks and underwear, and recreational habits, and then contrasted this standard of luxury with the stark privation which faced the butcher workmen and -women and their families. Perhaps most damaging to the packers' case were the union's statistics on the question of family budgets. W. Jett Lauck of the Bureau of Applied Economics provided a detailed annual budget of $1,434.64 required for a family of five to live in minimum health. Florence Nesbitt of the United Charities introduced her agency's minimum budget for a pauper family of five—$1,106.82. The average annual income for a packinghouse laborer was about $800. The city was stunned. Union lawyers drove home the point that charity cases received considerably more than men and women working long hours at difficult, dangerous work in order to supply the nation and its soldiers with their food. "Has American industry ever shown a greater shame?" asked Foster. "Workers paid less than paupers!"[28]

The union contrasted living conditions in Packingtown with skyrocketing corporate profits and argued persuasively that introduction of the eight-hour day, far from disrupting production as the packers contended, would actually lead to higher productivity. Frank Walsh, who pleaded the unions' case, was a former director of the U.S. Commission on Industrial Relations and a liberal Democrat with strong labor connections in Kansas City. He emphasized the conflict between high profits and decent living standards. Using the language of the Clayton Anti-Trust Act, Walsh insisted that "labor is not a commodity or article of commerce."[29]

The people of Packingtown and the organized labor movement hailed the first round of arbitration and Judge Alschuler's award of March 1918 as a great victory. And indeed, the practical gains were considerable. The award established a basic eight-hour day and seven paid holidays; provided overtime rates, paid lunches, and a guaranteed forty-eight-hour week; and required that women doing the same work as men receive equal pay. Best of all, the award granted the full one-dollar-per-week raise demanded by the union as well as a proportional increase for all piece-rate workers. The workers and their families held a celebration rally in Davis Square, a small park just across from the packing plants.[30]

But the award was a victory not simply in the sense that the workers had achieved a number of practical reforms. Addressing the large, racially mixed crowd in Davis Square, John Fitzpatrick was jubilant. "It's a new day, and out in God's sunshine you men and you women, Black and white, have not only an eight-hour day, but you are on an equality." The packers' policies stood condemned by the public and the government. Symbolic of the new atmosphere of hope in the neighborhood was a row of benches near the University of Chicago Settlement House. After the award these were called the "eight-hour benches" because the shorter workday allowed packinghouse laborers to sit out in the sun with their children on their knees.[31] Humanity, it seemed, had finally been vindicated in Packingtown.

But the glow sparked by the 1918 award faded gradually as workers realized that not all decisions would be in their favor. Wages began to fall behind the cost of living. In November 1919 Alschuler awarded a minor wage increase but denied demands for a forty-four-hour week, double time for overtime, and abolition of piece rates in the packers' railroad car shops. The system of arbitration also tied the union leadership directly into the drive for production and minimized the collective strength of rank-and-file workers on the shop floor.[32] Arbitration not only *gave* authority and legitimacy to the union, but also *took away* the right to strike and drew union officials into the effort to discipline workers and maintain production. There would be no standing grievance committees. With productivity at a premium and high profits at stake, the packers wanted to avoid the department stoppages and restriction of output which shop-floor organization seemed to breed. The arbitration made the union leadership responsible for controlling such action, for holding the workers in line.[33]

When union leaders left for Washington to testify before the National War Labor Board in July 1918, Judge Alschuler admonished them to "not stay there too long. Get down to the Yards; keep things smooth and help things along." "We have been doing that in the Yards from morning to night," John Kikulski said. "The record shows that 1,000 cars per day was [*sic*] shipped to our army, and this has been raised since the beginning of the arbitration to 1,800 cars per day. This is the kind of agitators we are."[34]

By settling grievances at the plant level, union officials helped management avoid spontaneous stoppages, which could grow from a variety of disputes with management on the shop floor. Martin Murphy, president of the Stockyards Labor Council, estimated that an average of thirty disputes per day were settled at the plant level. Often a superintendent, sensing a high level of tension which might result in strike action, would contact union officials, who would come down to the plant to defuse the situation *before* a stoppage had actually taken place. "We would go down there and keep them working," Murphy said, "settle whatever dispute there was."[35]

In spite of union and government strictures against such action, however, some unofficial strikes continued to break out. The high point came in June and July, 1919, when at least a dozen strikes occurred in several different plants. The hog-killing gang at Wilson and Company, a hotbed of illegal strike activity, erupted three times between July 3 and July 19, 1919.[36] Once the workers stopped, the role of union officials as peacemakers was even more crucial; it was they who got the men or women back to work.[37]

Shop-floor organization also emerged once again in spite of official union opposition. In order to handle the sort of day-to-day grievances that were inevitable products of the mass-production system, workers in the various departments and plants elected "floor committees" of three rank-and-file workers each to bring issues before foremen and superintendents. Such committees were elected in many shops within a year of the arbitration agreement, if not earlier, even though the agreement specifically outlawed them. For several months the union itself was not even aware of their existence. When officials went to some plants in the spring of 1919 to settle a series of strikes led by the committees, they were "introduced to shop committees we never knew before, that were elected automatically by the men as spokesmen on that floor."[38]

The union's own structure, by separating skilled from unskilled, actually encouraged the growth of such committees. Some vehicle was needed to represent all the workers in a department. Local unions could not fulfill this need, since they were organized on the basis of skill, race, and ethnicity, so the shop committees functioned as the unofficial leadership in emergency situations. The committees' composition in any given department was a cross-section of the labor force, though two groups were particularly prominent—Poles and blacks.[39] The fact that the committees were *ad hoc* structures developed on the shop floor is suggested by the bewildering range of titles by which committee members were known. Most were called "floor committeemen," but Steve Zielinski of the dry salt gang at Boyd-Lunham was elected "shop steward," while Anton Zientara was chosen by the laborers in the sweet pickle department of the same plant as their "president."[40]

The existence of the floor committees in some departments and the outbreak of strikes in the summer of 1919 suggest a continuity between this period and the union organization of 1900–1904. There is little doubt, however, that the responsibilities of the union leaders under the arbitration agreement placed severe limitations on the growth of shop-floor organization. During the war years the union put all emphasis on the hearings before Judge Alschuler, and the floor committees remained relatively weak by comparison to the house committees of the 1900–1904 era.

DISINTEGRATION: RACE

In his excellent study of the July 1919 Chicago race riot and its relationship to labor organization, William Tuttle has argued that the union campaign in the stockyards was a major cause for the disturbance. A legacy of racial conflict from earlier strikes and a massive influx of black migrants, seemingly impervious to the union's efforts, combined with such factors as the shortage of housing and political competition to heighten the atmosphere of racism among white workers. The packinghouses occupy a central position in Tuttle's analysis. Here the class consciousness of white immigrants collided with the race consciousness of black migrants in the course of a campaign for "100 percent union." The growth of class consciousness, Tuttle argues, stimulated the growth of racism. Blacks became identified as a "scab race," tools of the packers.[41]

For all of its subtlety in sorting out the complicated influences that provided a fertile ground for the 1919 race riot, Tuttle's argument regarding the interplay among community, workplace, and organization is misleading in some respects. It homogenizes both black and white packinghouse workers, ignoring crucial differences within each group. Tuttle underplays a turbulent conflict within the black community between union and nonunion workers, while he equates the mentality and behavior of the new immigrants with that of the more acculturated Irish-American population. Convinced of the importance of the link between unionism and racism, Tuttle has also underrated the importance of the Stockyards Labor Council's determined fight against prejudice among white workers and its efforts to bring the two races together. Notwithstanding the real tension that existed over the question of union membership, Tuttle has overestimated the importance of workplace confrontations. The social ecology of three bordering South Side communities—Packingtown, Canaryville, and the Black Belt—provides a different view of the riot. Finally, race relations among the workers must be placed within the context of class relations in the industry. One comes away from Tuttle's description of the riot feeling that racism was an inevitable, if tragic, outgrowth of the situation in Chicago in the summer of 1919. In reality the packers played an extremely active and important role, in the plants and in the communities, dividing black and white workers from one another and creating an atmosphere ripe for racial conflict.

In the spring of 1919, when the end of federal mediation and a confrontation with the packers seemed imminent, the SLC launched an organizing drive to bolster its demand for recognition. The campaign was kicked off with a mass demonstration addressed by the council leadership. In the following weeks the SLC sponsored open-air meetings, and street-corner agitators harangued workers going to and from the plants. A three-piece band of Musicians' Union volunteers played from a flatbed truck. Packingtown took on the atmosphere of a Baptist camp meeting. Seven large trucks equipped with loudspeakers were parked near the various entrances to the yards, and organizers mounted the truck platforms like evangelists, carrying the union gospel in a babel of languages to the crowds of workers. The "converted" then climbed onto the trucks and were whisked to the Labor Council's Columbia Hall at Forty-seventh Street and Ashland Avenue, where they signed cards and received the SLC's special campaign button. The button, pinned to thousands of overalls and workshirts in the course of June, read, "100% UNION OR BUST!" Special organizing committees badgered black workers on the elevated platforms near the yards and on the train ride home to the Black Belt. Eight thousand workers joined in the last two weeks of June alone, and on July 12 a giant parade wound its way through the stockyards district to an open-air meeting of thirty thousand union faithful. Yet the drive was only partly successful. About 95 percent of the white workers had joined by July, but most recruits came from the immigrant neighborhoods immediately adjacent to the yards. Estimates of the proportion of organized black workers vary, but it was certainly never more than one-third and may have been less than a fourth. The SLC was still not reaching the mass of black packinghouse workers.[42]

This failure was not the product of neglect. The actions as well as the rhetoric of the SLC leadership indicate a dedication to the goal of a progressive, interracial union. They were opposed at every turn by the packers, who tried in a variety of ways to create tension and keep the workers divided.[43]

Black workers played important roles during the SLC organizing drive. Both the Amalgamated and the AFL employed black organizers. G. W. Downing, a member of black Local 651, was vice president of the Stockyards Labor Council. In January 1918, when Fitzpatrick brought a delegation to present the workers' demands to President Wilson, another member of Local 651, Joseph Bell, was there to represent black workers. SLC leaders insisted that they vigorously followed up complaints of racial discrimination, and the disproportionate number of grievances filed by the Labor Council on behalf of black workers supports the claim. Rank-and-file white workers also supported blacks through their shop-floor organizations. They frequently elected black stewards, and in at least one case threatened a strike, forcing the dismissal of a foreman accused of physically and verbally abusing a black laborer. The Urban League's industrial secretary found that blacks were treated most fairly in those departments with strong shop-floor organizations.[44]

The SLC also made attempts to draw major institutions and leaders from the black community into the campaign. Representatives appeared before the Baptist Ministers' Alliance and African Methodist Episcopal Sunday School Convention to explain how unionization could help black workers. Union witnesses appearing before the Chicago Commission on Race Relations reported after the riot that union men had also spoken before several other organizations. In September 1918 the Amalgamated invited a spokesman from the Equal Rights League and *Chicago Defender* editor R. S. Abbott to appear before a union conference in Chicago. Both speakers were well received, and the audience cheered Abbott's expressions of admiration and support for the union. During July 1919 T. Arnold Hill, secretary of the National Urban League, addressed a mass meeting of black and white workers.[45]

Recognizing that the lack of any interracial social contact was a primary obstacle to uniting the workers, the SLC had sponsored a number of meetings and parades during 1918 in order to bring the races together. At mass meetings black and white union speakers emphasized interracial solidarity. Some of the SLC's efforts to bring the races into contact in fact appear quite bold in light of the growing strength of racism in Chicago during the immediate postwar period. On July 6, 1919, during the 100 percent campaign, the Council planned a giant "stockyards celebration." This was to begin with an interracial march from Forty-seventh and Paulina in Packingtown, proceed through the heart of the Black

Belt, and end at Beutner Playground at Thirty-third Street and
LaSalle. The packers succeeded in having the march banned at
the last minute, ostensibly for fear of a racial confrontation. Instead two separate parades, one black and the other white,
marched along the same route. The black community lined the
streets and cheered both parades. One of the marchers carried a
placard reading, "The bosses think that because we are of different color and different nationalities we should fight each other.
We're going to fool them and fight for a common cause—a square
deal for all."[46]

The crowd that gathered around the speakers' stand at the
playground was jubilant, as was Jack Johnstone of the SLC. "It
does me good to see such a checkerboard crowd—by that I mean
all of the workers are not standing apart in groups, one race huddled in one bunch, one nationality in another. You are all standing shoulder to shoulder as men, regardless of whether your face
is white or black."[47]

The packers' intervention to prevent the July 6 march was only
one part of their effort to divide the labor force along racial lines.
During the organizing drive which preceded the July race riot, the
packers hired three hundred mounted police, who rode directly
into audiences to disrupt street-corner meetings. Labor Council
organizers were arrested daily.[48]

Three weeks after this successful interracial rally, Chicago's
South Side exploded in a bloody race riot, claiming the lives of
twenty-three blacks and fifteen whites, including several packinghouse workers.[49] The Stockyards Labor Council had succeeded in
organizing only a small proportion of the black packinghouse
workers by the time of the riot. One major reason for this failure
lay in the physical and social separation of the two major communities of stockyards workers, Packingtown and the Black Belt.
If unionization was to take place, two groups of workers with very
different attitudes and experiences had to be brought together.
Both groups lived in neighborhoods which were segregated from
"respectable" Chicago. In the case of Packingtown, the division
was based largely on class lines, while for the Black Belt the line
was racial.

Though many of the skilled Irish and German butchers who
built the 1904 union movement had left the industry, some of the

Slavic workers who had lived through the experience and come to appreciate the importance of organization remained. Like millions before them, those who came to Packingtown faced a difficult process of adjustment to life in an industrial slum. While ethnic cultures remained strong, the union provided the most important avenue for the assimilation of thousands of immigrants who stayed in America rather than returning to the old country.

In a community like Packingtown, overwhelmingly working-class in composition, isolated from native-American middle-class influence, and dominated by one huge industry, work and work-related problems were powerful influences on the mentality of immigrant workers. "Here," an economist observed, "the specter of meatpacking hung over every waking hour of most residents."[50] During the SLC organizing drives the neighborhood was saturated with union leaflets in half a dozen languages, and loudspeakers carried the message in words the people could understand. The saloons and halls lining Ashland Avenue were given over to the organizing efforts, and even the parish priests lent their support to the cause. What one labor organizer described as the process of acquiring an "industrial discipline"—developing a collective morality or ethic and a commitment to a common struggle for common goals—was well advanced in Packingtown. Its residents shared more than employment in the slaughterhouses and stockyards. They shared also a tradition of organization and militancy and a sullen resentment of the Meat Trust.

It was this tradition which made Packingtown the strongest political base for the new Cook County Labor Party in the municipal election in spring 1919. In spite of powerful Democratic and Republican organizations there, the Twenty-ninth Ward showed a higher proportion of Labor voters than any other in the city. Thirteen percent of the voters supported Fitzpatrick for mayor; 20 percent supported SLC president Martin Murphy for alderman. Within the ward, Labor made its strongest showing in those precincts closest to the yards, which were populated largely by Lithuanian and Polish immigrants. Given the close relationship between the Stockyards Labor Council and the Labor Party, the strong turnout was not surprising. John Kikulski appeared as a candidate on Labor's citywide ticket and the party's ward organization was run out of the Labor Council's office.[51]

The union upsurge in Packingtown, then, was part of a broader community mobilization which also included independent labor politics. The packers had ruled the industry ruthlessly since the 1904 strike, but the lessons of that era had not been forgotten. When the call was sounded, the community rose up.

About one mile east of the stockyards, stretching between Eighteenth and Fifty-seventh streets and bounded on the east and west by Cottage Grove and Wentworth avenues, a different kind of community had developed (see map 1, p. 70). Like Packingtown, the Black Belt was the product of residential segregation, but what made the Black Belt an "undesirable area" was its racial rather than its class composition. Packingtown was created when thousands of immigrants from various ethnic groups came together for employment. The strongest bond in the Black Belt, however, was race, not occupation. People from a variety of social and economic backgrounds came to live in the Black Belt because they found it difficult and even dangerous to live in any other part of the increasingly segregated city. Here they created for themselves a distinctive black urban culture. Black packinghouse workers were a large and important part of this community, but they were well integrated into it.[52]

A minority of workers in the Black Belt shared similar attitudes concerning work and organization with the people of Packingtown. Whites referred to these people as "northern negroes." In the case of packinghouse workers, this meant that they had worked in the industry for some time; some had probably gone through the same labor experiences as the Poles and Lithuanians who remained after the 1904 strike. The daily earnings of the small group of black butcher workmen were actually higher than those for Polish and Lithuanian immigrants before the Great Migration, and by 1917–18 labor shortages had forced the packers to move some blacks up into the more skilled positions.[53] Like the "Americanized" Slavic immigrants, they had been exposed to the values of the union's "industrial morality." David Brody concludes, "The prewar Negroes, forming a permanent part of the packinghouse force, responded to the wartime organizing drive in the same manner as the whites." By early 1918, 90 percent of these workers were union members, about the same proportion as that for whites.[54]

This generation of more experienced black workers created the types of institutions commonly associated with stable working-class communities—unions, cooperatives, fraternal groups, and an independent political organization. Local 651 of the Amalgamated became a focal point for this portion of the community. Union members established their own cooperative grocery store and co-sponsored educational meetings with white locals. Black butchers were instrumental in forming a Colored Club of the Cook County Labor Party in the spring of 1919 and served as delegates from the party to a national Labor Party convention the following fall. Like most other Chicago unions, 651 passed resolutions calling for an end to British imperialism in Ireland and could be counted on to turn out its share of marchers on Labor Day and in Free Tom Mooney demonstrations.[55]

Robert Bedford may have been typical of these union blacks. Born in the North, he had migrated to Chicago and worked in the Wilson plant for several years before being elected one of three floor committeemen in the cattle-killing gang during the winter of 1918–19. He was quite articulate and popular among both whites and blacks.[56]

Bedford and other black unionists emphasized union solidarity. Like many of the Slavic laborers living over on the other side of the yards, they recognized that the only hope for change lay in collective action across the racial line. For example, a bulletin issued by Federal Labor Union Number 15805, composed of black stockyards workers, was addressed to "Fellow Colored Workers" and concluded, "So you see, Brothers, that the slogan amongst the stockyard workers is 'Each for all, and all for each, irrespective of race, creed, color, nationality or sex.' So come and hear what we are demanding from the packers in conjunction with our white Brothers who are thoroughly organized and going down the line with us."[57] "The truth is," said Charles Ford, a black Amalgamated organizer, " . . .there ain't no negro problem, any more than there's a [*sic*] Irish problem or a Polish problem or a Jewish or any other problem. There is only the human problem."[58]

Men and women like Robert Bedford could not forget they were black, however; in Chicago, in the summer of 1919, this would have been impossible. Union blacks clearly demonstrated a degree of race consciousness. Frank Custer, Bedford's partner on

the floor committee on Wilson's killing floor, feared the consequences of growing racial hostility in the months following the
end of the war and worked for understanding between the black
and white butcher workmen. But if the dreaded race riot should
occur, Custer knew where his loyalty lay. "Supposing trouble
starts—I am a colored man and I love my family tree, and I ain't
going to stand for no white man to come imposing on my
color. . . . There is going to be a fight."[59]

The great mass of black packinghouse workers, moreover, did
not share the experiences and values of the unionized minority.
Most were newcomers to the urban industrial environment, and
like the Slavic immigrants they faced a difficult period of transi-
tion. In the case of the white immigrants, the unions played an
important role in this process and had a profound effect on the
way in which many immigrants viewed their situation. In the case
of the black migrants, this formative experience was shaped by
individuals and institutions whose interests were far removed
from and sometimes hostile to those of organized labor. More important, the migrants often viewed the migration process itself
and the chance for industrial employment differently than did the
white immigrants.

A wide range of community institutions and organizations, what
Allen Spear has called the "institutional ghetto," addressed themselves to this problem of adjustment.[60] The black migrant lived in
a community which was little more than eight blocks from Packingtown physically but a world apart from it socially. The attitudes and behavior espoused by black community leaders and
institutions—and not the SLC's street-corner speeches, leaflets,
and parades—shaped the migrants' responses to unionization.

The most important institution in the migrant's adjustment to
the northern city was the Urban League, which set about in 1915
to facilitate "the adjustment of Blacks to city life and promote
equal industrial opportunity." The league's representatives met
the migrants on the platform of the Illinois Central Station, and it
was to the league that friends and relatives would refer the
newcomer. The Urban League successfully placed a large proportion of the migrants in homes and jobs. Between the spring of
1917 and the summer of 1919 about fifty-five thousand people
came to the league, which placed about twenty thousand of them.

In essence, its task was to persuade white employers that the migrants would be assets to their businesses. This involved overcoming racist attitudes which were widely held by employers and promoting values and behavior among the migrants which would make it easier for them to be successfully placed. According to Arvarh Strickland, the league's historian, "the agency's reputation depended upon the successful assimilation of Negro workers into the employer's plant. To a great extent, the organization became the agent of the employer. It tried to insure him against inefficient, indolent, and troublesome workers."[61]

The organization's social workers never forgot to "urge upon applicants the necessity for strict application to duties, punctuality, efficiency and proper deportment."[62] Like white immigrants, the migrants had to develop an "industrial morality," but the morality espoused by the league and other institutions upon which the migrant depended was often that of the packer and his personnel manager, not the union organizer. The league's activities in this area were supplemented by the work of the Negro Workers' Advisory Committees set up regionally under the auspices of the Negro Economics Division of the Department of Labor. The committees also aimed to make the migrant a better worker. Committee representatives visited the plants to lecture black workers on efficiency and punctuality.[63]

The league's campaign, however, encompassed far more than the migrant's industrial experience. More urbanized, "respectable" elements within the community worried that "Southern" habits would reflect badly on the community at large. "It's no difficult task to get people out of the South," the *Chicago Whip* observed, "but you have a job on your hands when you try to get the South out of them."[64] Therefore, the league's program included a serious effort to impart to the migrant a concept of acceptable social behavior which reflected middle-class values and goals. A community worker lectured them in their churches on "thrift, civic pride, personal hygiene, deportment, and other civic virtues." She also followed them into their homes with her "practical message" of discipline and self-help. Block clubs were organized to give the campaign a community basis.[65]

The Urban League and several other major black organizations and institutions were somewhat ambivalent in their attitude toward organized labor. In the case of the Urban League, its leaders seemed to recognize that the long-range welfare of blacks lay in collective action with their white fellow workers. They saw the need for some mechanism to protect workers' rights within the factory. In those plants with large numbers of black workers, "welfare secretaries" tried not only to discipline workers, but also to ensure suitable working conditions. But given the league's immediate goal of placing the migrants in bitterly antiunion plants, it would have been extremely difficult for the organization to be anything but antilabor in the event of conflict.[66]

Besides relying on industrialists' goodwill in its efforts to place migrants in jobs, the Urban League also had to rely upon them financially. The league's second largest contributor during the war era was the Stockyards Community Clearing House, the welfare arm of the Big Five packers. By 1919 the packers contributed about 20 percent of the league's total budget. It would be misleading to suggest that the league's policies were determined solely by this economic relationship, but the packers clearly saw the organization as one way to undermine the unions. Significantly, packer contributions closely paralleled the Stockyards Labor Council's organizing drives. Donations peaked in late 1917 (during the council's period of greatest growth), during the immediate postwar period (at the time of the campaign for "100 percent union"), and during the months leading up to the disastrous 1921 strike. Once that strike was lost, financial support fell away sharply.[67]

Partly because of such financial support but also in a genuine effort to serve the best interests of its black migrant constituency, the Urban League changed its position on unionism significantly between 1919 and 1921. Its official stand as of early 1919 encouraged black participation where unions did not practice discrimination and condoned strikebreaking "only where the union affected had excluded colored men from membership." As late as the summer of 1919, the league seemed to be supporting the Stockyards Labor Council's organizing drive. In the wake of that summer's riot, however, with unemployment beginning to climb and labor clearly on the defensive, the league's support began to waver. By 1921 some officials saw a need to advance black employment prospects by providing strikebreakers. Testifying before the Chicago Commission on Race Relations that year, a league spokesman emphasized race over class interests. "The League is not opposed to unionism," he said, "but is interested primarily in the welfare of colored workers."[68]

Chicago's two influential black newspapers, the *Defender* and the *Whip*, went through a comparable change. Although originally skeptical, Robert Abbott, the *Defender*'s popular editor, supported the goal of interracial unionism throughout the period 1918–20. In the course of 1921, however, Abbott concluded that the union effort was a lost cause and that the black community's interests lay in loyalty to the packers.[69]

Many community institutions were notably less ambivalent and in some cases stridently antiunion. The Wabash Avenue YMCA, one of the black Belt's most important cultural centers, was a focal point for propacker and antiunion activity. The Y was headed by Mr. A. L. Jackson, whom William Tuttle describes as "intellectually and emotionally sympathetic to the packers, and decidedly hostile to the unions."[70] Once again, the packers used financial support to influence policy. Armour gave an annual membership in the organization to each black worker after one year's service, and "plant loyalty" became a goal of the Y's industrial program. This program consisted of a number of "efficiency clubs" organized and financed by the various packers. It was at efficiency club meetings, claimed Jack Johnstone of the SLC, that "Black workers were lectured and taught that the thing to do is to keep out of organized labor."[71] According to the packers, the clubs' purpose was to "instill a sense of responsibility on the part of the industrial worker and a sympathetic understanding and goodwill on the part of company officials." But the National Urban League's Industrial Secretary, William L. Evans, agreed with Johnstone that the clubs were designed to discourage union activity and that the Y was instrumental in this strategy.[72]

Other important sources of public opinion in the Black Belt underscored the message. A few black ministers spoke up for the unions, but the rest, some of whom depended on direct contributions from the packers, either ignored or condemned organized labor. The city's only two black aldermen also sided with the packers, while the *Broad Axe*, with the city's second largest black circulation, urged readers to be industrious and shun strikes.[73] The

Chicago Federation of Labor's charge that the "packers subsidized colored politicians, ministers and YMCA secretaries to prevent the colored workmen at the stockyards from entering the union" contained more than a grain of truth. There were some elements in the black community, William Z. Foster concluded, who would oppose the Stockyards Labor Council regardless of its policy on black workers.[74]

The packers supplemented their community strategy with one aimed at disrupting organization within the plants. There were, indeed, as Tuttle argues, confrontations between blacks and whites during the drive for "100 percent union" in the summer of 1919. But confrontations also occurred between union and nonunion blacks. The fundamental issue was one of labor organization.

In the middle of June, when a rash of unofficial strikes broke out in various departments of the Hammond and Wilson plants, management filed a grievance with the federal arbitrator, claiming that these were part of the union's drive for recognition. Clearly, most of the strikes *were* related in some way to the issue of nonunion workers. At Hammond, for example, there were only two nonunion men left by mid-June in a hog-killing gang of seventy-nine. The hog butchers killed several animals, started the cutting process, and then stopped the line, demanding that the two scabs join or be fired. When management refused to fire the men, the strike spread throughout the pork house, tying up between seven hundred and nine hundred workers, and from there to the sausage department. Similar strikes closed down almost the entire Wilson plant at just about the same time. It seems that some workers, sensing their strength as well as the desperate need to win full recognition, seized the initiative and struck to enforce a *de facto* closed shop. But testimony from foremen and supervisors as well as from union officials and rank-and-file workers all suggests that, while the timing and effectiveness of the strikes was based upon considerable organization, they were not ordered by the union officials, who were as much surprised by the developments as were the packers.[75]

Both white and black unionists denied that the issue was race per se. "I can get along with these colored fellows," said smokehouse worker Louis Michora. "We all can get along with them just like brothers with these fellows that have the buttons on."[76] Union members claimed that the strikes were provoked by small groups of black nonunion "agitators" in several plants who had been ridiculing, harassing, and threatening union members, particularly black union activists, for months. The workers claimed that this agitation was part of an effort to stir racial violence in the plants and disrupt the union.[77]

The trouble at Wilson's started on the cattle-killing floor, where there were from 12 to 14 nonunion workers, black and white, and about 140 union men, also racially mixed. The floor committee-men—two blacks, Robert Bedford and Frank Custer, and a German-American, William Bremer—appeared before Judge Alschuler to explain an unofficial strike which broke out among unskilled laborers in the plant's smokehouse and dry salt cellars and then spread to the cattle butchers. Each of the three men identified a group of black "agitators" who received preferential treatment and led the attack on the union. "We get it on the street and anywhere else," Robert Bedford claimed. "This Williams is the leader of some men to raise a line of prejudice, and show the white men, the colored man is not with him, and show the colored man, the white man is not with him and he wants to raise a dissention on that footing."[78] Several of these alleged agitators were experienced butcher workmen who had come together from a packinghouse in Texas, joined the union, and then dropped out in a body for unknown reasons. These men are interesting in part because they do not fit the stereotype of the black migrant sharecropper, freshly transplanted to the factory from southern soil.[79]

Austin "Heavy" Williams was the group's leader. Robert Bedford and Frank Custer acknowledged that Williams, though illiterate, was a persuasive speaker and quite popular among black workers. Williams had joined the union shortly after his arrival from Texas in 1916. The Stockyards Labor Council's organizing campaign had not even begun; it was a risky time to take out a union card. Williams dropped out in 1918 along with the others who had come with him from Texas. Why? Frank Custer believed that Williams and his fellow Texans were paid agents from the beginning, sent to Chicago to discourage organization among black workers. "As I say, they will take the pick, it seems, take my people—that is, the highest class of my race, and use them for a big stick."[80]

Williams's own explanation for his change of heart was simple enough: it became clear to him that the union could not win and that his own interests would be better served by siding with the packers. He quit, he said, "Because I seen it was going down. . . . I wanted to see which way my money was going." The union's hard-sell 100 percent campaign seems only to have deepened his resolve to stick with management. He resented the pressure being applied by the union men and openly defied it. "Heavy" was given a job as straw boss over the black laborers on the gang, a position which allowed him to make sure that only nonunion men were hired and gave him an opportunity to influence new workers against joining. Williams also became a leader and recruiter for the Wilson Efficiency Club at the Wabash Avenue YMCA, which vied with the union for the black migrants' loyalty.[81]

Although Williams himself was never accused of violence against union members, several of his followers were. Some carried guns and knives. One man was accused of throwing bricks at a group of Poles who were soliciting for the union outside the yards gate. Another was defended by an attorney from Wilson's own legal staff when he was arrested for attacking a black union man with a heavy "pritching iron" normally used to turn cattle carcasses. This small group of half a dozen men kept up a steady torrent of abuse.[82]

Evidence from the testimony of workers from other packinghouses suggests that the situation at Wilson's was not unique. There was a hard core of black scabs and also a nucleus of black union activists, serving on floor committees and recruiting for the Stockyards Labor Council. Most migrants were probably caught in between. On the one hand they faced an aggressive union and on the other the alternating threats and promises of a small group of black leaders who seemed to enjoy some special status in the plants.

The most extreme and the most fascinating of these elements was the American Unity Labor Union (AULU), founded by Richard E. Parker in the summer of 1916. The organization remained active into the early 1920s. Besides being leader of the

AULU, Parker was also a labor recruiter for the packers and steel mills in and around the city and a promoter of the Race Publishing Company, which sometimes published his newspaper, the *Chicago Advocate*. Parker was a "race man"—"the man who was always with his race, right or wrong." He claimed that he had distributed twenty thousand leaflets in the yards at his own expense because of a "personal interest" in his race. Illinois state investigators were skeptical. Their report established financial links between Parker and the Big Five packers.[83] Parker variously refered to the AULU as "the only colored labor union at the yards" and as a "race employment agency." Quite apart from the confusion it must have caused for organizers trying to explain the union issue, the AULU competed directly with the SLC for the loyalty of the migrants. While the Stockyards Labor Council was explicitly enjoined from organizing within the plants, AULU organizers solicited openly in at least one house from a choice spot near the timekeeper's office.[84]

The Chicago Federation of Labor dismissed the AULU as a tool of the packers, and it is difficult to dispute the claim, as far as it goes. But the real importance of the organization is that it struck a responsive chord in some black workers. Their identification with its appeal suggests something of the migrant's attitude toward unions. The organization's pronouncements appealed to three important elements in the experience of many black workers: a distrust of white unions, an identification of common interests based on race rather than class, and a basic belief in the packers' benevolence.

Parker's warning not to "join any white man's union" appealed to a legacy of distrust even among urbanized black workers. One skilled butcher argued that his union card was not honored outside the Chicago stockyards, as were those of white men at the same skill level. Another remembered how those blacks who had stood by the union in the 1904 strike suffered from discrimination in rehiring afterward.[85] To such experiences one must add memories of racial hostility surrounding labor violence in Chicago, riots in which innocent bystanders as well as scabs could be attacked simply because they were black.[86] Hostility to unions was stronger among the migrants. Some had had experience with racist southern unions. "Unions ain't no good for a colored man," said one migrant; "I've seen too much of what they don't do for him." For others, the problem was one of ignorance. Irene Goins, a black organizer in the stockyards who worked for the Women's Trade Union League, complained, "My people . . . know so little about organized labor that they have a great fear of it, and for that reason the work of organizing has proceeded more slowly than I anticipated."[87]

Related to this distrust was a tendency for black workers to define their interests in racial terms. This explains the appeal of Parker's all-black AULU. "Get a Square Deal with Your Own Race," one of his advertisements urged. "Get together and stick together . . . make your own way; other races have made their unions for themselves. . . . Make a union of your own race."[88] A nonunion black worker put the point across more crudely. "You are nothin' but a lot of white folks' niggers," he hollered at a group of black union activists.[89] Given a fairly high level of suspicion on the part of black workers toward unions run by whites, the AULU's appeal was obvious.

Finally, many migrants were genuinely grateful for the opportunity packinghouse work represented. To men and women who had lived with racial oppression and grinding poverty in the rural South, migration north meant more than a good job; it represented a measure of liberation.[90] Packinghouse wages were extremely high by southern standards. *Crisis*, the journal of the NAACP, reported in December 1918 that some black women in the Chicago packinghouses earned as much as $33.00 per week, while black butchers often made $9.00 per day. In the South the migrants had lived on the edge of subsistence, but in Chicago they found themselves being courted by the packers, who offered not only steady employment and good wages but also gymnasiums and life insurance policies, baseball teams and choral groups. "Blacks, after all," writes William Tuttle, "felt that they had received fair treatment at the hands of Armour, Swift, Sears and other industries and corporations," which also made special efforts to support black community institutions.[91] "The name of Armour," the *Chicago Defender* noted, "has always been a sign of justice so far as our race is concerned."[92] The packers might be viewed as the avaricious Meat Trust in Packingtown, but in many Black Belt homes they were seen as genuine benefactors. Mary

McDowell told the story of a migrant approached by a union organizer who proceeded to explain all the benefits to be gained by
union membership. "It sounds pretty good to me," the migrant
said, "but what does Mr. Armour think about it?"[93]

Yet the organization of black workers was still a viable goal until
the race riot of July 1919. In spite of the various obstacles, the
SLC remained optimistic, and the strong showing at the interracial march just three weeks before the riot suggests that it was
making some headway. The riot itself finally smashed any hope of
bringing black and white workers together, but it was not simply
the product of poor race relations in the stockyards. It was also
the culmination of a reign of terror directed against the black
community by Irish street gangs which had emerged from the
neighborhood sandwiched between the Black Belt and Packingtown. This was Canaryville, the most dangerous neighborhood in
the city and the one with the strongest traditions of racism.

Both of those labor conflicts which had provoked the most extensive racial violence prior to 1919—the 1904 packinghouse
strike and the 1905 teamsters' strike—involved direct engagements between black strikebreakers and large numbers of Irish or
Irish-American workers. The teamsters' strike, in particular,
mobilized the Bridgeport Irish community in attacking scab
wagons. If, as William Tuttle suggests, these conflicts left deep
scars, they were etched most deeply in the collective consiousness
of the second- and third-generation Irish-Americans raised in the
neighborhood immediately adjacent to the Black Belt.[94]

There were two fairly distinct Irish neighborhoods in Bridgeport: Hamburg, which ran between Thirty-first and Thirty-ninth
streets, and Canaryville, which stretched several blocks south from
Thirty-ninth Street (see map 1). Although all of Bridgeport was
known as "a pretty tough hole," Canaryville had by far the worst
reputation. For years it had represented what one University of
Chicago sociologist called "a moral lesion on the life of the
city."[95] The Irish-American population of the neighborhood
tended to be transient, and the frequent evictions were often accompanied by violence. Fistfights and even gunfights were fairly
common occurrences. The Cook County State's Attorney noted
that more bank robbers, payroll bandits, automobile bandits,
highwaymen and strong-arm crooks had been produced by the

"Canaryville School of Gunmen" than by any other neighborhood in the city during his seven years of service.[96] Blending into this hardcore criminal population were a number of large Irish street gangs which euphemistically described themselves as "athletic clubs." "It is in this district," wrote Frederick Thrasher, "that the athletic clubs and other organizations of young toughs and gangsters flourish, and where disreputable poolrooms, hoodlum-infested saloons and other criminal hang-outs are plentiful."[97]

When they were not fighting one another, the clubs launched assaults on the Black Belt. Young black men were not as apt in the era of the Great Migration to form such organizations. The black groups which engaged the Irish were of a defensive type rather than anything like a street gang. Police called Wentworth Avenue, which separated the black and Irish neighborhoods, the "dead line." Trespassers were often greeted with cries of "He is from the east side!" or "Hit him, he is from the west side!" and promptly beaten. When the young black poet Langston Hughes unknowingly wandered across Wentworth on his first Sunday in the city in 1918, he was set upon by an Irish gang who said "they didn't allow niggers in that neighborhood."[98]

Canaryville was the home of Ragen's Colts, an athletic club formed under the political patronage of Democratic alderman Frank Ragen and reputed to have two thousand members. The Colts' involvement in the attacks on blacks represented, in part, the political dimension of the conflict between the two neighborhoods. In 1915 and again in the spring municipal elections of 1919, the Black Belt's staunch support had been the decisive factor in "Big Bill" Thompson's victories. Turnouts were massive and heavily Republican. "The Black Belt of Chicago," Carl Sandburg wrote in 1919, "is probably the strongest effective unit of political power, good or bad, in America."[99] Facing the powerful black political machine across Wentworth Avenue was Bridgeport's strong, aggressive Irish Catholic Democratic organization. More than votes or even patronage was at stake. The Irish saw Thompson as an incarnate social and political evil. Tinged with anti-Catholicism and corruption, he seemed to be stealing Irish political influence through treachery, and his means of doing this was the black migrant. As the military arm of the Irish political machine, the Colts campaigned with their fists. Confrontations occurred throughout the spring of 1919 and reached a crescendo during June. Finally, at the end of the month two black men were murdered on the same night by gangs believed to be connected with the Colts. The attacks were followed immediately by notices posted along Garfield Boulevard (Fify-fifth Street) and neighboring streets warning that all blacks would soon be driven out of the South Side. A pattern of racial attacks had already emerged, then, by July. The Colts were only waiting for a chance to escalate the war.[100]

At the end of July, a racially motivated brawl on Twenty-ninth Street Beach provided the opportunity, and the Irish gangs took to the streets. "But for them," the Chicago Commission on Race Relations concluded, "it is doubtful if the riot would have gone beyond the first clash." Collusion of police and courts allowed gangs to perpetrate most of the violence associated with the riot. "Gangs operated for hours up and down Forty-seventh Street, Wells, Princeton, Shields and Wentworth Avenues and Federal Street without hindrance from the police," the commission reported. One municipal court judge claimed that "they [gang members] seemed to think they had a sort of protection which entitled them to go out and assault anybody."[101]

The Stockyards Labor Council and the Chicago Federation of Labor worked continuously to maintain order during the two weeks of the riot. The Labor Council claimed that the packers intentionally portrayed the riot as a labor-related incident in order to discredit the unions, even though there was no connection. The council and the CFL issued statements asking their members to remain calm and not to go back to work until the trouble had passed. An editorial in the Federation's *New Majority* underlined the importance of white workers disassociating themselves from the racist attacks. "Right now it is going to be decided whether the colored workers are to continue to come into the labor movement or whether they are to feel that they have been abandoned by it and lose confidence in it."[102] The SLC took the unusual step of calling an interracial mass meeting, probably the only large meeting of blacks and whites in the city during the riot. Again the leadership instructed members not to return to work until order was restored. Ironically, the riot may have brought those blacks who remained loyal even closer to the unions. White union

members provided moral and material support for black brothers
and sisters injured or left homeless by the rioting in their neighborhoods.[103]

The SLC's attempts to keep its membership united were fairly
successful. One black worker was attacked within the stockyards
by a group of Slavic laborers, but this was the only example of
violence at work uncovered by the Commission on Race Relations. What struck many observers about the riot was the conspicuous absence of the large population of immigrant stockyards laborers from the crowds that attacked blacks. "It was evident during the riot," Mary McDowell later wrote, "that our Polish neighbors were not the element that committed the violence; it was
committed by the second and third generations of American born
young men from the 'athletic clubs' which had grown under the
protection of political leaders in this district, themselves mostly
American born."[104]

Most attacks occurred either within the Black Belt itself or just
across Wentworth Avenue, in the Irish neighborhood. The assaults within the limits of Packingtown occurred around the entrances to the yards, and these too were the work of Irish gangs.[105]
Hannah O'Day, a veteran of the stockyards labor movement,
described to Mary McDowell how Ragen's Colts stood at the
yards gate, armed with clubs. As black workers emerged after
their day's labor, the Colts pounced on them.[106]

On Saturday, August 2, one week after the start of the riot, a
fire destroyed forty-nine frame tenements occupied largely by
Lithuanian packinghouse laborers and their families. The tragedy
left 948 immigrants homeless. Rumors spread that the fire, which
was clearly the work of arsonists, had been started by blacks who
came into the neighborhood during the night. At this point,
Packingtown's involvement in the violence might have increased,
but it did not. Neighborhood priests worked to keep their par-
ishioners from wreaking vengeance. In condemning the riot, Father Louis Grudzinski used carefully chosen terminology which
his flock was sure to understand. He called it a "black pogrom"
and implied that someone was trying to draw the Slavic community into the violence. The evidence suggests that Grudzinski was
right. It is extremely unlikely that blacks were responsible for the
fire. To get to Packingtown from the Black Belt, arsonists would

have had to pass directly through the Irish neighborhood—where most of the attacks on blacks had taken place—in large enough numbers to accomplish the task. Governor Lowden of Illinois, Mary McDowell, and a grand jury all agreed that it was the Irish athletic clubs again, this time with blackened faces. The only other allegations were made by the *New Majority* and the Polish newspaper *Dziennik Zwiazkowy*. Both claimed the fire was part of the packers' effort to stir racial hostility. If either the Irish gangs or the packers saw it as necessary to alienate the immigrants from the blacks with such extreme measures, this would underscore the general impression that racism was not nearly so strong in Packingtown as in the more "Americanized" neighborhoods near the yards.[107]

Union, company, and government observers all agreed that race relations in the packing plants themselves were generally good during and immediately after the First World War. Indeed, a committee from the U.S. Department of Labor's Negro Economics Division which looked into the quality of race relations in Illinois factories in the fall of 1918 contrasted the unsatisfactory situation in other industries and regions with the good relations in meat packing at Chicago. Managers from the various plants corroborated these findings and were struck by the good relations, particularly between Polish and black workers, *after* the riot. The crucial factor in the Chicago slaughterhouses, the committee found, was unionization. A report from the director of the Negro Economics Division to the Secretary of Labor following the riot noted that whatever shop-floor hostility did exist seemed to be between the blacks and those Irish-American workers who remained in the industry, and this was a carryover from conflicts within the community. "This did not seem to have any connection with the union situation," the report added, "but with individual contacts."[108]

The Labor Council's drive for 100 percent organization in the summer of 1919 undoubtedly increased the level of tension in the plants between union and nonunion workers, and there were many blacks among the latter group. But the emergence of racist violence was due more to factors in the community and particularly to the conflicts in various spheres between the Irish-American and black communities. The strength of racism among the Irish as well as its relative weakness among Slavic immigrants suggests that race prejudice was something which immigrants learned over time as part of the process of becoming "Americanized." The subsequent history of relations between blacks and precisely those immigrant groups which were the backbone of the union movement in the World War I years shows that in time the new immigrants learned the lesson only too well.[109]

But the history of race relations among packinghouse workers was intimately bound up with the nature of class relations in the industry. As in steel towns, whatever racial antagonism did exist between whites and blacks was accentuated by a conscious corporate strategy to keep the two groups divided and hostile to each other. In the community this included the subsidizing of institutions, organizations, and perhaps even individuals who opposed unionization. Such support was intended to undercut unionism among blacks and therefore increase the level of tension between the races. In the plants the packers used a variety of strategies, including partial treatment of individual blacks, discrimination toward white and black union members, and verbal and physical intimidation, to reinforce whatever racial divisions already existed. The resulting racial conflict was one of the most important factors leading to a fragmentation of the packinghouse workers' movement.[110]

DISINTEGRATION: NATIVISM AND FACTIONALISM

In the summer of 1919, just at the point when racial hostility was tearing the packinghouse workers' movement apart, ethnic and skill divisions and a bitter factional struggle between the Stockyards Labor Council and the Amalgamated accelerated this process of disintegration. While these racial, ethnic, and skill barriers were often the products of forces outside the workplace and the union, they were aggravated and reinforced by the movement's structural weaknesses. Central to the factional dispute was the question of whether the unions should renew the arbitration agreement, postponing once again the inevitable confrontation with the packers, or force the issue, demanding recognition and backing up the demand with strike action.

To some extent a potential for conflict was inherent in the relationship between the SLC and the Amalgamated. Although organized into mass locals of the Amalgamated, most immigrant workers looked to the SLC for leadership, especially because of Kikulski's stature among the Slavic workers. With the SLC directing the organizing and leading the movement in the yards, many of the Amalgamated's immigrant members remained beyond its reach. There was some feeling that Johnstone's and Kikulski's more aggressive attitude toward the packers had helped to produce the rash of unofficial strikes, and indeed the SLC seemed more tolerant of such actions than the Amalgamated. Also, proportional representation of the huge immigrant locals at the union's policy-making conventions threatened to swamp the Amalgamated's department-based and meat cutter locals. The fact that the department locals were composed mostly of the native-born and older immigrant skilled butchers, while the SLC's laborers' locals were composed largely of more recent Slavic immigrants, meant that the factional lines between the two bodies were reinforced by skill and ethnic divisions.[111]

In the long run, however, the most important distinction between the SLC and the Amalgamated was strategic in nature. The two sides in the dispute suggest the options which the labor movement faced in the immediate postwar era. The leadership of the Labor Council, with strong roots in the prewar syndicalist agitation, pushed for a confrontation with the packers. Arbitration, they argued, would continue only as long as the packers saw some advantage in it. Sooner or later, there would have to be a showdown over the question of recognition and it would be better that this come while the momentum of the movement remained strong. The workers' power should be consolidated through an aggressive drive for 100 percent organization; then the unions could demand recognition and strike immediately if necessary. Only in this way could permanent organization be brought to the yards.[112]

In contrast, the Amalgamated's approach was not that different from what it had been in the early twentieth century, and was also characteristic of the more conservative AFL leaders, who, faced with an aggressive business class, sought some way to avoid conflict. The war had institutionalized the arbitration principle in the form of the Alschuler hearings, and Dennis Lane, the

Amalgamated's secretary-treasurer and editor of the union's journal, clung tenaciously to the stability and prosperity which the arbitration system seemed to offer. The course charted by the SLC, he argued, was reckless and irresponsible.[113]

At the end of April 1919, without consulting the union's rank and file, the Amalgamated officers signed an agreement for the packinghouse workers.[114] The Stockyards Labor Council attacked the Amalgamated for selling out its membership. In July 1919, Lane decided to move against the SLC, in spite of a plea from the Chicago Federation of Labor that he wait until the yards were fully organized and the racial turmoil had subsided. In the midst of the riot and of strikes against the resulting military occupation of the yards, Lane announced the formation of District Council 9, with jurisdiction over all butcher workmen in the stockyards region. The international union had created a direct rival of the SLC.[115]

To compensate for the numerical superiority of the large immigrant locals, the new council allowed five representatives per union, regardless of size. This assured the department-based locals and the meat cutter locals, which were also included in the council, a majority of delegates. District 9's strongest support came from these meat cutter locals, which resented the dominance of the packinghouse unions in the international. Most packinghouse workers, however, including many in the department-based locals, rejected the plan and remained loyal to the SLC. As a result, fourteen local unions, representing the overwhelming majority of butcher workmen and virtually all of the Slavic common laborers, were expelled from the Amalgamated.[116]

The confusion which the conflict caused can only be imagined. The important cattle butchers' local, for example, was claimed by both District 9 and the Labor Council. An ethnic split in the hog butchers' union, which remained loyal to the SLC, provided an opportunity for the Amalgamated to charter a rival union. In September 1919 the Labor Council turned out fifteen thousand men and women to demonstrate opposition to the new council. The following month both councils put out newspapers called *The Packing House Worker* in which they attacked one another as traitors to the butcher workmen's cause. At this point, most of the

skilled allied trades which had been affiliated with the Labor
Council seceded to establish the Mechanical Trades Council.
Now there were three separate labor councils in the yards. To
further complicate matters, the leaders of the two black packinghouse locals went with District 9, providing another potential
source for racial conflict just at the time when the Labor Council
was working for a diminution of the hostility generated by the
riot.[117]

Underlying the factional dispute between the two councils was
a growing nativism within some sections of the Amalgamated.
The union's 1917 convention, anticipating an influx of immigrant
packinghouse workers, had ratified a resolution allowing the publication of organizers' reports in Polish, Lithuanian, and Bohemian as well as German and English. Eventually, as Mexicans
started entering the industry, a Spanish column was added to the
union's journal. The 1920 convention, however, bolstered by
delegates from District 9, passed a "100 percent American" resolution. This stipulated that all officers, local as well as international, must be U.S. citizens. At the end of 1921, with the
union's packinghouse base eroding rapidly, the immigrant
foreign-language columns disappeared from the *Butcher Workman*.[118]

Factionalism among the stockyards unions was symptomatic of
a broader conflict which divided Chicago's labor movement and
others throughout the country in what has come to be called the
Red Scare.[119] In Chicago the progressive leadership and majority
of the city's labor federation were challenged by an increasingly
vocal conservative faction identified with "patriotic" forces in the
postwar years. While the progressives remained firmly in control,
incessant conflict within the federation certainly weakened the labor movement at a time when it was under attack in many industries.

Chicago labor's factional conflict is reflected in the columns of
the *New Majority*, the federation's official journal, and *The Unionist*, an opposition paper. The *New Majority* called for recognition
of the Soviet government, establishment of a workers' republic in
Ireland, and an independent labor government for Chicago. *The
Unionist* attacked the federation's leadership and the *New Majority*,
which it portrayed as part of the "Bolshevist movement in Chi-

cago." The paper counseled workers against strikes and warned of a "Bolshevist conspiracy" to destroy the city's labor movement. "*The Unionist* has always hewn to the straight line," the paper editorialized, "standing up for decency, conservatism, and arbitration in all controversies between capital and labor. . . . It has always been opposed to the red flag, to bomb throwing, anarchy and that sort of proceeding."[120]

Financial backing for *The Unionist* is not clear, but the paper was certainly sympathetic to the labor federation's right wing. Editorials blasted Fitzpatrick but defended Simon O'Donnell, the corrupt president of the Chicago Building Trades Council. The paper also printed ads for Standard Oil, the Endicott-Johnson shoe company, and other large corporations. Many of these dealt with company unions and corporate welfare measures. For an article on industrial relations, the paper turned to John Calder, architect of the personnel program at Swift and Company. Many columns were filled with reprinted articles by conservative intellectuals and labor leaders.[121]

At the beginning of 1920 it looked as though a compromise engineered by Fitzpatrick and the CFL might end the conflict between District 9 and the SLC. The two councils agreed to dissolve so that an election could be held to constitute a new District 9. An election, the federation reasoned, would wipe the slate clean and allow for a new organizing campaign to rebuild the badly splintered movement.[122] The workers voted overwhelmingly to retain the SLC leadership, and a special convention was held to plan the reconstruction process. Speaking before the convention, Jack Johnstone called for reconciliation and hard work. "We have all buried the hatchet and we have nothing left before us except to organize the packing industry and we are going to do the job up right."[123]

The Amalgamated, however, refused to accept the results and continued to support the old District 9. Before this problem could be worked out, a new scandal hit the movement. Johnstone came before the CFL with charges filed by a member of Kikulski's own local that the Polish organizer had embezzled a substantial sum of money raised by the Polish and Lithuanian laborers' locals to support striking butcher workmen in Detroit. Kikulski had left Chicago with $7,000 but never showed up in Detroit. Brother

Szafranski, treasurer of Local 554, who had also been involved in the transaction, resigned shortly after Kikulski's departure and returned to Poland. The exact details of the embezzlement remained obscure because the local's books were locked in a safe for which no one could find the key. [124]

In the midst of all the confusion, Kikulski suddenly changed sides. Resigning from the Stockyards Labor Council and taking a large proportion of the council's Polish and Lithuanian membership with him, he was immediately elected president of the Amalgamated's old District 9. Now he turned on Johnstone with countercharges of mismanagement. A CFL trial committee exonerated Johnstone and found Kikulski guilty, but this seemed to have little effect on his following among the Slavic laborers, who remained loyal to their leader. Charges and countercharges flew until, in the spring of 1920, the conflict became deadly. Kikulski was shot to death in broad daylight on the street near his home. He was replaced by Stanley Rokosz, who had organized Polish steelworkers during the 1919 strike, but Rokosz was also killed— beaten to death with a baseball bat near the stockyards. Responsibility for the murders was never established. Leaders on both sides were shot at and slandered as the packinghouse workers' struggle for organization sank into a series of personal vendettas. [125]

Although the SLC had established a solid reputation in the immigrant community, much of its success in retaining the loyalty of the immigrant laborers was bound up with Kikulski's position in the community and his charismatic leadership. His defection and subsequent death left a gaping hole in the movement. Disillusioned by unfavorable arbitration awards, the unsuccessful organizing drive, the riot, and factional conflict, many immigrant workers dropped out. Those who remained had shifted their allegiance to District 9 when Kikulski became its president. In February, under pressure from the AFL Executive Council, the SLC locals voluntarily resigned from the Chicago Federation of Labor. Having lost its mass immigrant base by the summer of 1920, the Stockyards Labor Council faded away. [126]

In practical terms the factional conflict resulted in a rapid degeneration of organization in the yards. The union treasury fell from almost $150,000 in August 1919 to less than $35,000 in May

1920, while membership declined from about 68,000 in November 1919 to less than 40,000 one year later. Most disastrous was the total failure to organize black workers. By December 1921, on the eve of a general strike in the industry, the membership of black Local 651 had fallen to 112, of whom only 49 were in good standing. In the vacuum created by the race riot and the conflict between the Amalgamated and the SLC, the packers consolidated their position in the black community and prepared to run their industry free of union influence. [127]

The war years offered butcher workmen and -women a splendid opportunity to organize and fight for improvements in the quality of life, and their short-term achievements were considerable—the eight-hour day, increases in real wages, and some reassertion of shop-floor power. In the two years following the war's end, however, their organization splintered along racial, ethnic, and factional lines.

From its inception, the structure of union organization had reinforced divisions inherent in the labor market and in the community. Unlike the departmental structure of the 1900-1904 period, which mixed workers of various racial and ethnic backgrounds and skill levels, the Labor Council's community-based locals divided black from white and new immigrant from old, while most of the skilled butchers entered the department locals. This separation inhibited the kind of socialization which had successfully integrated Slavic immigrants into the movement in the early twentieth century. The structure also accentuated the objective differences in wages and conditions between skilled and unskilled.

The most dramatic example of this fragmentation appeared in the 1919 race riot, which certainly retarded unionization. Yet the racial conflict of the postwar years was rooted as much in community as in work-related problems. Competition between Canaryville and the Black Belt for housing and political power, as well as the violent legacy of black-Irish confrontations in earlier labor disputes, set the stage for the race riot. This tense situation was manipulated by the packers, who maximized their influence in the Black Belt through paternalism and disrupted interracial organization in the plants through victimization of union members.

Paternalism solidified propacker sentiment in the black community, while the agitation of antiunion blacks increased racial tensions in the plants. The Stockyards Labor Council, the CFL leadership, and many rank-and-file activists—black and white—fought the rising tide of racism, but lost.

Finally, government arbitration weakened the butcher workmen's movement in the long run. By focusing all attention on a temporary institution—the arbitration court—the hearings drew energy away from the vital trask of organizing and from the inevitable conflict over recognition. The arbitration agreement outlawed shop-floor organization and enlisted the efforts of union leaders in avoiding strikes and maximizing production. Since the Stockyards Labor Council and the Amalgamated were divided over the question of extending the agreement, the question of arbitration also fueled the bitter factional conflict between the two groups. When the struggle with the packers finally came in the winter of 1921, the butcher workmen's movement was at its weakest, and the packers moved in for the kill.

NOTES

1. Arbitration hearings, June 21, 1919, records of the U.S. Department of Labor, Mediation and Conciliation Service (RMCS), Case 5/66:41, Box 42, 221, Federal Records Center, Suitland, Maryland.

2. Ibid., 346–47.

3. George Soule, *Prosperity Decade: From War to Depression* (New York, 1975), 78; David Brody, *The Butcher Workmen* (Cambridge, Mass., 1964), 77; Rudolf Clemen, *The American Livestock and Meat Industry* (New York, 1923), 473–74; Chicago Commission on Race Relations, *The Negro in Chicago* (Chicago, 1922), 357–58.

4. *Historical Statistics of the United States* (Washington, D.C., 1975), 119.

5. Memorandum, George Haynes to Hugh Kerwin, Mar. 14, 1921, RMCS, RG 280, Case 170/1365, Box 130. For figures on the growth of black and women's employment, see chapter 2.

6. William Tuttle, *Race Riot: Chicago in the Red Summer of 1919* (New York, 1970), 124–25; Alma Herbst, *The Negro in the Slaughtering and Meat Packing Industry of Chicago* (Boston, 1932), 30.

7. Ray Stannard Baker, *The New Industrial Unrest* (Garden City, N.Y., 1920), 112, quoted in Tuttle, 141.

8. William Z. Foster to John Fitzpatrick, June 22, 1918, John Fitzpatrick Papers, Chicago Historical Society.

9. On Fitzpatrick, see John Kieser, "John Fitzpatrick and Progressive Labor" (Ph.D. diss., Northwestern University, 1965); David Brody, "John Fitzpatrick," *Dictionary of American Biography*, supp. 4, ed. John A. Garraty (New York, 1974), 279–80; Gary M. Fink, ed., *Biographical Dictionary of American Labor* (Westport, Conn., 1984), 225–26.

10. Keiser, 11–19; William Z. Foster, *American Trade Unionism* (New York, 1947), 20–21.

11. Brody, *Butcher Workmen*, 69–70, 73–74.

12. "Labor Turnover in Chicago," *Monthly Labor Review* 9 (Sept. 1919): 44–59.

13. William Chenery, "Packingtown Steps Forward," *Survey* 40 (Apr. 13, 1918): 35–36; *Butcher Workman* (hereafter, *BW*) 2 (Oct. 1917): 3; 2 (June 1916): 4; 2 (July 1916): 3; *Naujienos*, Apr. 27, May 11, 18, 1916, Chicago Foreign Language Press Survey, Chicago Historical Society; *Chicago Tribune*, Feb. 27, 1918; Mary McDowell, "In the Stockyards District, 1917," Mary McDowell Papers, Folder 15, Chicago Historical Society.

14. Chicago Federation of Labor minutes, July 15, Aug. 5, Nov. 4, Dec. 2, 1917, Chicago Historical Society; Foster, *American Trade Unionism*, 21–22; *BW* 5 (Nov. 1919). See also *BW* 8 (Apr. 1922).

15. William Z. Foster, *From Bryan to Stalin* (New York, 1936), 90–92.

16. Olive Anderson, "The Women's Part in the Stockyards Organization Work," *Life and Labor* 7 (May 1918): 102–4; Brody, *Butcher Workmen*, 86.

17. Chicago Federation of Labor minutes, Aug. 19, 1917; Chicago Commission on Race Relations, 428–29; Foster, *American Trade Unionism*, 22–23; Tuttle, 143; Herbst, 30–32. Mr. Claude Lightfoot notes in his unpublished autobiography that Local 651 was somewhat integrated. He recalls seeing white workers enter the union hall, which was a few doors down from his family's house, but these men may have been labor officials. (Claude M. Lightfoot, "From Chicago's Ghetto to World Politics: The Life and Struggles of Claude M. Lightfoot," unpublished ms., 1983, in the author's possession, 40.)

18. Brody, *Butcher Workmen*, 78; *Report of the President's Mediation Commission* (Washington, D.C., 1918).

19. Typescript notes of interview with Dennis Lane, president, Amalgamated Meat Cutters and Butcher Workmen of North America, "Americanization Study," David J. Saposs Papers, Box 26, Folder 2, Wisconsin State Historical Society; *BW* 3 (Dec. 1917): 5; 4 (Jan. 1918).

20. Olive Anderson, "Chicago League Organizing Stockyards Women

Workers," *Life and Labor*, Apr. 1918, 84, and "The Women's Part"; Brody, *Butcher Workmen*, 76–77.

21. *BW* 3 (Nov. 1917): 4; 5 (Nov. 1919): 2, 5; Chicago Federation of Labor minutes, July 18, 1904, Nov. 18, 1917; *Dziennik Zwiazkowy*, Nov. 6, 1921, Chicago Foreign Language Press Survey, Chicago Historical Society; Herbst, 30, 45; *Dziennik Narodowy*, Nov. 21, 1917 and Jan. 28, 1918. (My thanks to Joe Hapak for these citations.) I have been unable to locate any copies of Kikulski's paper.

22. Herbst, 29; *National Provisioner* 59 (Oct. 19, 1918): 131.

23. *Chicago Tribune*, Feb. 23, 1918; *BW* 4 (Mar. 1918): 3; Sherman Rogers, "Clearing the Jungle: What Has Been Happening in Packingtown," *Outlook* 136 (Oct. 6, 1920): 230; Brody, *Butcher Workmen*, 77. For a full description of management reform strategies, see chapter 7 of this study.

24. Telegrams, John Fitzpatrick, Dennis Lane, and William Z. Foster to Samuel Gompers, Nov. 29, 1917, and Dennis Lane to John F. Hart, Nov. 28, 29, 1917, files of the office of the president, General Correspondence, *American Federation of Labor Records: The Samuel Gompers Era* (Sanford, N.C., 1979, microfilm), Reel 90; Brody, *Butcher Workmen*, 78; *Dziennik Narodowy*, Nov. 30, 1917.

25. T. P. Reynolds to Samuel Gompers, Dec. 3, 1917, *American Federation of Labor Records*, Reel 90; Brody, *Butcher Workmen*, 79–80; *Report of the President's Mediation Commission*.

26. Soule, 75.

27. Verbatim testimony from managers, workers, and economic experts on the problem of living standards and family budgets is contained in RMCS, RG 280, Case 33/864, Boxes 40 and 41.

28. William Z. Foster, "How Life Has Been Brought into the Stockyards," *Life and Labor* 7 (Apr. 1918): 63–66.

29. Ibid., 69; Foster, *American Trade Unionism*, 28. Walsh's closing argument, published by the Chicago Federation of Labor as a pamphlet in Polish and English, became a bestseller "back of the yards." See Frank Walsh, *Over the Top at the Yards* (Chicago, 1918). A copy is on microfilm at the Chicago Historical Society.

30. Mary McDowell, "Easter Day After the Decision," *Survey* 40 (Apr. 13, 1918): 38.

31. *New Majority*, Nov. 22, 1919, 11; Mary McDowell, "Easter Day," 38.

32. *New Majority*, Dec. 6, 13, 1919; RMCS, RG 280, Case 33/864, Box 46.

33. RMCS, RG 280, Case 33/864, Box 42, arbitration hearing dated June 23, 1919; Brody, *Butcher Workmen*, 80.

34. National War Labor Board Records, RG 2, Docket no. 80, National Archives and Record Service, Washington, D.C.

35. RMCS, RG 280, Case 33/864, Box 46.

36. RMCS, RG 280, Case 33/864, Boxes 42 and 46.

37. The Amalgamated already had strict rules against any official war-time strikes and a complicated grievance process established to avoid unofficial ones. See *Constitution of the Amalgamated Meat Cutters and Butcher Workmen of North America, Revised and Adopted at Fort Wayne, Indiana, July, 1917* (Chicago, 1917), 27–31.

38. RMCS, RG 280, Case 33/864, Box 41.

39. By tabulating the ethnicity of each floor committeeman who testified at the Alschuler hearings, I came up with the following breakdown: Polish—9; black—5; Bohemian—3; German—3; Irish—3; Lithuanian—2; total—25.

40. RMCS, RG 280, Case 33/864, Box 41.

41. Tuttle, chap. 5, 155–56 and passim.

42. *New Majority* 5 (June 14, July 5, July 19, 1919); *BW* 5 (June 1919 and July 1919); Tuttle, 134–39.

43. One of the SLC's formal demands read, "There shall be no discrimination against any employee because of creed, color or nationality" (Sterling Spero and Abram L. Harris, *The Black Worker* [New York, 1931; reprint, New York, 1974], 271).

44. *BW* 3 (Nov. 1917); 5 (July 1919); 6 (Jan. 1918). On the question of grievances, see William Z. Foster's testimony before the Chicago Commission on Race Relations, 428–29. See also William L. Evans to John T. Clark, Oct. 7, 1920, Archives, Pittsburgh Urban League. My thanks to Peter Gottlieb for directing me to this letter.

45. Chicago Commission on Race Relations, 413; *BW* 4 (Oct. 1918); 5 (July 1919); Herbst, 56.

46. Herbst, 42; H. R. Cayton and G. S. Mitchell, *Black Workers and the New Unions* (Chapel Hill, N.C., 1939), 247. For other union efforts to discourage racism among white workers, see *New Majority*, July 5, July 12, 1919; *BW* 4 (Oct. 1918); Mary McDowell, "Easter Day," 38.

47. Quoted in Herbst, 42.

48. *New Majority*, July 5, 1919; Tuttle, 138–39; Spero and Harris, 275.

49. For descriptions of the rioting, see Tuttle, chap. 1; Allen Spear, *Black Chicago: The Making of a Negro Ghetto* (Chicago, 1967), 214–22; Chicago Commission on Race Relations, chap. 1; Carl Sandburg, *The Chicago Race Riots* (New York, 1919; reprint, New York, 1969).

50. Walter A. Fogel, *The Negro in the Meat Industry* (Philadelphia, 1970), 37.

51. Reports, Cook County Board of Election Commissioners, City of Chicago, Municipal Reference Library; David F. Simonson, "The Labor Party of Cook County, Illinois, 1918–1919" (M.A. thesis, University of Chicago, 1959). See also Roger Horowitz, "The Failure of Independent Political Action: The Labor Party of Cook County, 1919–1920" (bachelor's essay, University of Chicago, 1982), esp. pp. 32–33, 40.

52. Fogel, *Negro in the Meat Industry*, 37–38. The best social and economic profile of the Black Belt in this era is Spear, 129–200, but see also Tuttle, chap. 2, and the Chicago Commission on Race Relations, chap. 4.

53. Cayton and Mitchell, 242; U.S. Immigration Commission, *Reports*, part 11, *Immigrants in Industry*, vol. 13, *Slaughtering and Meat Packing* (Washington, D.C., 1911), 213. See also chapter 2 of this study.

54. Brody, *Butcher Workmen*, 85. See also Spero and Harris, 271.

55. *BW* 4 (Oct. 1918); *New Majority*, Mar. 15, Apr. 26, Aug. 2, 1919; George Haynes, *The Negro at Work during the World War and during Reconstruction*, U.S. Department of Labor, Division of Negro Economics (Washington, D.C., 1921), 75; broadside for the Colored Club of the Cook County Labor Party, Graphics Collection, Chicago Historical Society.

56. RMCS, RG 280, Case 33/864, Box 46.

57. Quoted in Spero and Harris, 274.

58. *BW* 5 (July 1919).

59. RMCS, RG 280, Case 33/864, Box 46.

60. Allen Spear, "The Rise of the Urban Ghetto, 1870–1915," in *Key Issues in the Afro-American Experience*, ed. Nathan Huggins, Martin Kilson and Daniel Fox (New York, 1971).

61. Spear, *Black Chicago*, 169–74; Tuttle, 99–100; Arvarh Strickland, *History of the Chicago Urban League* (Urbana, Ill., 1966), 48–49.

62. Ibid., 49.

63. See Haynes, 71, 76.

64. *Chicago Whip*, Oct. 23, 1920, quoted in James R. Grossman, "A Dream Deferred: Black Migration to Chicago, 1916–1921" (Ph.D. diss., University of California, Berkeley, 1982), 208. On friction between the migrants and more urbanized ghetto residents, see Grossman, 203–12.

65. Strickland, 44–45.

66. Tuttle, 99, 148; Chicago Commission on Race Relations, 147; Cayton and Mitchell, 255. For a forthright statement of the league's strikebreaking policy by its Industrial Secretary, see William L. Evans, "The Negro in Chicago Industries," *Opportunity* 1 (Feb. 1923): 15–16. See also Spero and Harris, chap. 7.

67. Strickland, 38, 74; Tuttle, 147–48. See also Grossman, 360.

68. Grossman, 353–62.

69. Ibid., 343–53. See also Herbst, 52.

70. Tuttle, 151.

71. RMCS, RG 280, Case 33/864, Box 42, arbitration hearing dated June 23, 1919.

72. Cayton and Mitchell, 392; George Arthur, "The YMCA Movement among Negroes," *Opportunity* 1 (Mar. 1923): 16; William L. Evans to John T. Clark, Oct. 7, 1920, Archives, Pittsburgh Urban League.

73. Spear, *Black Chicago*, 174; Spero and Harris, 268; Herbst, 52; Brody, *Butcher Workmen*, 85–86; Grossman, 340–42.

74. *New Majority*, Aug. 9, 1919, 1; *Crisis* 18 (Oct. 1919): 294; Spero and Harris, 268; Chicago Commission on Race Relations, 429.

75. RMCS, RG 280, Case 33/864, Box 46, testimony of Jack Johnstone, John Kikulski, Martin Murphy, William Brennan, George Williams, James F. Towle. See also *New Majority*, June 28, 1919, 9.

76. RMCS, RG 280, Case 33/864, Box 42, arbitration hearing dated June 20, 1919, 92.

77. For considerable evidence submitted in support of the unionists' claims, see ibid., 63–375, from which much of the verbatim testimony cited here is drawn.

78. Ibid., 177.

79. For the conflict at Wilson and Company, see the testimony of Robert Sobyro, ibid. (109–48), Robert Bedford (148–92, 220–43), William Bremer (193–220), William Ghee (243–58), Frank Custer (258–99), and Frank Guzior (302–48), and, for similar problems at Hammond and Armour, 8–39 and 54–58.

80. Ibid., 294.

81. On Williams, see the testimony of Robert Bedford, Frank Custer, and Austin "Heavy" Williams, ibid. The quotation is on p. 429.

82. See the testimony of Robert Bedford and Frank Custer, Box 42, and Jack Johnstone and Joseph Hodges, Box 46, ibid.

83. Spero and Harris, 271–73; Chicago Commission on Race Relations, 59–61; Herbst, 35–36.

84. RMCS, RG 280, Case 33/864, Box 46, Johnstone testimony; Herbst, 35–36.

85. Cayton and Mitchell, 241; William Evans to John T. Clark, Oct. 7, 1920, Archives, Pittsburgh Urban League. See also Tuttle, 145–46.

86. Spear, *Black Chicago*, 36–41; Tuttle, 112–24.

87. Spear, *Black Chicago*, 160; Goins quoted in Tuttle, 127. See also *BW* 5 (Oct. 1918): 5.

88. Quoted in St. Clair Drake and Horace R. Cayton, *Black Metropolis*, vol. 1 (New York, 1962), 305.

89. RMCS, RG 280, Case 33/864, Box 42, testimony of Robert Bedford, 221.

90. Florette Henri, *The Great Migration* (Garden City, N.Y., 1977); "Letters of Negro Migrants, 1916–1918," ed. Emmett Scott, *Journal of Negro History* 4 (July 1919): 290–340. See also Grossman, 365–70.

91. Tuttle, 38.

92. Quoted ibid., 151.

93. Spero and Harris, 130, 269; Tuttle, 153.

94. Tuttle, 117–23; Spear, *Black Chicago*, 36–40; Steven Sapolsky, "Class-Conscious Belligerents: The Teamsters and the Class Struggle in Chicago, 1901–1905" (University of Pittsburgh, typescript, 1974); Spero and Harris, 132.

95. Frederick Thrasher, *The Gang*, abridged ed. (Chicago, 1963), 278–79.

96. Quoted in Chicago Commission on Race Relations, 8. See also Sandburg, 4.

97. Thrasher, 279. For an overview of the neighborhood, see Myron Davis, "Canaryville," University of Chicago research paper, 1927, in Chicago Historical Society, "Documents: History of Bridgeport," Document 1a.

98. Thrasher, 139; Chicago Commission on Race Relations, 11–17; Tuttle, 102–3; Davis, 20–21; Langston Hughes, *The Big Sea* (New York, 1963), 33.

99. Sandburg, *Chicago Race Riots*, 2, quoted in Tuttle, 184. On Thompson's machine in the Black Belt, see Harold Gosnell, *Negro Politicians: The Rise of Negro Politics in Chicago* (Chicago, 1967), 37–62. See also John Allswang, *A House for All Peoples: Chicago's Ethnic Groups and Their Politics, 1890–1936* (Lexington, Ky., 1971).

100. Chicago Commission on Race Relations, 53–59; Tuttle, 197–200.

101. Chicago Commission on Race Relations, 15.

102. Drake and Cayton, 307; Spero and Harris, 276; Cayton and Mitchell, 248–49; *New Majority*, Aug. 2, 1919.

103. Drake and Cayton, 307.

104. Mary McDowell, "Prejudice," in Caroline Hill, ed., *Mary McDowell and Municipal Housekeeping* (Chicago, 1938), 32–33. See also Thrasher, 50–51.

105. See the spot map following page 8 in the Chicago Commission on Race Relations, *Negro in Chicago*, which pinpoints the locations of physical attacks.

106. Howard E. Wilson, *Mary McDowell, Neighbor* (Chicago, 1928), 175. The Chicago Commission on Race Relations report described the

same or similar attacks *(Negro in Chicago*, 45) but blamed them on the Aylwards, another Irish-American gang.

107. *Chicago Tribune*, Aug. 3, 1919; Chicago Commission on Race Relations, 20–21, 539–40; Tuttle, 60–61; McDowell, 33; Herbst, 46–47; Dominic Pacyga, "Villages of Packinghouses and Steel Mills: The Polish Worker on Chicago's South Side, 1880–1921" (Ph.D. diss., University of Illinois, Chicago, 1981), 292–301; *Chicago Defender*, Aug. 19, 1919.

108. Haynes, 67, 69. See also Herbst, 49–51.

109. Joseph Parot, "Ethnic versus Black Metropolis: The Origins of Polish-Black Housing Tensions in Chicago," *Polish-American Studies* 29 (1972): 5–33. In his study of five serious race riots which occurred in Chicago between 1947 and 1957, Arnold Hirsch found that the white crowds involved in the attacks were predominantly Irish and eastern or southeastern European. See Arnold Hirsch, "Race and Housing: Violence and Communal Protest in Chicago, 1940–1960" in *The Ethnic Frontier: Essays in the History of Group Survival in Chicago and the Midwest*, ed. Peter D'A. Jones and Melvin Holli (Grand Rapids, Mich., 1977), 350–55.

110. For a similar argument regarding the origins of racism among white steelworkers, see Neil Betten and Raymond Mohl, "The Evolution of Racism in an Industrial City, 1906–1940: A Case Study of Gary, Indiana," *Journal of Negro History* 59 (1974): 51–64.

111. Brody, *Butcher Workmen*, 89.

112. Herbst, 41; Foster, *American Trade Unionism*, 26.

113. *BW* 5 (Aug. 1919).

114. *New Majority*, May 10, 1919, 1, 11.

115. Brody, *Butcher Workmen*, 90. The right-wing analysis of the factionalism which followed is reflected in the January through April issues of *The Unionist*. For a left perspective, see an article by an anonymous packinghouse worker, "Making and Breaking the Packing House Unions," *Labor Herald*, Mar. 1922.

116. Herbst, 43; Chicago Federation of Labor minutes, Oct. 5, Oct. 19, and Nov. 2, 1919, and Jan. 8, 1920; *The Unionist*, Jan. 22, 1920, 1, and Feb. 5, 1920, 1.

117. *BW* 6 (Jan. 1920); 5 (Aug. 1919); Chicago Federation of Labor minutes, Jan. 8, 1920; Herbst, 41.

118. Amalgamated Meat Cutters and Butcher Workmen of North America, *Proceedings, Ninth General Convention, July, 1917* (Chicago, 1917), 114–15, 139, and *Proceedings, Tenth General Convention, July, 1920* (Chicago, 1920), 13; Herbst, 44.

119. Robert K. Murray, *Red Scare: A Study in National Hysteria* (New

York, 1964). As home of the IWW and the birthplace of two separate communist organizations in the summer of 1919, Chicago was a focal point for antiradicalism. See Donald F. Tingley, *The Structuring of a State: The History of Illinois, 1899–1928* (Urbana, Ill., 1980), 217–24.

120. *The Unionist*, June 7, 1919, 1, 3; July 26, 1919, 1; Aug. 2, 1919, 5.

121. Ibid., June 7, 1919, 3, 5; Aug. 28, 1919, 5; May 20, 1919, 1, 2, 7; Jan. 22, 1920, 3. On corruption in the Chicago building trades in this era, see John Hutchinson, *The Imperfect Union: A History of Corruption In American Trade Unions* (New York, 1972), 53–61. On the *Unionist–New Majority* conflict, see also AFL Executive Council minutes, Nov. 13, 1920, 17–18, *American Federation of Labor Records*, Reel 6.

122. *New Majority*, Feb. 21, 1920, 12; *The Unionist*, Feb. 19, 1920, 1.

123. *New Majority*, Feb. 28, 1920, 8.

124. Chicago Federation of Labor minutes, Apr. 18, 1920, May 2, 1920; *New Majority*, Apr. 24, 1920, 13; May 8, 1920, 13; May 22, 1920, 13.

125. *The Unionist*, Apr. 22, 1920, 1; *Chicago Tribune*, May 18, 1920; Foster, *American Trade Unionism*, 30–31; Chicago Federation of Labor minutes, May 2 and 16, 1920.

126. Brody, *Butcher Workmen*, 91. The AFL supported the Amalgamated during the conflict. See AFL Executive Council minutes, Oct. 19, 1919, 54–55; Dec. 15, 1919, 5, 50; Feb. 27, 1920, 28, *American Federation of Labor Records*, Reel 6.

127. Herbst, 63; Brody, *Butcher Workmen*, 95.

7

The Packers' Offensive, 1921–22

World Events of the past few years demonstrated as never
before that co-operation is one of the greatest factors in achieving
anything worthwhile. The meat packing industry has reached the
point where there must be greater co-operation between employers
and employees.

J. Ogden Armour,
March 17, 1921[1]

The patrolmen have been instructed not to shoot unless
necessary. They have been advised to use their clubs and fists
freely. However, they have also been told that if the occasion
should arise for shooting, they must shoot quickly and accurately.
That policy has had excellent results already.

Captain Russell, Stockyards Police,
December 8, 1921[2]

Frederick Winslow Taylor and other proponents of the reform
movement we now associate with the term "scientific management" argued for their views with the enthusiasm common to all
visionaries. And in the early years of this century, Taylor and
other management reformers won a small following among American employers, notably in the metal trades. Hoping to neutralize
unions in their shops and, of course, to increase productivity,
these businessmen welcomed a new breed of professional managers. Welfare specialists designed schemes to improve the quality

of the work environment as well as the public image of their corporations. Personnel experts studied labor relations to pinpoint problem areas and reduce labor turnover. Production engineers studied the work process itself, and many firms adopted new incentive pay systems.[3]

Until the World War I years, however, scientific management was largely a failure. Instead of bringing labor peace into shops where they were introduced, the reforms frequently precipitated conflict. Most employers, like the packers, simply ignored the ideas. Yet by the early 1920s, all of the major packers and corporations in most sectors of the economy had not only introduced many of these reforms but had gone beyond them to implement elaborate employee representation systems.[4] What accounts for this rapid transformation of management theory and practice?

The packers' neglect of scientific management principles was rooted in the favorable employment conditions they enjoyed, along with other employers of unskilled labor, throughout most of the early twentieth century. The 1904 strike had brought a flurry of piecemeal reforms in its wake but nothing like a comprehensive personnel policy.[5] The normal situation in packing— thousands of workers searching for jobs and little or no trade union organization—meant that the packers had little interest in new ideas. Having created a huge pool of common labor and crushed the Amalgamated, they had little need or desire to experiment.

Like many other employers in manufacturing industries, the packers discovered a new interest in management reforms during World War I. Their sudden burst of interest sprang from the labor problems they faced during and immediately after the war. The labor shortage, the Stockyards Labor Council's aggressive recruiting, and the reemergence of shop-floor organization all pressed the packers to devote more attention to winning and holding their employees' loyalty, if only to regain the upper hand. In this sense, workers' organization helped to reshape management psychology and to produce the first major wave of personnel management reforms in the industry's history.[6]

But the new strategy turned on more than a benevolent image. Management practice had indeed changed, but its opposition to labor unions had not. If the new welfare and incentive systems represented one side of the so-called American Plan, the other was a ruthless suppression of all independent labor organization.

The war years had presented the packers with a dilemma: tremendous increases in demand offered the opportunity for unusually large profits, but the labor shortage and trade union organization brought threats to management control. In the case of packing, government arbitration offered a temporary solution, but the early 1920s brought a constriction in the market for meat products and a sharp decline in prices. If wages were to be reduced, it was imperative to rid the industry of unions and to supplement them with a more tractable form of employee representation. The new departure in management psychology signaled by the advent of the American Plan throughout industry combined sophisticated welfare policies and company unions with a firm decision to destroy trade union organization.

THE ECONOMIC CRISIS

Rather than collapsing under the weight of rapid deflation and the speedy return of four million men to the labor force, the American economy boomed in the first year after the war. Prices continued to rise in 1919, though at a somewhat slower pace than during the war, and investment remained steady. Both prices and investment began to fall the following year, however, and by 1921 the country had entered a serious depression which threw hundreds of thousands of men and women out of work.[7]

A short-term decline in meat consumption as well as prices aggravated conditions in packing. Prices fell hard in the course of 1920 and reached 1917 levels by the following year. Employment also declined precipitously to prewar levels. The number of packinghouse workers in Chicago fell from forty-five thousand in 1919 to twenty-seven thousand in 1921, a decline of 40 percent. Now many Packingtown families reentered the familiar world of unemployment and poverty. For those working, however, wages remained at the highest level in the history of the industry— fifty-three cents per hour for common labor. These high wage levels were largely the result of the upward pressure exerted by labor organization and government arbitration. Industry analysts claimed that by the end of 1920, profits had fallen to a 1.5 percent return on investment. One large packer reported losses of thirty million dollars by the end of the following year, while another claimed eight million. The main problem, the packers argued, was high wages. The *National Provisioner* spoke for the industry in the summer of 1921: "The element of wages is one of the big factors, if not the biggest, that will have to be taken into consideration in any solution of the operating cost problem."[8]

So long as government arbitration served their purposes, the big packers saw little need to develop special strategies to pacify their workers. Arbitration undercut any large-scale strike action and gave the packers time to consolidate their strength. With the financial pressure generated by falling prices in the course of 1920, however, arbitration became an obstacle to cutting costs. Judge Alschuler rejected the packers' November 1920 demand for a return to the ten-hour day, and packinghouse labor costs remained steady while those in many other industries declined. In February 1921 the Big Five repudiated their agreement with the Mediation Commission and the following month announced an eight-cent-per-hour wage cut and reintroduction of the ten-hour day.[9]

Despite strong rank-and-file pressure for a strike, the Amalgamated's leadership appealed once again to the government to mediate a settlement. A strike authorization vote and the pledge of support from ten craft unions with jurisdiction in the yards strengthened Secretary Lane's bargaining position. Government officials worked out a compromise: the unions would accept the wage cut in exchange for maintenance of the eight-hour day and an extension of the arbitration agreement for six more months. Once again the union postponed the inevitable conflict over recognition. Judge Alschuler's rejection of a request for a further wage reduction in July 1921 only strengthened the packers' resolve to gain a free hand in dealing with the industry's financial problems. Both sides prepared for a confrontation when the Alschuler administration closed up shop in September.[10]

THE WELFARE STRATEGY AND EMPLOYEE REPRESENTATION

The experience of the wartime labor shortage and union organization, followed immediately by this postwar depression, en-aged a fundamental reform of packinghouse labor policies. Most of the major packers had established their own industrial relations departments by 1917 to direct welfare work and develop more systematic personnel management policies. In 1920 the Institute of American Meat Packers, the industry's national trade association, set up its own standing Committee on Industrial Relations, which coordinated the activities of industrial relations departments in each of the firms and commissioned an extensive study of "labor waste" in the industry. The committee also served as a forum for professional personnel managers who advocated a more "scientific" approach to the industry's labor problems.[11]

By far the most innovative of the large packers, Swift took the lead and designed an industrial relations department characteristic in strategy and structure of those eventually adopted by most of the Big Five. The department was divided into five divisions: Employment, Medical, Training, Working Conditions, and Social Service. The Employment Division developed standard job descriptions, maintained a "demand list" of positions open in the plant, and coordinated hiring, placement, advancement, and dismissal in an effort to "find the right man for the right job." This division also analyzed labor turnover figures to pinpoint problem areas in the firm's policies and to stabilize the work force.

The Medical Division presided over an expanded health and safety program, while the Training Division concentrated on instructing plant management in more modern techniques. John Calder, Swift's personnel mastermind, developed an elaborate foreman training program. By the fall of 1920, 3,200 Swift supervisors and foremen had completed a sixteen-week course and 1,400 more were just beginning.[12]

The Working Conditions Division had only limited prerogatives during the period of government arbitration, but greatly expanded its activities following the development of an employee representation plan. This division was primarily responsible for improving the quality of the work environment.

The broadest range of activities was reserved for the Social Service Division, which was responsible for housing and community activities, the Stockyards Community Clearing House, social surveys, the pension program, Americanization, and recreation. It was this division which established the Stock Yards Day Nursery on Ashland Avenue near the entrance to the yards, where sixty children of working mothers were cared for daily. Swift's Premiums, 1920 champions of the Colored YMCA Baseball League, were supported with Social Service funds, as were the Swift Efficiency Club at the Wabash Avenue YMCA and the Efficiency Club Singers. For immigrant workers, the Social Service Division offered free Americanization classes at noontime in various departments throughout the plant. By May 1922 nearly five hundred workers had been taught by volunteers from the United Americans. This patriotic group considered Swift's to be the most successful of the fifty plant programs in which it conducted classes. [13]

The struggle between the packers and the union for the loyalty of the butcher workmen and -women was fundamentally ideological. The packers sought to prove not only that harmonious relations were possible but that, indeed, workers' interests were tied to those of their employers. To accomplish this end, the packers marshaled a whole range of programs aimed at shaping the consciousness of their employees.

There were, of course, economic strategies. One way in which a worker might come to identify more closely with his employer was through stock ownership. Introduced by Swift at the turn of the century, such plans were adopted by most of the major packers by the early twenties. By 1909 Swift already had two thousand employee shareholders, though most of these were white-collar and salaried employees. In 1909 the firm announced a new stock option plan specifically designed to attract production workers, particularly the more skilled and stable portion of the work force. Employees could buy shares with a 10 percent cash down payment and were given two years in which to pay the balance. Five percent interest was due on this, but the employee shareholder received quarterly dividends while paying on it. While the option price was considerably lower than the market price, the amount of stock each employee could subscribe for varied with his or her weekly wage. The plan also required a worker to be employed with the firm continuously for at least six months in order to take part. These rules made it impossible for some common laborers to

own stock even if they thought they could pay for it. Yet a substantial number of workers did become "part-owners" of Swift
and Company. Louis Swift announced at the corporation's annual
meeting in 1921 that, counting those still paying for shares under
the stock option, half of the firm's forty thousand shareholders were employees, meaning that one-third of Swift's sixty-
thousand workers owned stock. The *National Provisioner* explained how the plan not only encouraged thrift and planning but
also helped to stabilize industrial relations. "A union man is not so
quick to strike," the journal observed, "when he owns stock in
the company against which he is striking."[14]

The other packers followed Swift's lead. Morris and Company
established a profit-sharing plan just after the war, which set aside
5 percent of the company's net earnings for distribution to employees. Workers subscribed a portion of their paychecks and received profit-sharing certificates in return. A quarter of a million
dollars was dispensed in the course of 1919. "It is a combination
of thrift and the wages system," the *National Provisioner* explained, "designed to give the workers a 'stake' in the business
and to establish closer human contact between the working force
and the company." Armour followed with a stock option plan in
1923 and Wilson fell in line the following year.[15]

In addition to these financial strategies, the packers tried to socialize workers with a barrage of propaganda booklets, leaflets,
talks, classes, and plant newspapers. Both Swift and Armour put
out pamphlets explaining their employee representation systems
and urging workers to participate. Swift set up a social training
program for its representatives. In the fall of 1921, Armour
distributed to each of its employees a special leaflet, printed in
five languages, complete with simple graphs and statistics, to
demonstrate that a wage cut was essential if the firm was to survive and workers were to save their jobs. Executives and personnel managers addressed employees on company time to explain
policies and argue for closer cooperation between workers and
bosses.[16]

Americanization programs proliferated in the plants. The spectacle at Wilson and Company on Flag Day in 1920 is suggestive of
activities elsewhere. The drive for "100 percent Americanism"
was launched with a brass band, a big parade, and patriotic songs.

Thousands of loyalty leaflets were distributed. (The scene was fraught with irony, however. Disappointed organizers noted that few of the immigrants joined in the songs—presumably because they did not know the words—and many of the leaflets went unread, since they were printed in English.) Americanization and citizenship classes emphasized not only the importance of naturalization, participation in the electoral process, and separation of church and state, but also the central position of private property in the American system and the threat to it posed by Bolshevism. Professional "Americanizers" employed the "same methods as the Reds" but to combat radicalism.[17]

By far the most ambitious propaganda projects were the plant newspapers that most large packers established during 1921 in the same period when they introduced employee representation systems. What did such papers actually contain? Much of the *Swift Arrow* during the early twenties was taken up with announcements of births, deaths, marriages, anniversaries, retirements, and vacations. The paper also publicized the firm's various welfare programs, so many columns were filled with baseball and bowling scores, the dates and times of club meetings and classes, company union election results, and announcements of employee awards for continuous service and efficiency.[18]

But the company newspaper had a far more important function than simply presenting news and information. It was designed to carry the packers' message to their employees, to argue for a community of interest between labor and capital, and to extol the virtues of the American economic system. "This is the first edition of YOUR NEWSPAPER," the *Swift Arrow* declared as if to convince itself as well as its readers. "It is YOUR PAPER in every respect. . . ."[19] The claim begins to sound hollow, however, as one looks beyond the papers' mundane news and announcements to analyze their more substantive articles. These clearly suggest that such papers were the voices not of the industry's workers but of its management.

Swift put its message across in a number of ways. A serialized novel told the story of a Russian immigrant who, rejecting the Bolshevism of his fellows, made good through a life of hard work. The story of a Swift executive who had worked his way up from the bottom ran alongside the news that a black machine operator had set a new production record for sewing bags in the company's glue plant. The moral, apparently, was that the journey from glue factory to boardroom was only a matter of time and hard work. Throughout the early twenties, in the midst of the industry's financial crisis, the *Arrow* ran a fascinating popular economics series designed to introduce workers to the problems faced by management. The series, entitled "The Truth about Swift and Company," happened to appear for the first time on the occasion of the company's November 1921 wage cut. Later articles were entitled "Business Trend Must Affect All: Workers and Management Have Common Interests in Prosperity and Depression" and "Role of Manager Vital: Russia Learns Mistake of Trying to Run Enterprise Without Leadership." A March 1922 article was illustrated with a representation of Swift's financial statement in Polish and Lithuanian as well as English. Several articles were devoted to the theme of work as the basis of civilization and progress. [20] The packers had long tried to counter calls for government regulation with advertising campaigns aimed at consumers. Now they felt the need to sell their employees on their management and on the whole system of American enterprise. While the most dramatic engagements of the packers' offensive were fought in the streets of Packingtown during the winter of 1921–22, this ideological dimension of their conflict with unionism was no less significant.

The cornerstone of the packers' drive against the unions was employee representation, or company unionism. While welfare work was designed to minimize workers' grievances and increase their identification with the firm, company unions provided a nominally representative structure which could compete directly with the union for workers' loyalties. Ideally, these company unions would provide an aura of industrial democracy, a feeling among workers that they could exert some influence over company policy or at least be consulted in its formulation.

The idea of company unionism was not a product of the twenties. International Harvester, John D. Rockefeller's Colorado Fuel and Iron Company, and a few other large firms had introduced company unions before World War I. During the war, the War Labor Board ordered 125 employers to set up representative shop committees, and some corporations retained these committees after the conflict. The President's Industrial Conference Board strongly supported employee representation in its October 1919 report, and by the end of that year 145 companies had set up programs covering 403,765 workers. The concept really took hold, however, in the following three years, so that by 1922 almost 700,000 workers in 385 companies were covered by employee representation systems. The greatest growth came among the country's largest employers. Of the 1,400,000 workers in company unions by 1927, 850,000 worked for firms employing 15,000 or more workers.[21]

In packing too the roots of company unionism lie in the wartime labor situation. In 1917, Wilson and Company set up "progress committees" in its Chicago plant, composed of equal numbers of management representatives and production workers. This committee system was extended to all of the company's plants the following year. Progress committees only handled those problems not included under the jurisdiction of the government arbitrator, but with the end of arbitration in the fall of 1921 they were reconstituted as Joint Representative Committees and mandated to consider all matters involving the welfare of Wilson employees. In 1918 Swift began experimenting with representation systems at its Jersey City, Toronto, and Winnipeg plants, which were not covered under the government mediation agreement.[22]

The real emergence of company unionism in packing, however, came only with the decline of the government arbitration plan. The packers used the period between February 1921, when they signed their last arbitration agreement, and the following September, when the government withdrew completely, to set up structures parallel to the unions. These employee representation systems would fill the vacuum left when the packers destroyed labor organization in the industry. The final arbitration agreement was signed in February, and the first of the company-wide plans appeared at Armour within a few weeks. Over the next several months, plans were introduced and refined at all the other major firms with the exception of the ailing Morris and Company.[23]

On the surface at least, the plans appeared to be little models of democracy. While the packers gave them different names, their general characteristics were similar. Most consisted of a national body with jurisdiction over the entire system (at Armour, the General Conference Board) and subordinate bodies based at the plant (Plant Conference Boards) and department (Divisional Committees) levels, all of which consisted of equal numbers of salaried and wage representatives. While the salaried delegates were appointed by management, those representing the employees were elected. Any person exercising managerial authority—foremen and timekeepers, for example—could not run for office. Representatives were elected for one-year terms and could be recalled. Any worker had the right to bring a problem before the Divisional Committee or Plant Conference Board by submitting the case to a supervisor, either directly or through his or her representative. It was the supervisor's responsibility to bring the case to the attention of the department superintendent. The case might be settled at this stage or referred to either the Divisional Committee or Conference Board. In case of a tie, the matter was referred to the general superintendent, who alone had the power to convene the company's General Conference Board. If this body became deadlocked, the matter was referred to arbitration by a mutually acceptable third party, though this seems rarely to have happened.[24]

Yet the plans were much less democratic in practice than they at first appear to be. How representative were the representatives, for example? In her study of industrial relations in packing Edna Clark found that representatives tended to be drawn from among the most loyal production workers. Those elected at Armour were particularly unpopular because of their reputation as "company men." While the qualifications for nomination appear minimal, they were fairly restrictive within the context of the packinghouse labor force. In effect, they excluded large numbers of workers. To run for office one had to be a wage worker, a citizen of the United States, at least twenty-one years of age, and an employee of the company continuously for six months to a year before the election. The prospective candidate had also to speak, read, and write English. The combined effect of seasonal layoffs, the citizenship provision, and the literacy requirements excluded many immigrant workers from participation. And it is clear that the union had its strongest base among the very group most unlikely to be nominated—the recent immigrants.[25]

Employee representatives at the various plants were remarkably similar in terms of personal characteristics. At Swift's Chicago plant, the average age was a bit over thirty-seven, at Armour's Chicago plant, forty-one and a half, and at Cudahy's four plants nationwide, forty-three. Average length of service for these same three groups ranged from seven and a half years at Swift to eleven years at Cudahy. In spite of the large proportion of eastern Europeans in the industry's labor force in these years, few Slavic names show up in the lists of employee representatives. Of the twenty-four men (no women) elected as representatives to the first committee which set up the system at Armour, fifteen were born in the United States. (See appendix B.) Of the nine foreign-born, two came from Canada, two from Ireland, and three from Germany. One was an American born in Mexico. Of the three representatives with Slavic names, only one was foreign-born, a Russian Pole who was a laborer in the butterine department. The preponderance of native-born representatives in an industry staffed largely by immigrants can be explained in part by the plan's restrictions, but the virtual absence of Polish and Lithuanian immigrants might also reflect the strength of union loyalty among these groups. Of the twenty-four representatives, eighteen were at least forty years old. Fourteen had worked for Armour a minimum of ten years, and eight of the men in the group were thirty-year veterans. In an industry characterized by high turnover and including large numbers of recent immigrants and migrant blacks, these workers clearly represented only the most stable element in the labor force. They were hardly representative of the typical packinghouse workers.[26]

Participation in and support for company unions is difficult to gauge. The packers claimed that 80 to 90 percent of those eligible to vote in the initial elections in May and June 1921 did so and that the general reaction was one of enthusiastic support. The unions insisted that participation was much lower. The whole idea of company unionism, they argued, violated the spirit of the government arbitration agreement. Clearly, some of those workers who did participate in the elections did so under duress. Voting was often done under the watchful eye of the timekeeper, who recorded the check numbers of those who refused to vote. In some cases balloting was personally supervised by foremen, policemen, and assistant general managers. Some workers still refused to take part. In one cattle-killing department, only two skilled butchers and twenty-one laborers (less than half of the gang) voted. The union claimed that the superintendent cursed the men, saying, "Someone here is going to get fired."[27]

Yet some workers did support the plans, so these organizations must have served some purpose. What were the functions of the company union so far as workers in the plants were concerned? To the select few who became representatives, the company union offered an avenue of upward mobility, a ladder that might carry one off the bench and into, if not the boardroom, perhaps at least a foreman's position. While there are no data available on the advancement of employee representatives, the packers clearly saw the plans as a source for the recruitment of lower-level management. Such recruitment was in the packers' interests not only because it provided a psychological bridge between the role of production worker and that of foreman, but also because it stimulated participation in the plans by enhancing the position of the representative in the eyes of other workers. There were also more immediate benefits. Regular meetings, occasional trips to other plants, and emergencies offered the "company man" respites from his labor on the killing floor or in the freezer. The representatives also wielded a measure of real power over their fellow workers. They were in a position to "put in a good word" for those who curried their favor and to even scores with those who crossed them. An extreme example of this is the authority given to the Armour Conference Board following the 1921–22 strike to decide which strikers should be rehired and which black-listed. Company unions in other industries did the same kind of work for their employers, and this underscores the influence which representatives could exercise over the fates of their fellow workers. While such influence undoubtedly earned them the undying hatred of some, it probably won them the envious support of others.[28]

What did the company union offer the average worker who was not a representative? An analysis of cases submitted for consideration by plant assemblies gives some clues. Data for cases filed at the Swift and Armour plants in Chicago in the period immediately following the introduction of the plans suggest that some workers saw the company union as a viable means of settling their grievances and improving their work environment. Workers used the grievance procedure in both plants. One hundred and forty-nine matters were handled by the Armour Conference Board in its first four months of existence, while the Swift representatives settled a total of 865 cases in approximately two years. Swift claimed to have settled 1,800 cases by 1925. The data also suggest that workers gained some satisfaction from the system. According to the companies' tabulations, 56 percent of the cases were settled in the employee's favor at Armour, 68 percent at Swift.[29]

It is important, however, to consider the *types* of cases handled by company unions within the context of power relations in the plants. Most of the cases can be broken down into two broad categories: the innocuous ones which lent themselves to fairly simple and inexpensive solutions and which were often not really grievances at all; and conflict cases, those which clearly pitted worker against management over an issue of importance to both parties. Examples of the first sort of case are requests or suggestions concerning safety, recreation, and food service, questions about pensions, and problems with workmen's compensation. Examples of the more provocative cases are disputes with foremen, protests regarding work rules, problems regarding lateness and absenteeism, and claims for adjustments in hours and wages. In both firms, well over one-third of the cases may be classified as innocuous. At Swift, more than 300 of the 865 cases involved employee accommodations or health and comfort. Almost 400, however, involved disputes over wages, hours, or management policy and practice. Without exact figures on how many of the more important cases each side won, it is impossible to say whether workers exercised any influence at all over fundamental aspects of their work situations. It may be that employees won most of those cases involving health and safety and lost most of those involving hours, wages, and discipline.[30]

One firm conclusion that can be drawn from an analysis of the programs is that the balance of power was tipped decisively in the packers' favor. Aside from the more or less subtle influences affecting the psychology of workers making decisions in the presence of their bosses, there were structural characteristics of the systems which assured management control. Management and employees voted separately but as units. A majority in both units made the vote unanimous. In case of a tie between the units at the department or plant level, the general superintendent decided whether or not the case should be referred to the General Conference Board. While employee representatives were elected and might represent a spectrum of worker views, management representatives were appointed and were certainly expected to vote according to company policy. Management also chaired meetings of the various representative bodies.[31]

Hence, while company unions did provide workers with a way to affect their working conditions, management continued to control the most fundamental aspects of production. In packing, as in the economy in general, company unionism conveyed an image of industrial democracy but "sustained a system that granted management full authority over the terms of employment."[32]

PACKER PATERNALISM IN THE BLACK COMMUNITY

The packers also tailored their welfare programs to conditions among black workers in their efforts to retain blacks' loyalty in the event of a strike. The Efficiency Clubs were particularly effective tools for influencing black migrants, many of whom found themselves in a strange, hostile environment, searching for recreation and sociability. The clubs served as the basis for choral groups, picnic outings, Liberty Loan campaigns, and sports programs. Many black workers organized their social lives around them. The Wabash Avenue YMCA's Industrial Baseball League included eight teams of black packinghouse workers, who played before twelve thousand spectators in 1918. There can be little question but that the clubs, which advocated efficient work and employee loyalty, had an influence in the community. Attendance at their regular meetings during the first nine months of 1920 alone was over five thousand.[33]

Far more important than such cultural influence, however, was the direct economic control which the packers wielded in the Black Belt. By the end of the war, one-half of all black industrial workers earned their livelihoods at Union Stockyards. The role of packinghouse wages became especially critical in the face of heavy unemployment during the 1921–22 depression, when perhaps as many as twenty thousand black workers were unemployed. Packinghouse employment represented a good job at a time when any kind of job was hard to find.[34]

It is true that as a confrontation with the packers approached black trade unionists once again rallied to the cause. Six hundred attended a mass meeting called by the Amalgamated at Unity Hall, in the heart of the Black Belt, and established an organizing committee which included representatives from the Brotherhood of Sleeping Car Porters, the Hotel and Restaurant Employees, and the Musicians, as well as the Butcher Workmen.[35]

But such groups represented only a small minority in the community. The union found few supporters among the "respectable elements" in the Black Belt. Most middle-class and professional blacks urged workers to remain loyal to the packers. Ministers preached about the dangers of unionism and the benevolence of the employers. Reverend Charles Dixon, a black minister himself, claimed that preachers and editors cleared their sermons and editorials with the Wabash Avenue YMCA, which also served as a conduit for packer subsidies. On the Sunday before the strike started fifteen black unionists visited the fifteen largest churches in the Black Belt and found that in all but one the minister read a letter from the packers urging workers to disregard the strike call. The following Thursday a union organizer went to the home of each of the fifteen ministers in the hopes of presenting the union's side of the story, but he found none of them home. Finally, a housekeeper explained that all of the ministers had been called to an urgent meeting with representatives of the packers at the offices of Armour and Company.[36]

In the end, the combined burden of black middle-class opposition, employer paternalism, high unemployment, and the legacy of the race riot proved too much. The Amalgamated's efforts and those of its allies in the black community had little lasting effect. Just before the strike Local 651's membership stood at just over one hundred. The butcher workmen and -women faced the prospect of a long, bitter strike with their ranks divided on the issue of race.[37]

THE 1921–22 STRIKE

As the economy contracted in the course of 1921, placing pressure on employers to cut costs and driving national unemployment up

to over 20 percent, the wartime labor upsurge of which the packinghouse workers' movement was a part collapsed. Now management assumed the offensive. Nineteen twenty-two was a year of
wage cuts and the extension of employee representation plans,
but it was also a year of strikes and lockouts. The number of
striking and locked-out workers, which had declined since 1919,
rose sharply in 1922 to 8.3 percent of the industrial work force. A
total of 1,613,000 workers struck to preserve their organizations
against employer attacks. Many strikes which were nominally over
the issue of wages were, in effect, life and death battles for the
unions involved. More often than not, such battles were lost. So
it was with the strike of 45,000 workers in thirteen packing
centers across the country. The strike started at the end of 1921
and dragged on through February of the new year.[38]

The packers' version of the American Plan, like those in many
other industries, employed a stick along with the carrot of welfar-
ism. With their reorganized industrial relations departments and
employee representation plans in place, the packers turned on the
unions. The Amalgamated held a national packinghouse conference in mid-August and developed a set of demands calling for
maintenance of the wages and conditions in effect and arbitration
of any disagreements, demands that were minimal and in keeping
with the Amalgamated's reliance on arbitration. The union submitted them in early September to the packers, who simply ignored them. When the long-awaited wage cut finally came in November, it was as much a declaration of war on the union as a
financial expedient. Rather than simply announce the cuts, most
large packers presented them to their company unions. After being subjected to an intensive media campaign designed to demonstrate the industry's dire financial straits, employee representatives dutifully approved the cuts on November 17. (Their
response was typical of employee representatives at the time. A
1922 National Industrial Conference Board study noted only two
cases out of more than three hundred studied in which representatives had rejected pay cuts during the 1921–22 recession.) The
National Provisioner was ecstatic over the "mutual confidence"
which had been displayed by the conference boards. "The remarkable feature of this wage cut," the journal noted, "was [that]
it was made by the employees themselves through their own or-

ganizations." This enthusiasm was echoed in the pages of the company newspapers. This was a system which conveyed the impression that the employees themselves, after due consideration of the facts, had democratically voted themselves a substantial pay cut. Here indeed was a major breakthrough in the development of personnel management![39]

The precise formulation of the cut was sharply regressive, with those who could least afford it being hit with the largest cuts. The common labor rate was reduced more than 15 percent, from forty-five cents to thirty-seven and a half cents per hour. Semi-skilled workers, those earnings between forty-five and fifty cents, lost a nickel, while the tiny minority of valuable skilled workers who earned fifty cents per hour or more lost only three cents from their hourly rate.[40] Aside from occasional remarks about the weakness of organization among the skilled workers during the strike, there is little evidence regarding the effect which this regressive wage cut had on worker relations. But it could have done little to heal the breach between skilled and unskilled which had opened since the end of the war.

The wage cut left union leaders little option but to fight. The packers had rejected their final appeal for arbitration. Faced with a weakened union, the employers preferred to settle the matter of labor organization once and for all. The wage cuts went into effect on November 28, and the Amalgamated called a national packinghouse strike to begin December 5.

It is difficult to imagine a labor conflict more unequal than the 1921 packinghouse strike. On one side stood the packers, united by an economic crisis, their influence in the plants and in the community consolidated as a result of their welfare activities and employee representation plans. On the other side stood the butcher workmen and -women, deeply divided along racial, ethnic, and skill lines, their organization wracked by factional conflicts and virtually bankrupt. Following its triumph over the Stockyards Labor Council, the Amalgamated itself was plagued by disputes among its officers and by regional breakaways.[41] As in 1904, the packers chose the timing of the strike so that economic conditions favored them. High unemployment allowed them to draw on a large casual labor pool and minimized the resources upon which the working-class community depended. In this context, it is not difficult to understand the strike's failure. One is more impressed by the devotion of those who answered the call and by the community's persistent support of the strike. Packingtown rose once again in rebellion against the Meat Trust.

As in 1904, Packingtown's ethnic communities closed ranks in support of the strike, especially Polonia, which contributed the greatest number of strikers and so had the most at stake in the conflict. Funds rolled in from parish welfare societies in Packingtown and throughout the city as well as from both major Polish fraternal groups, the clerical Polish Roman Catholic Union and the Polish National Alliance. Other religious, fraternal, and athletic organizations in various Polish neighborhoods also helped. Father Louis Grudzinski, pastor of Packingtown's largest Polish parish, was outspoken in support of the strike, as were several of the community's Polish bankers and other businesspeople. The Businessmen's Association of the Town of Lake contributed nearly one thousand dollars in cash and food. White Eagle Dairy Company gave away fifty quarts of milk each day during the month of January, and a Lithuanian bakery provided hundreds of loaves of bread. Polish newspapers reflecting various political viewpoints followed strike activity sympathetically.[42]

The situation was far different over in the Black Belt. Having carefully cultivated their image and connections and increased their economic influence there during and immediately after the war, the packers relied heavily on the loyalty of black workers and community leaders to make it through the strike. Blacks represented a much more important source of strikebreakers in the 1921–22 strike than they had in 1904. As soon as the union's call went out, Morris and Company opened an employment office in the heart of the Black Belt. Other firms sent out recruiters to railroad stations, elevated platforms, and throughout the community, collecting workers from poolrooms and street corners. The companies provided free truck rides to the Union Stockyards.[43]

The success of the packers' efforts is reflected in the employment statistics for the period during and immediately after the strike. Black employment at the yards rose in the months following the race riot, fell sharply between 1920 and 1921 with the onset of the postwar depression, and then rose to a new high point of one-third of the total labor force in 1922 at the time of the strike. Payroll records for one large Chicago packer show a dramatic rise in the proportion of black employees from about one-fourth to more than a third of the total labor force in January 1922, the first full month of the strike. This proportion fell somewhat during the following month but remained high throughout the early 1920s, when black workers enjoyed a reputation for loyalty to the packers. Seasonal layoffs and depression conditions during 1921 and 1922 had allowed the packers to reconstitute their labor force once again, this time replacing many immigrant unionists with nonunion blacks. Workers and union officials complained bitterly of this victimization, particularly of Polish unionists, as early as the summer of 1919. Such tactics not only ensured the packers an adequate labor supply during the strike but also reinforced racial divisions among the workers.[44]

The state intervened much more extensively and more decisively on the side of the packers than it had during the 1904 strike. Early in the strike Judge Dennis Sullivan handed down a sweeping injunction, basing his decision on a recent Supreme Court ruling which had dramatically expanded the enjoining powers of local authorities in labor disputes. "I have come to the conclusion," Sullivan ruled, "that there are no absolute rights in society today. All rights are relative. . . . As I understand the law in Illinois, there is no such thing as 'peaceful picketing.' "[45] In effect, all picketing was outlawed.

Two thousand policemen, many of them mounted on horseback and motorcycle and heavily armed, invaded Packingtown to enforce the judge's order. The force which they directed against the crowds of strikers and their sympathizers considerably escalated the level of violence in the strike. Captain Russell of the Stockyards Police Station explained the orders under which his men were to act. "The patrolmen have been instructed not to shoot unless necessary. They have been advised to use their clubs and fists freely. However, they have also been told that if the occasion should arise for shooting, they must shoot quickly and accurately. That policy has had excellent results already."[46]

Packingtown was engulfed in bloody riots during the first several days of the strike. On the afternoon of December 7, crowds gathered at Forty-fourth Street and several other spots along Ashland Avenue across from the packing plants, gathering rocks and shouting at the mounted police. When the rocks began to fly, the police opened fire, killing one striker and wounding nine others. Mounted policemen rode their horses and motorcycles directly into the crowds and up the steps of wooden tenements. Running battles raged throughout the community. "The entire locality from 51st Street to 31st Street and from Wood to Halsted Streets was filled with strikers and riots," a Polish newspaper reported. Police estimated that fifteen thousand men, women, and children took part in the violence.[47]

Rioting continued the following day. This time much of the action was concentrated in the Polish and Lithuanian neighborhood just west of the yards. Showers of rocks and bottles hit police during a four-hour battle in the vicinity of Davis Park, just across from the Armour plant. Housewives threw bottles and scalding water down on the police. Snipers fired from the rooftops and windows of tenements, and the patrolmen returned the fire. Police fired at least fifty shots into a frame house at the corner of Fifty-fifth Street and Ashland Avenue. Forty people were injured when a crowd scaled an elevated track and pelted a train with bricks. Newspaper accounts of the number killed in the rioting conflict. Dennis Lane of the Amalgamated claimed that police had killed three or four and had beaten or shot hundreds of strikers. It is clear that by the time the strike ended at least one person was dead, and dozens were seriously injured.[48]

One reason for the high level of violence was clearly the aggressive posture the police assumed, but the large number of strikebreakers who lived in and around Packingtown was also a contributing factor. Rather than the small skirmishes with isolated strikebreakers which had characterized the 1904 strike, there were now large-scale confrontations involving strikers, scabs, and police. The packers complained of widespread intimidation of those who wished to work, but the show of police force eventually held the crowds in check.[49]

Judging from newspaper accounts and lists of those injured and arrested in the disturbances, women were especially prominent in the riots. Of twenty-three people arrested on the first day, over half were women. They attacked the mounted police with rocks, bottles, and red pepper, shouting "Cossacks, Cossacks!" Housewives surrounded the homes of scabs. One of the women arrested demanded an all-female jury, claiming that she could not get a fair trial with men.[50] Women had played an important role in packinghouse strikes since the late nineteenth century, but now they made up a much larger proportion of the labor force and of union membership than ever before. Their participation was not only more apparent but also more organized. Polish women were particularly prominent in an auxiliary group which drew more than five thousand to one of its meetings and staged a strike parade of nearly fifteen thousand. Mary Janek, "the Polish Mother Jones," was the matriarch of the strike in Polonia. Her photographs show a middle-aged woman wearing a heavy black overcoat, a babushka, and a look of grim determination.[51]

Estimates of the strike's effectiveness vary widely. The union claimed that 12,000 went out in Chicago and 29,000 in other packing centers on December 5, the first day of the strike. The Amalgamated also maintained that the strike had spread and that 25,000 workers (over 90 percent of the labor force) had been drawn in at Chicago by the end of January. The packers insisted that only 1,100 Chicago workers responded to the call and that the larger plants were operating close to maximum production. Harvey Ellerd, head of Armour and Company's personnel department, later wrote that only 352 of the Chicago plant's 10,523 workers were absent on the first morning of the strike. This was only slightly higher than the normal 1.5 percent rate of absenteeism. The positions of those who did walk out, the companies claimed, were easily filled. A realistic assessment would fall somewhere between the conflicting claims. There is evidence that the packers considerably understated the strike's effects. A photograph of a mass meeting near the yards shows thousands of workers, including some blacks, with banners and signs. Thousands of people took part in the rioting. Finally, livestock market figures documented the impact which the strike had, at least in the short run. December purchases of both hogs and cattle were unusually low for what should have been the busy season. Armour bought no hogs at all for four days, and it was rumored that some cattle were shipped back to the feedlots. Certainly the packers' claim that they could eventually replace most or all of the strikers was true, given the high level of unemployment in the city; still, to-

ward the end of December government conciliators reported
"strikers holding out firmly."[52]

The strike was crippled from the outset, however, not only by
the weakened condition of the union and the hostile economic climate but also by a lack of support from organized labor. Again, as
in the 1904 strike, the most strategic skilled auxiliary workers—
the stationary firemen and engineers—stayed on the job. This
time, moreover, even the packinghouse teamsters failed to honor
the picket lines and, in effect, helped to keep the industry on its
feet. In contrast to the massive outpouring of support during the
1904 strike, financial help from outside of Packingtown was
meager.[53]

Once again the Amalgamated leaders appealed to Washington
for help, but on January 23 federal mediators urged Secretary
Lane to declare an end to the strike. Balloting on January 26
showed a strong majority for continuing the struggle, but the total
number voting was small, reflecting defections from the strikers'
ranks. The Amalgamated executive board called the strike off on
February 1, 1922, and those packinghouse workers who had not
been blacklisted returned to their jobs.[54]

The story of the packinghouse workers in the postwar years provides a case study of the American Plan in action. Like those in
other industries, management reforms in packing must be understood within the context of the shifting power relations in the
industry. The welfare measures of the war years were largely a
defensive response to a tight labor market and strong trade union
organization, while the employee newspapers and company unions of the postwar years were part of an offensive directed at a
crumbling workers' movement. Employee representation was
designed to convey a sense of industrial democracy, but its primary function was to consolidate the packers' power through organizations which they could control. This control within the
plants was reinforced in the black community through an extensive paternalistic welfare network. The separate social worlds of
migrant black and immigrant white packinghouse workers grew
even further apart as the packers tightened their grip in the Black
Belt. The disastrous effects of this racial division among the

workers can be seen in the collapse of the 1921–22 strike, in which Packingtown lined up with the union and the Black Belt with the packers.

As in the past, the defeat of the packinghouse workers' movement came in the midst of a hostile economic and political environment. With unemployment over 20 percent during 1921, employers throughout the country went on the offensive, locking out unionized workers or forcing their organizations into disastrous strikes, while thousands of unemployed poured into the plants. In a political climate dominated by the Red Scare and the rising tide of nativism, immigrant workers fought to preserve their hard-earned gains. More than in 1904, government also played an important role in this defeat. Sullivan's sweeping injunction, enforced by thousands of policemen, made it clear that the state controlled the streets.

In the short run at least, the American Plan was a great success in packing. Labor organization was destroyed for more than a decade, and the packers embarked on an ambitious program of progressive management reform. Yet many of the problems which had brought the diverse population of butcher workmen and -women together and created the need for unionization at the turn of the century and during the World War I years still remained. During the late 1930s, Chicago's packinghouse workers rose once again along with workers throughout the United States to create a giant industrial union movement which finally brought lasting union organization to the industry.

NOTES

1. *Armour Oval* 3 (Mar. 17, 1921): 1.

2. Quoted in Benjamin Stolberg, "The Stockyards Strike," *Nation* 114 (Jan. 25, 1922): 92.

3. Harry Braverman, *Labor and Monopoly Capital: The Degradation of Work in the Twentieth Century* (New York, 1974); David Montgomery, "Immigrant Workers and Scientific Management," in his *Workers' Control in America: Studies in the History of Work, Technology, and Labor Struggles* (London and New York, 1979); Daniel Nelson, *Managers and Workers: The Origins of the New Factory System in the United States, 1880–1920* (Madison, Wis., 1975), 55–162. See also John R. Commons et al.,

History of Labor in the United States (1918; reprint, New York, 1935), 3:303–96; Richard Edwards, *Contested Terrain: The Transformation of the Workplace in the Twentieth Century* (New York, 1979), 97–104.

4. See Montgomery, "Immigrant Workers and Scientific Management" and "Whose Standards?" both in *Workers' Control in America;* David Brody, "The Rise and Decline of Welfare Capitalism," in his *Workers in Industrial America: Essays in the Twentieth Century Struggle* (New York, 1980); Nelson, 161–62; Commons et al., 3:336–58.

5. See Rudolf Clemen, *The American Livestock and Meat Industry* (New York, 1923), 704–12.

6. For comparable developments in steel, electrical manufacturing, and munitions production, see Brody, *Steelworkers in America: The Non-Union Era* (New York, 1969), 147–98; Ronald W. Schatz, *The Electrical Workers: A History of Labor at General Electric and Westinghouse, 1923–60* (Urbana, Ill., 1983), 20–21; and Montgomery, *Workers' Control in America*, 113–38.

7. George Soule, *Prosperity Decade: From War to Depression* (New York, 1975), 81–105.

8. Clemen, 720; Alma Herbst, *The Negro in the Slaughtering and Meat Packing Industry of Chicago* (Boston, 1932), 151; James R. Barrett, Peter Rachleff, Robert Ruck, and Steven Weiner, "Race, Class and Union in the Chicago Stockyards, 1900–1940" (University of Pittsburgh, typescript, 1975), 95; *National Provisioner* (hereafter *NP*) 64 (Mar. 19, 1921): 25; 64 (Mar. 25, 1921): 1–3, 20; and, quotation, 64 (June 25, 1921): 15. For figures on the drop in domestic meat consumption and the dramatic decline in meat exports, see Institute of American Meat Packers, *Reference Book on the Meat Packing Industry* (Chicago, 1929), 12, 21.

9. David Brody, *The Butcher Workmen: A Study in Unionization* (Cambridge, Mass., 1964), 96–97.

10. Ibid., 96–98; *Butcher Workman (*hereafter *BW)* 7 (Mar. 1921): 1–2; *NP* 64 (Mar. 26, 1921): 20; 65 (July 16, 1921): 20.

11. *NP* 63 (Sept. 25, 1920): 17.

12. *Chicago Tribune*, Feb. 23, 24, 1918; *BW* 6 (Mar. 1918); Clemen, 713.

13. *Swift Arrow* 1 (June 3, 1921): 2; 1 (Mar. 31, 1922): 1; 1 (May 12, 1922): 1, 3; 2 (June 9, 1922): 4; 2 (Jan. 19,1923): 4; 2 (Jan. 5, 1923): 1. For a summary of similar programs at Armour, see Kate J. Adams, *Humanizing a Great Industry* (Chicago, 1919).

14. *Chicago Tribune*, May 20, 1919; *NP* 40 (Feb. 13, 1909): 18; 64 (Jan. 8, 1921): 28. See also *NP* 65 (Oct. 1, 1921): 39.

15. *NP* 62 (Jan. 17, 1920): 18; 70 (Feb. 9, 1924): 26. See also U.S.

Bureau of Labor Statistics, Bulletin no. 208 (Washington, D.C., 1917) and Robert F. Forester, *Employee Stock Ownership in the United States* (Princeton, N.J., 1927), 165–66.

16. Ernest Burton, *Employee Representation* (Baltimore, 1926), 211–12; *Swift Arrow* 1 (Aug. 12, 1921): 1; 1 (Mar. 31, 1922): 3; 1 (Apr. 14, 1922): 3. This and another multilanguage leaflet are contained in the records of the U.S. Dept. of Labor, Mediation and Conciliation Service (RMCS), RG 280, Case 170/1365a and Case 170/1365c, Box 132, National Archives and Records Service, Suitland, Md.

17. *NP* 63 (Sept. 25, 1920): 18–19, 25–26, 42–43; *Swift Arrow* 1 (Mar. 31, 1922): 3; 1 (May 12, 1922): 5; RMCS, RG 280, Case 33/864, Box 44, 632–82.

18. This and the following paragraph are based largely on a reading of the *Swift Arrow* between May 1921 and May 1923 and scattered issues of the *Armour Oval* for these years which are contained in RMCS, RG 280, Case 170/1365, Box 132. For a discussion of the proliferation of employee newspapers during the early 1920s, including those of the packers, see National Industrial Conference Board, *Employee Magazines in the United States* (New York, 1925).

19. *Swift Arrow*, 1 (May 27, 1921): 1. The emphasis is in the original.

20. *Swift Arrow* 1 (Nov. 18, 1921): 1; 1 (Sept. 9, 1921): 1; 1 (Sept. 23, 1921): 1; 2 (May 11, 1923): 1.

21. Stuart D. Brandes, *American Welfare Capitalism, 1880–1940* (Chicago, 1976), 121–26; Nelson, 156–62; Robert Ozanne, *A Century of Labor-Management Relations at McCormick and International Harvester* (Madison, Wis., 1967), 41–42, 117–18; Schatz, 22, 40–41; S. Howard Patterson, *Social Aspects of Industry* (New York, 1935), 480–82; Robert W. Dunn, *The Americanization of Labor* (New York, 1927), 129–30; Commons et al., 3:336–57. For a careful, sympathetic analysis of company unions in various settings, see Daniel Nelson, "The Company Union Movement, 1900–1937: A Reexamination," *Business History Review* 56 (1982): 335–50.

22. Clemen, 723; Herbst, 57; Brody, *Butcher Workmen*, 99; Wilson and Company, *Yearbook, 1921* (Chicago, 1922), 29–31. See also Clemen, 735–36, for a description of another early plan at the Dold Company in Buffalo.

23. Brody, *Butcher Workmen*, 99–100.

24. *Armour Oval* 3 (Mar. 17, 1921): 1–2; Clemen, 728–29; Brody, *Butcher Workmen*, 99–100. For descriptions of the plan at Swift, which was slightly different, see *NP* 65 (July 30, 1921): 20, 36; 65 (Aug. 13, 1921): 131–32; and Paul H. Douglas, Curtice Hitchcock, and Willard E. Alkins, *The Worker in Industrial Society* (Chicago, 1923), 754–59.

25. Edna Clark, "History of Controversy between Labor and Management in the Slaughtering and Meat Packing Industries in Chicago" (M.A. thesis, University of Chicago, 1922), 196; Clemen, 726–27; *Armour Oval* 3 (Mar. 17, 1921): 2.

26. Clemen, 726, 734–35; *NP* 65 (July 30, 1921): 20, 36; *Armour Oval* 1 (Mar. 17, 1921): 3; Clark, 196; Stolberg, 92. See also *Swift Arrow* 1 (June 3, 1921): 1.

27. *BW* 7 (July, 1921); 7 (Apr. 1921); *NP* 65 (Sept. 17, 1921): 18; 65 (Sept. 24, 1921): 23; Clark, 196; *Swift Arrow* 1 (June 3, 1921): 1; 1 (Feb. 17, 1922): 1; 2 (June 9, 1922): 1; Catherine Lewis, "Trade Union Policies in Regard to the Negro Worker in the Slaughtering and Meat Packing Industry of Chicago" (M.A. thesis, University of Chicago, 1945), 36–37, 67. See also affidavits concerning management intimidation written by workers in several plants and presented to Judge Alschuler by union officials, in RMCS, RG 280, Case 170/1365, 15–37.

28. Ozanne, 126–27.

29. Clemen, 728–30; *Swift Arrow* 3 (Sept. 28, 1923): 1; *NP* 72 (Jan. 31, 1925): 22. See also *Monthly Labor Review* 19 (July 1924): 37–38.

30. *Swift Arrow* 3 (Sept. 28, 1923): 1; Clemen, 730, 734–35; *Monthly Labor Review* 19 (July 1924): 37–38.

31. Clemen, 728–29; *NP* 65 (Nov. 26, 1921): 20.

32. Brody, "The Rise and Decline of Welfare Capitalism," 57.

33. Chicago Commission on Race Relations, *The Negro in Chicago* (Chicago, 1922), 147–48; William Tuttle, *Race Riot: Chicago in the Red Summer of 1919* (New York, 1970), 151. Attendance at Efficiency Club activities had fallen off by the mid-1920s. See "Statistical Summary of Activities, January–June 1926," Box 3, papers of the Wabash Avenue YMCA, University of Illinois, Chicago.

34. Arvarh Strickland, *History of the Chicago Urban League* (Urbana, Ill., 1966), 70–71; Walter A. Fogel, *The Negro in the Meat Industry* (Philadelphia, 1970), 29.

35. Herbst, 56–57.

36. Ibid., 63–65.

37. Ibid., 63.

38. Commons et al., 4:399–400; Montgomery, *Workers' Control in America*, 96, 100.

39. *NP* 65 (Nov. 26, 1921): 19–20, 25; *Swift Arrow*, Special Assembly Edition, Nov. 23, 1921, 1. See also *NP* 65 (Nov. 12, 1921): 22; 67 (Aug. 5, 1922): 27; Nelson, 162. See also Commons et al., 3:357–58.

40. *NP* 65 (Nov. 26, 1921): 19.

41. Brody, *Butcher Workmen*, 91–96.

42. *Dziennik Ziednoczenia*, Feb. 4, 15, 1922; *Dziennik Chicagoski*, Jan. 1, 3, 5, 7, 9, 10, 11, 12, 23, and Feb. 4, 10, 1922, Chicago Foreign Language Press Survey, Chicago Historical Society (hereafter CFLPS). See also Dominic Pacyga, "Crisis and Community: Back of the Yards, 1921," *Chicago History* 6 (Fall 1977): 167–77.

43. Clark, 201; Herbst, 64–65.

44. Barrett, Rachleff, Ruck, and Weiner, 94–95; Herbst, 34–35, 64–65, 72, 75, 77; Horace Cayton and George Mitchell, *Black Workers and the New Unions* (Chapel Hill, N.C., 1939), 231; Chicago Commission on Race Relations, 361; Brody, *Butcher Workmen*, 96; Clark, 201–2. On the matter of victimizations, see the Mediation Commission cases for two strikes against William Davies Company, which discriminated against union members with considerable seniority and in one case hired black women at a lower hourly rate. Both cases were settled in favor of the employees and the unionists were reinstated (RMCS, RG 280, Case 170/1386, Box 133). The black workers' loyalty to the packers is also indicated in the small sample of women's employment records which Alma Herbst reproduced in her study. These include reasons for termination. Of ten white women employed in December 1921, four went out on strike, while six remained at work. All nine of the black women employed at the time of the strike remained at their jobs (*Negro in Slaughtering*, 157–65).

45. Quoted in Clark, 203. See also Chicago *Herald Examiner*, Dec. 9, 1921; Claude M. Lightfoot, "From Chicago's Ghetto to World Politics: The Life and Struggles of Claude M. Lightfoot," unpublished ms., 1983, in the author's possession, 37–38.

46. Stolberg, 92.

47. *Dziennik Chicagoski*, Dec. 8, 1921 (CFLPS); *Chicago Tribune*, Dec. 8, 1921.

48. Chicago *Herald Examiner*, Dec. 9, 1921; Dennis Lane to Frank Morrison, Dec. 10, 1921, AFL National and International Union File, *American Federation of Labor Records: The Samuel Gompers Era* (Sanford, N.C., 1979, microfilm), Reel 40.

49. Sherman Rogers, "Employee Representation and the Stockyard Strike," *The Outlook* 129 (Dec. 28, 1921): 681–82.

50. *Dziennik Chicagoski*, Dec. 8 and 9, 1921 (CFLPS); Chicago *Herald Examiner*, Dec. 8 and 9, 1921; Chicago *Evening American*, Dec. 9, 1921.

51. *BW* 8 (Jan. 1922): 1–2.

52. *Chicago Tribune*, Dec. 6, 1921; *BW* 8 (Jan. 1922); 8 (Feb. 1922); *NP* 65 (Dec. 10, 1921): 17; 65 (Dec. 17, 1921): 19; 65 (Dec. 31, 1921): 23; Harvey Ellerd, "Our Experiences with Employee Representation,"

ings of the Academy of Political Science 13 (June 1928): 116; O. F. Nelson to H. L. Kerwin, Dec. 22, 1921, Labor Department Records, quoted in Brody, *Butcher Workmen*, 103. See also Herbst, 58–59.

53. Brody, *Butcher Workmen*, 104–5.

54. Ibid., 105; *Dziennik Chicagoski*, Feb. 4 and 13, 1922 (CFLPS).

Conclusion

The early twentieth century is often remembered as an era of rationalization. Bankers and executives restructured the nation's economy, concentrating capital in much larger firms run by modern, efficient corporate bureaucracies. Manufacturers transformed systems of production, introducing extreme division of labor, mechanization, and assembly-line organization of work. According to this formulation, industrial relations also underwent a process of rationalization. Chastened by the waste and violence of titanic late nineteenth-century labor struggles, important business and union leaders worked together to create new, more rational systems of industrial relations. Mediation and arbitration were proposed as substitutes for strikes and lockouts.[1]

Whatever resistance working people might have raised to the changes that swept their society were muted, we are told, because the American working class was hopelessly fragmented. Race, nationality, wage, and skill differentials and their inability to create an autonomous, radical labor movement rendered American workers "lumpen people in a lumpen society." "It is no wonder," one of our leading historians of the period concludes, "that workers, the poor, and the oppressed counted for little in determining the fate of the first century of modern American history." Facing the giant corporations, the churning assembly lines, and the esteemed arbitration boards, real American workers were much like Sinclair's fictional characters in *The Jungle*—weak and in disarray.[2]

But this is only one perspective. Consider the world of the assembly line, that great symbol of industrial efficiency, from the vantage point of the killing floor, rather than the boardroom. Laboring in one of the most highly rationalized industries in the world, the butcher workman's economic life was chaotic. There were slow seasons, slow weeks, and slow days; low wages and crooked foremen; high accident rates and a wide range of occupational diseases. At times it must have seemed as though the whole industry was so structured as to deprive the laborer of his or her bread.

In fact, the idea of work "rationalization" itself is at best a relative concept. The direction of the process and its ultimate effects depended in large part on the balance of power in the industry's production relations. Whether a particular organization of work was rational depended on who was doing the rationalizing; management's efficiency could be labor's chaos and vice versa. If we are to grasp the evolution of mass-production work, it is not sufficient to focus exclusively on new technology and management theory and practice. This is the perspective which has given us our image of early twentieth-century industry as a world of reason and enlightenment—an image which few industrial workers of the era would recognize. We need to consider more carefully the relationship between management's initiatives and those of labor; to study the sorts of organizations and strategies created by workers in response to mass-production work and, in turn, how these shaped the nature of management reforms. In particular, we must consider changes in the organization of work and in management practice within the context of production relations and the struggle for power within the workplace. Rather than the manifestation of some neutral process of modernization, scientific management and other early twentieth-century management reforms often represented efforts by employers to maximize their power at the "frontier of control."[3]

Nor is it possible to comprehend the full impact of work-related problems if we study only what happened within the walls of the factory. Another look at Sinclair's "jungle"—the community of Packingtown—demonstrates an old generalization: The quality of workers' lives, in the community as well as in the workplace, was shaped in large part by work-related problems—low wages, chronic unemployment, dangerous health and safety conditions.

Within this context, such concepts as family strategies, life choices, and even property mobility take on new meanings. Family structure and behavior did influence social and economic conditions and even power relations in Packingtown, but this occurred within rather narrow perimeters of choice and not always in positive ways. The mass-production factory and the big-city neighborhood clearly left their marks on the immigrant family. The family economy, for example, was not simply a holdover from peasant society; it was just as much a product of wage labor status in the New World. Boarding was an important strategy in the effort to make ends meet, but it also subsidized the industry's low wage by providing cheap meals and lodging for boarders and supplementary income for the host families. Likewise, home ownership was not necessarily an indication of surplus income, as some historians of social mobility have assumed. Often it was an integral part of the struggle for existence. In Packingtown, the sacrifices which home ownership required had more to do with a realistic desire for family security in a hostile and uncertain world than with new or old world values regarding property as a status symbol. Ethnic cultural values and demographic factors certainly influenced family behavior, but whatever choices Packingtown's families made were severely circumscribed by the harsh economic realities which dominated life in the neighborhood.[4]

Because the quality of life in Packingtown was closely related to conditions in the industry, the bitter struggles which butcher workmen and -women waged against the packers represented efforts to gain a greater control over their lives in the community as well as in the plants. The only real breakthroughs in living standards, during the early years of the twentieth century and the First World War era, came largely through union organization and conflict. Indeed, it was a deep concern for the welfare of the community and its families that lent packinghouse strikes their desperate quality. In assessing the motivation of industrial workers, particularly recent immigrants with a strong sense of family and community identification, it is essential to consider the neighborhood as part of the context for class relations. Only when we

look down the filthy streets of Packingtown and into its crumbling, overcrowded tenements can we begin to appreciate what
was at stake in these struggles and in countless others in communities throughout the country in these years. When the men
and women of Packingtown organized and fought the packers
they did so to protect the security of their families and the in-
tegrity of their communities. Far from insulating them in ethnic
ghettoes, this deep desire to protect and defend what they valued
most led immigrant packinghouse workers to an appreciation for
the value of working-class organization and struggle. Values which
are often considered "traditional" immigrant values became the
basis for class action.[5]

Such organization and struggle would have been impossible
without some measure of solidarity among workers from quite
diverse social backgrounds, and this brings us to the complex
problem of class formation and fragmentation. The experience of
the packinghouse workers suggests that the question of working-
class fragmentation in the early twentieth century remains a
matter for investigation. The significance of the findings lies both
in the obvious potential for such fragmentation in the stockyards
and in the considerable success which the butcher workmen and
-women had at various times in uniting on job issues. What were
the factors contributing to and discouraging this class cohesion?

On one level, the experience of the packinghouse workers provides substance for economic and cultural theories of fragmentation. Labor economists have explained class fragmentation by
focusing on the divisive effects of segmented and hierarchical labor market structures. Where these objective differences in wage
rates, benefits, and employment security overlapped with
significant racial, ethnic, and gender divisions—as was so often
the case in American industry—their divisive effects were accentuated.[6]

The labor market in meat packing was representative of such
segmentation in several respects. The transformation of work in
the industry allowed the packers to reorganize the labor market,
creating a status hierarchy and a wide range of wage rates among
the skilled knife men as well as a large pool of casual laborers to
do the unskilled work. As a succession of immigrant and later
black and Mexican men and women settled into these common

labor positions, skill levels reinforced racial and ethnic divisions. The existence of a large, heterogeneous population of casual laborers; the fact that Poles, blacks, and other new groups were often first introduced into the labor market as strikebreakers; and the threat which this population represented to the wages and status of the more experienced butchers in the industry all heightened the danger of interethnic and interracial conflict and at times inhibited the development of class solidarity among the packinghouse workers. Not surprisingly, the packers developed personnel policies which accentuated such divisions—pensions, profit-sharing, and other fringe benefits for permanent employees; differential wage cuts which favored the skilled; and company unions based on older, more loyal workers.

It is a mistake, however, to analyze fragmentation in purely structural terms, as labor economists have done, focusing entirely on labor market segmentation. The story of Packingtown, Canaryville, and the Black Belt demonstrates that fragmentation was also rooted in the neighborhood. The diversity of the labor market was reflected in and accentuated by separate racial and ethnic communities, each of them with its own social structure and cultural institutions. On Chicago's South Side, the varied work experiences of skilled Irish butchers, recent Slavic immigrants, and black migrants were reinforced by the physical and social barriers separating these groups.

Yet this study also suggests that such divisions can easily be overdrawn. In opposition to the clear tendencies toward fragmentation in this era, there were countervailing pressures inherent in the changing character of manufacturing and neighborhood life. Huge plants with finely integrated production systems linked the fates of very large, socially diverse groups of workers who might otherwise have had little in common with one another.[7] In packing, a significant intensification of work, the downward pressure on wages caused by casual hiring methods, and the army of unemployed at the yards gate provided a rationale for more skilled, Americanized workers to reach out to the unskilled black and Slavic newcomers. In a peculiar way, the hiring practices of the packers and the structure of work in the industry actually facilitated this effort. Rather than Balkanizing the various social groups which made up the labor force, mixed work gangs brought them together, presented them with shared grievances, and offered the opportunity to begin an informal process of socialization.

Likewise, the effects of social and cultural heterogeneity in the community were complex. The existence of strong racial and ethnic subcultures was not necessarily an impediment to class formation. As Victor Greene and David Brody have shown for Slavic coalminers and steelworkers, the strong cohesion of such communities often facilitated organization and mobilization during strikes.[8] This was clearly the case with the new immigrants in packing during both periods of organization. As in the workplace, there were also points of contact among immigrant workers and between them and native-born whites in the community. Some institutions of big-city life—the saloon and the settlement house, for example—provided a common ground and facilitated the acculturation of newcomers.

In Chicago, "Americanization from the bottom up" took place within a mature working-class community with a strong labor movement and long traditions of militancy, rather than a company town dominated by a single corporation. The organizational fortunes of the packinghouse workers rose and fell with those of the labor movement as a whole. Fragmentation and decline came within the context of economic depression, unemployment, and employer and government attacks on the metropolitan and national labor movements. Under such pressures, the racial, ethnic, and skill "fault lines" in the broader working-class community contributed to the disintegration of the class movement. But such diversity is not sufficient in and of itself to explain working-class fragmentation in the early years of the corporate political economy.

The strategy and structure of the unions themselves also helped to determine the prospects for successful organization across racial and ethnic lines. As in other industries of the era, the packers and the unions contended for the loyalty of the new immigrants and the black migrants. Considering the extreme diversity of the labor force, the unions were remarkably successful at integrating the immigrants during both periods of organization. Particularly in the 1900–1904 period, the Amalgamated's department-based locals maximized interethnic contact and provided the institutional context for Americanization from the bottom up. The union's success in this regard should encourage scholars of immigration to investigate an aspect of immigrant acculturation which has heretofore been virtually ignored—the role of working-class institutions and informal contact at work and in the community among workers from diverse ethnic backgrounds.

Although the butcher workmen's unions also won some support among blacks, the labor movement was generally far less successful in the Black Belt than it had been in Packingtown. In the ghetto, paternalistic personnel policies, continuing discrimination in the labor market, racially segregated neighborhoods, and a lingering suspicion of the "white man's union" combined to keep most blacks out of the union camp. In the crucial era from 1919 to 1922, race consciousness obscured the mutual interests of both Packingtown and the Black Belt in class organization. But this failure was not preordained by the skin color of those involved; the time, the place, the specific strategies of the unions and the employers, and other factors all played a role. Because of the diversity of the American working-class population, a careful analysis of the conditions under which various minorities settled into the urban industrial environment is essential to understanding the problem of class formation and fragmentation.

There were also patterns in the character of working-class protest in these years, but none that a simple distinction between "premodern" and "modern" behavior can explain.[9] What is most striking about the highly developed movement in packing during both periods of union activity is the workers involved. Shop-floor organization and restriction of output have generally been associated with mature groups or workers, those who had "learned the rules of the game" and created organizations and strategies suited to their problems.[10] Legislation and collective enforcement of work rules, for example, were common among highly skilled metalworkers in late nineteenth-century Britain and America. Often such rules were designed to guard against just the sort of rationalization that occurred in packing.[11]

In the case of the packinghouse workers, however, we are looking at a strong, sophisticated, and relatively successful shop-floor movement encompassing a very large proportion of recent immigrants, including women and male common laborers without industrial work or trade union experience—just the sort of "premodern" workers who ought not to have behaved in this way. The key to the paradox lies in the relationship between the earlier generation of Irish and German butchers, with their craft traditions and sense of solidarity, on the one hand and recently arrived Polish and Lithuanian common laborers on the other. The "butcher aristocracy" temporarily overcame nativism and craft sectionalism, consciously integrating newcomers into its movement. The Slavic laborers responded enthusiastically and soon became good union men and women. Indeed, in the second round of unionization, Poles became the most cohesive group in the movement. Part of the importance of the packinghouse workers' organizational and protest behavior, then, lies in our view of the immigrant workers themselves. Given the right situation—a work process which linked the interests of the skilled and unskilled and a union structure and strategy which encouraged interethnic class solidarity—recent immigrants were quite capable of developing a class perspective and helping to build strong working-class movements. This view of immigrant workers and their relations with groups of older skilled workers might suggest how craft traditions and strategies were transformed by a new generation of workers and how these new forms provided a useful legacy for the industrial union movement of later years.

On the other hand, crowd violence, often considered a premodern form of protest, remained an important element in packinghouse strikes from the 1870s to the 1920s. Here the character of meat packing as an industry and of Chicago as a city can tell us a good deal more than the premodern/modern dichotomy. Meat packing employed mostly unskilled labor from the 1880s on, while Chicago was a veritable clearinghouse for such labor. Packinghouse workers' organizations were particularly vulnerable in periods of depression, when the city was flooded with unemployed and casual laborers. Any movement hoping to score a victory under such conditions had to employ aggressive picketing, and this imperative often drew the crowd into strikes. Even the ecology of the city's South Side played a role in the persistence of the strike riot. Originally built on the outskirts of the city, by the turn of the century the Union Stockyards were surrounded by densely populated working-class neighborhoods. Central to neighborhood life even in normal times, the yards became the focal point of activity during strikes, attracting large crowds determined to prevent the entry of strikebreakers.

Finally, the story of the packinghouse workers underscores the importance of production relations to our understanding of class relations in American society as a whole during the "Progressive Era." Notwithstanding the conservative rhetoric of the labor officials involved and the welfare reforms of the leading packers, conflict within the plants was frequent and generalized, revolving around matters of control as well as wages and conditions, and representing a serious threat to the packers' managerial prerogatives. Nor were such conflicts peculiar to packing. As research moves from the study of unions and union leaders to empirical work on strike activity and shop-floor relations, it becomes more difficult to sustain the notion of a business-labor consensus during the "corporate liberal" era.[12] The persistence of workplace conflict undermined any lasting ideological rapprochement between corporate leaders and America's immigrant workers.

The increasingly intrusive state bureaucracy played an important role in mediating such conflict, particularly during the war years and immediately after. Wartime arbitration provided a measure of recognition for the unions and resulted in significant improvements in wages, working hours, and conditions. On the other hand, the arbitration also outlawed shop-floor organization and called on union leaders to discipline their own members and to help maximize production. Thus the system stabilized industrial relations during the war years when the union was in a relatively strong bargaining position and collapsed just at the point when the union was weakest. State intervention at the local level—in the form of a sweeping injunction and massive police force—was resolute and decisive in the defeat of the 1921–22 strike.

The failure of the packinghouse workers to build a durable interracial, interethnic industrial union in the course of the early twentieth century is hardly surprising. The odds were certainly against them. Far more significant is the progress they made toward that goal. And yet even this is not so difficult to understand, once we have seen their work situation and its effects on their community.

The most compelling reason they had for uniting was the simplest of all: Only their own collective efforts could bring them a greater degree of control over their individual lives. The significance of this struggle was etched in their daily fight for survival. For Packingtown was not a jungle, and its people were not without hope. Like millions before and after them, they fought for their own and to make their community a better place to live. The union and its attempts to transform the work situation brought the packinghouse workers, so many of them new to their industrial slum life, into the mainstream of a very old conflict.

NOTES

1. Robert Wiebe, *The Search for Order, 1877–1920* (New York, 1967); Louis Golambos, "The Emerging Organizational Synthesis in Modern American History," *Business History Review* 44 (1970): 279–90; Jerry Israel, ed., *Building the Organizational Society: Essays on Associational Activities* (New York, 1972), especially the essays by Hays, Eakins, and Radosh; Samuel Haber, *Efficiency and Uplift: Scientific Management in the Progressive Era, 1890–1920* (Chicago, 1964); Arthur Link and Richard L. McCormick, *Progressivism* (New York, 1983); Samuel P. Hays, *The Response to Industrialism, 1885–1914* (Chicago, 1957); James Weinstein, *The Corporate Ideal in the Liberal State* (Boston, 1968); Ronald Radosh, "The Corporate Ideology of American Labor Leaders from Gompers to Hillman," *Studies on the Left* 6 (1966): 66–88.

2. The quotations are from Gabriel Kolko's *Main Currents in Modern American History* (New York, 1976), which presents the most extreme formulation of the fragmentation theme (see chapters 3 and 5 and, for the quotations, pages 99 and 173). But the concept of working-class fragmentation in one form or another is widespread in the historiography and in attempts by social scientists in other fields to understand this period. See also Gerald Rosenbloom, *Immigrant Workers and American Labor Radicalism* (New York, 1968), and, for a brief discussion of the fragmentation theme in labor historiography and the work of labor economists, James R. Barrett, "Unity and Fragmentation: Class, Race, and Ethnicity on Chicago's South Side, 1900–1922," *Journal of Social History* 18 (1984): 37–39, on which this conclusion is in part based.

3. Carter Goodrich, *The Frontier of Control: A Study of British Workshop Politics* (New York, 1921; reprint, London, 1975); Harry Braverman, *Labor and Monopoly Capital: The Degradation of Work in the*

Twentieth Century (New York, 1974); David Montgomery, *Workers' Control in America: Studies in the History of Work, Technology, and Labor Struggles* (New York and London, 1979); Richard Edwards, *Contested Terrain: The Transformation of the Workplace in the Twentieth Century* (New York, 1977).

4. For studies of the problem of family economy see Virginia Yans-McLaughlin, *Family and Community: Italian Immigrants in Buffalo, 1880–1930* (Urbana, Ill., 1981), 159–79, and Tamara K. Hareven, *Family Time and Industrial Time: The Relationship between Family and Work in a New England Industrial Community* (New York and London, 1982), 89–112. In explaining immigrant family structure and behavior, Yans-McLaughlin emphasizes continuity in ethnic cultural values, while Hareven stresses the importance of family life cycle. In my own view, both tend to underestimate the pervasive influence of work-related problems in shaping the worldview and actions of immigrant workers and their families. For studies which tend to interpret home ownership in terms of upward mobility, see Stephen Thernstrom, *Poverty and Progress: Social Mobility in a Nineteenth-Century American City* (Cambridge, Mass., 1965); Josef Barton, *Peasants and Strangers: Italians, Rumanians, and Slovaks in an American City* (Cambridge, Mass., 1975); Caroline Golab, *Immigrant Destinations* (Philadelphia, 1977). John Bodnar, Roger Simon, and Michael P. Weber, *Lives of Their Own: Blacks, Italians, and Poles in Pittsburgh, 1900–1960* (Urbana, Ill., 1981) and John Bodnar, *The Transplanted: A History of Immigrants in Urban America* (Bloomington, Ind., 1985) analyze immigrant family life as the product of urban industrial conditions as much as of old world background.

5. Cf. John Bodnar, "Immigration, Kinship, and the Rise of Working-Class Realism," *Journal of Social History* 14 (1980): 45–65. Bodnar argues—rightly, I think—that the welfare of the family was the central concern of immigrant workers. But he sees this issue as divorced from what he views as more abstract issues regarding power and control in the workplace. I mean to suggest here a firm *link* between workplace and family concerns.

6. David M. Gordon, Richard C. Edwards, and Michael Reich, *Segmented Work, Divided Workers* (New York and London, 1982); idem, eds., *Labor Market Segmentation* (Lexington, Mass., 1975); Andrew Friedman, *Industry and Labour: Class Struggle at Work and Monopoly Capitalism* (London, 1978); Jill Rubery, "Structured Labor Markets, Worker Organization, and Low Pay," *Cambridge Journal of Economics* 2 (1978): 17–36.

7. Gordon, Edwards, and Reich, chapter 4.

8. Victor Greene, *The Slavic Community on Strike* (South Bend, Ind., 1968); David Brody, *Steelworkers in America: The Non-Union Era* (New York, 1969), 214–62.

9. Charles Tilly, "The Changing Place of Collective Violence," in *Social Theory and Social History*, ed. M. Richter (Cambridge, Mass., 1975); Herbert Gutman, *Work, Culture and Society in Industrializing America: Essays in Working-Class and Social History* (New York, 1976), chapter 1.

10. See E. J. Hobsbawm, "Custom, Wages, and Workload in the Nineteenth Century" in his *Labouring Men* (London, 1968), 344–70, from which the quotation is taken. On the work culture of this earlier generation of skilled workers in the United States, see Montgomery, *Workers' Control in America*, chapter 1. This discussion is based in part on James R. Barrett, "Immigrant Workers in Early Mass-Production Industry: Work Rationalization and Job Control Conflicts in Chicago's Packinghouses, 1900–1904," in *German Workers in Industrial Chicago, 1850–1910: A Comparative Perspective*, ed. Hartmut Keil and John Jentz (De Kalb, Ill., 1983).

11. Montgomery, *Workers' Control in America*, 15–18; James Hinton, *The First Shop Stewards' Movement* (London, 1973). In more recent times, such job control conflicts have been characteristic of some well-organized assembly line workers—notably British and American car workers. See Hugh Beynon, *Working for Ford* (London, 1975) and Nelson Lichtenstein, "Auto Worker Militancy and the Structure of Factory Life, 1937–1955," *Journal of American History* 67 (1980): 335–53.

12. On the widespread practice of restriction of output and other forms of job control among various trade groups, see U.S. Commissioner of Labor, *Eleventh Special Report, Regulation and Restriction of Output* (Washington, D.C., 1904). On the significance of control issues in the high level of strike activity throughout the early twentieth century, see Montgomery, *Workers' Control in America*, 20, 48–90, 97–101, 113–38; Bruno Ramirez, *When Workers Fight: The Politics of Collective Bargaining in the Progressive Era* (Westport, Conn., 1978), 3–13; and James R. Green, *The World of the Worker: Labor in Twentieth Century America* (New York, 1980), 67–99.

APPENDIX A

The Stewart Manuscript Census
of 1905

The data base referred to in the text as the Stewart Manuscript Census of 1905 ("Stewart Ms. Census, 1905") is derived from a unique door-to-door canvass of the Packingtown neighborhood conducted in 1905 under the auspices of U.S. Commissioner of Labor Ethelbert Stewart. Unfortunately, little is known about the census or the instructions given to enumerators. (Stewart's personal papers at the University of North Carolina, Chapel Hill, contain no information regarding the census.) It is most likely that the commissioner sought some insight into an area of chronic labor unrest. The neighborhood was the scene of disturbances in the 1902 and 1905 teamsters' strikes, as well as during the 1904 packinghouse strike.

Although it is clear from the selection of blocks studied that enumerators were careful to represent the various ethnic groups in the community, the census was apparently not conducted in a truly systematic fashion. Nine streets were included, and these seem to represent the three dominant nationalities in the neighborhood: Poles, Lithuanians, and Bohemians. A comparison of the census data with contemporary maps and with the 1900 and 1910 federal manuscript censuses indicates that enumerators were able to survey most but not all households on any given block. The defects in the census, then, are clear: It is neither a complete survey of Packingtown's total population, nor a random sample. With this in mind, I have tried to supplement my computer-assisted analysis of the Stewart census with a variety of other sources in drawing generalizations regarding the neighborhood and its inhabitants. Such supplementary sources were both quantitative—in the form of data from contemporary social surveys, government documents, and systematic samples (N = 200) from the 1900 and 1910 federal manuscript censuses—and qualitative—in the form of observations by contemporary writers.

There are, however, several strengths inherent in Stewart's census as well. The sample of 284 families is relatively large and includes fairly complete information regarding twenty-eight variables for each family—much more information than is available from the regular manuscript census schedules. These variables include address; number of rooms; type of dwelling (flat or house); number of rooms having beds; number of beds; age, ethnicity, occupation, and earnings for both husband and wife; age, sex, occupation, and earnings of children; sex and number of boarders and roomers; rate for boarding and meals; family expenditures on fuel, food, clothing, rent, and medical expenses; home ownership; amount of money sent to relatives in Europe; savings; time lost from work due to illness or accident; debts; and length of husband's residence in the U.S. and in Chicago. In addition, enumerators' comments about furnishings and living conditions, though clearly impressionistic, allow one to form an image of the *interiors* of homes.

All twenty-eight of these variables were coded for each family. Many of the data on household structure and family economy in chapter 3 were generated from frequency distributions and cross tabulations using this data base.

The original copies of the Stewart census are in a collection entitled the Ethelbert Stewart Miscellany, part of the Records of the Bureau of Labor Statistics (RG 257) at the National Archives and Record Service in Washington, D.C. Photostatic copies of the census are available at the Chicago Historical Society.

APPENDIX B

Personal Data on the First Group of Elected Employee Representatives at Armour & Company, Chicago Plant, March 1921

BEEF DIVISION

F. M. Daniel, sheep offal, 53 years old; 2 years' service; born in Tennessee; married; occupation, laborer.

Jordan McNary, beef loading, 43 years old; 4 years' service; born in Kentucky; married, 7 children; occupation, laborer.

Stuart Alexander, beef killing, 43 years old; 25 years' service; born in Mexico; captain in American Expeditionary Forces, awarded the "Croix de Guerre" for bravery.

John E. Johnson, cooper shop, 40 years old; 1 year's service; born in Georgia; formerly employed by International Harvester Co.

John C. O. Keating, freezer, 30 years old; 3 years' service; born in Chicago; single; occupation, scaler.

Roy Bishop, wool house, 34 years old; 3 years' service; born in United States; occupation, laborer.

Mathew P. Cody, dry salt department, 52 years old; 36 years' service; married; occupation, laborer.

PORK DIVISION

David Roberts, hog killing, 40 years old; 5 years' service; born in Mississippi; married, 2 children; occupation, grinder.

John Daverin, sweet pickle, 57 years old; 22 years' service; born in Ireland; married; occupation, inspector.

Dennis Lynch, dry salt, 51 years old; 5 years' service; born in New Jersey; occupation, laborer.

Bartholomew Dowling, packinghouse loading, 62 years old; 40 years' service; married, 4 children; occupation, laborer.

James Lonergan, pork-cutting department, 60 years old; 35 years' service; born in Ireland; married, 3 children; occupation, butcher.

PRODUCTION DIVISION

Joseph Chaloupka, fresh sausage department, 49 years old; 35 years' service; born in Ohio; married, 1 child; occupation, stuffer.

August Beckel, sausage department, 60 years old; 39 years' service; born in Germany; married; occupation, sausage maker.

John W.Wolniak, fruit preserving, 34 years old; 4 years' service; born in Illinois; married, 4 children; occupation, clerk.

August Pletzke, fertilitzer works, 66 years old; 37 years' service; born in Germany; married, 2 children; occupation, laborer.

Mathew Kleinbauer, canned chipped beef department, 61 years old; 1 year's service; born in Germany; married; laborer; former occupation, bricklayer.

Adam Cheimaski, butterine department, 45 years old; 13 years' service; born in Russia; married, 4 children; occupation, laborer.

M. J. McEllogett, lard refinery, 24 years old; 3 years' service; born in the United States; single; occupation, checker.

MECHANICAL DIVISION

Thomas J. Myler, cooper shop, 64 years old; 34 years' service; born in Newfoundland; married; occupation, cooper.

Michael McCarron, carpenter shop, 73 years old; 47 years' service; born in Canada; married, 6 children; occupation, carpenter.

Arthur T. Walsh, tin shop, 31 years old; 11 years' service; born in the United States; married; occupation, machinist.

George Merritt, pipe shop, 34 years old; 14 years' service; born in the United States; married; occupation, steamfitter.

John Deal, tractor department, 65 years old; 14 years' service; born in Ohio; married, 7 children.

Source: Armour Oval 3, no. 3 (Mar. 17, 1921): 3.

Index

A Note on the Author

James R. Barrett, a native of Chicago, received his Ph.D. in history from the University of Pittsburgh and now teaches history at the University of Illinois at Urbana-Champaign. He is the author of articles and essays in the *Journal of Social History,* the *Journal of Popular Culture, International Labor and Working-Class History,* and other journals and anthologies, and coauthor, with Steve Nelson and Rob Ruck, of *Steve Nelson, American Radical.*

Books in the Series
The Working Class in American History